Department
& Discipline

Department & Discipline

Chicago Sociology at One Hundred

Andrew Abbott

THE UNIVERSITY OF CHICAGO PRESS
Chicago & London

ANDREW ABBOTT is the Ralph Lewis Professor in the Department of Sociology and the College at the University of Chicago. He is the author of *The System of Professions: An Essay on the Division of Expert Labor,* published by the University of Chicago Press, which won the Sorokin Prize of the Americal Sociological Association in 1991.

The University of Chicago Press, Chicago 60637
The University of Chicago Press, Ltd., London

© 1999 by The University of Chicago
All rights reserved. Published 1999

08   07   06   05   04   03   02   01   00   99   1   2   3   4   5

ISBN: 0-226-00098-2 (cloth)
ISBN: 0-226-00099-0 (paper)

Library of Congress Cataloging-in-Publication Data
Abbott, Andrew.
    Department and discipline : Chicago sociology at one hundred.
        p.   cm.
    Includes bibliographical references.
    ISBN 0-226-00098-2 (cloth : alk. paper). — ISBN 0-226-00099-0
(paper : alk. paper)
    1. Chicago school of sociology—History.   2. American journal of
sociology—History.   3. University of Chicago. Dept. of Sociology—
History.   4. Sociology—United States—History.   5. Sociology—
United States—Periodicals—History.   6. Sociology—Illinois—
Chicago—History.   I. Title: Department and discipline.
HM22.U5A23   1999
301'.09—dc21   98-55981
                                                                      CIP

⊗The paper used in this publication meets the minimum requirements
of the American National Standard for Information Sciences—Perma-
nence of Paper for Printed Library Materials, ANSI Z39.48-1992.

For Woody

Contents

Preface

Sometime in 1992 Marta Tienda, then editor of the *American Journal of Sociology,* asked me to undertake a history of the journal, to be published during its centennial in 1995. Busy with other things, I declined. Truth to tell, I had a decidedly mixed attitude toward sociology journals. Like many people, I found most journal articles competent but dull. Certainly my own best papers—if "best" means most cited—had almost invariably been rejected by major journals, *AJS* conspicuous among them. But Professor Tienda was persistent and eventually prevailed upon me.

Once I headed for the archives, the project took on a life of its own. Diligent searches in attics and cellars failed to find any early *AJS* archives, so the early years had to be reconstructed from the personal papers of various faculty. But those faculty files challenged much of the Chicago lore that I had picked up over the years. It became necessary to think about the history of the department more broadly in order to envision that of the *AJS*. At this point I became involved in Gary Fine's edited volume on the second Chicago school, to which I ended up contributing a chapter—coauthored with Manny Gaziano—about the faculty during the postwar period.

By now the *AJS* centennial year was looming ominously. I had become a dean, and the project was going much slower than expected. I had also become chair of the American Sociological Association's Publications Committee, which gave me a bird's-eye view of sociological publishing and a much broader set of theoretical issues to consider. I produced a draft of the first half of the *AJS* history in 1995, a draft that showed how much our visions of this project had diverged. On their side, the *AJS* board were horrified by the length of the paper and by the fact that it didn't include formal theories and tests of hypotheses. Analytic history baffled them. For me, by contrast, the historical complexities demanded a monograph. Understanding the *AJS* meant understanding the department and, as gradually became clear, understanding the discipline as well. Studying the *AJS* was a way of rethinking how disciplines and schools develop, a task that seemed theoretical enough. Moreover, I was plowing what seemed virgin soil; there was almost no serious historical investigation of the institutional structures of modern scholarly publication.

But the *AJS* demanded massive cuts and a complete rewrite. There was much negotiation, but to little purpose. The medium had become the message; the centennial history itself had come to exemplify one of the things I was writing about—the metamorphosis of the *Journal* into a narrow, rigid structure, unable to reach beyond its fixed place.

By the time I had written something that I thought was a satisfactory and complete draft, there was a new editor at the *AJS*—Edward Laumann— and the centennial was two years gone. But the result was inevitable. Having asked me to write its history, the *AJS* decided that that history was not suitable for publication in its own pages. This sentence was true not only in the sense that the *AJS* turned down what I wrote, but also in the sense that the *AJS* in fact did not ultimately find its own history a suitable or legitimate topic for journal space. The *Journal*'s fiftieth anniversary had produced a saturnalia of articles about journal and discipline. But at one hundred, *AJS* did not dare reflect so much about itself. There were too many regressions to publish.

The *Journal*'s refusal made me rethink the whole project. In a sense, both the theme of my analysis and the meaning of my experience with the board were that the *AJS* had at some point ceased being the organ of a departmental vision and had become the organ of a discipline narrowly construed in intellectual terms if broad in geographical ones. As my data showed, in the 1920s and 1930s the *AJS* had been a central means through which the department and its intellectual program—a rather eclectic package that would come to be called the Chicago school—were constituted. In later years the move to truly national status brought standardization and, to some extent, intellectual sclerosis.

This theme converged with what had become the main theme of the chapter Gaziano and I had written on the Chicago faculty. For in the postwar period, the transformation of the department's retrospective self-image became complete, and the Chicago vision finally became identified in the minds of participants as something particularly Chicagoan rather than constitutive of sociology as a whole. It was only in the 1950s that the last survivors of the golden years began to admit that there had been a Chicago school. But admitting that meant admitting that there were other visions, that there was a larger discipline of which Chicago was only a part, not the center or epitome.

Thus the Gaziano-Abbott piece made a second leg to an analysis of departmental vision and disciplinary structure. The third leg to the tripod came from my American Sociological Association Sorokin Lecture, which had in 1993 become the latest in my long line of rejections from the *AJS*. In it I had argued that the theoretical essence of the Chicago school had been an insistence on the location of social facts in space and time. Indeed, as I found on rereading it, my paper made the claim that this kind of theory was more or less coextensive with sociology. I was in that sense stepping into the picture, making the old grandiose claims for the Chicago vision.

Thus it makes sense to bring these three pieces together into a book considering the changing relation between the Chicago school, its intellectual heritage, and the larger discipline. The two smaller pieces have already been published. Chapter 2 appeared in *A Second Chicago School?* edited by Gary Fine, under the title "Transition and Tradition." It has been slightly revised here. Chapter 7, under the title "Of Time and Place," was eventually published by North Carolina's *Social Forces*. I thank them for permission to reprint.

I have tied these three parts together with an introductory essay on the historiography of the Chicago school. This too was a project that grew like Topsy. Aiming to frame the book around the Chicago school, I began with the idea of producing a quick summary of "what the Chicago school had really been," but then I discovered that this particular "reality" was itself another mirage. So this piece too has become a substantive essay, a speculation on the nature of schools and on the relation between schools and their historiography.

The title of the book recycles a title already used by Stephen Diner for a paper on the early years of the Chicago department. I came up with it independently, but since I had read the Diner piece years ago, perhaps I was simply recalling it from some storeroom of the mind. It is a good title for what I am doing here, so I have retained it.

My thanks for this project are diverse. I have to thank the University of Chicago Press for some financial assistance on the *AJS* project. I must also thank my coauthor Manny Gaziano for letting me reuse our piece from the Fine volume; more important, I thank him for companionship in the archives. I thank Dan Meyer and the staff of the University of Chicago Special Collections Division for their unfailing support. Finally, the Warden and Fellows of Nuffield College in the University of Oxford provided intellectual hospitality that made writing chapters 5 and 6 an unmitigated pleasure.

I have also to thank the people who listened to the many horror stories the *AJS* project entailed: Colin Lucas, Richard Saller, Steve Pincus, Susan Gal, Steve Walt, Katherine Verden, and more than anyone else, my wife,

Susan Schlough. How Sue has stood my ranting about this affair I don't know, but I am sure it must have been very wearisome.

I cannot make the usual statement that my departmental colleagues have offered me help and support on this project. After all, most of this book consists of material they rejected in their character as the *AJS* board. But it is only fair to say that the editors of the *AJS* were very supportive, at least until they saw what I wrote. I therefore thank Edward Laumann and Marta Tienda, without whom this book would never have been published.

AMDG

Chicago, Illinois

31 August 1998

A brief note about the text: People got angry because the notes of my previous book were endnotes rather than footnotes. I have responded by placing the notes in this book at the foot of the page. However, the notes for chapters 2 through 6 use a specific and somewhat complex system of abbreviations. To avoid repeating my discussion of this system, I have placed the explanation in my comprehensive consideration of sources, which follows the epilogue. The reader will also find there some further acknowledgments, in particular of the research assistants who dug up astonishing amounts of information on our long-forgotten disciplinary colleagues.

Prologue

What exactly is, or was, the Chicago school? Was it a group of people or a set of ideas? Was it a brief moment or a long-running tradition? Was it produced by a confluence of larger forces or by the force of individual personalities? An enduring literature has worried these questions as a cat worries a struggling mouse. To be sure, the cat appears in no hurry to eat; these questions seem all the more fun because they remain unanswered.

Yet it is this unanswerability that is the key not only to our many images of the Chicago school, but to the Chicago school itself. For the Chicago school wasn't a thing at all, but rather a way of becoming a thing. Such was its theory, and such too was its practical reality. The book that follows may be taken as a meditation on the nature of the Chicago school and, through that, a meditation on the nature of social reality. Its real question—the one that underlies all those I have listed above—is the question of what it means to say that a social thing exists: that the Chicago school was or is something. Our linguistic conventions mislead us here, for the phrase Chicago school is a noun, and as such we assimilate it to model nouns like table or building and imagine for it a similarly fixed existence. But the Chicago school, I shall argue, was not a thing, a fixed arrangement of social relationships or intellectual ideas that obtained at a given time. It was rather a tradition of such relationships and ideas combined with a conception of how that tradition should be reproduced over time.

I shall investigate that tradition historically. This might seem a trivial point, but it is not. For I mean "historically" in its proper sense of "processually." The Chicago school is not some videotape, ever perfect, opening with a shot of Robert Park and Ernest Burgess engaged in timeless talk as they write up *Introduction to the Science of Sociology* in their Harper Library office and moving on through the great names and moments of the 1920s. One can all too easily create such teleological tales, in which the school springs almost inevitably out of the heady mix of early twentieth-century America. No, the Chicago school was contingent and accidental. Indeed, it is the school's refusal to be trapped that keeps the basic questions about it so open.

So I shall take a number of historical glances at the Chicago tradition

1

and try to capture the particular arrangements that make it a reality. I begin by reviewing the historiography of the Chicago school. To make sense of this bewildering literature, we must reconceptualize our idea of the school's "being." We have to rethink it as an intersection between a number of social strands and to imagine its "existence" as tied up in its ability to transform those social forces that constituted it.

I then turn, in chapter 2, to the reenactment of the Chicago tradition after the Second World War. Here I undertake an extremely detailed historical analysis, showing how the school in some sense emerged as a complex relation among constituent parts, rather than as a phenomenon instantiated in this or that person. The first section considers the details of faculty politics and departmental structure, trying to undermine our image of the Chicago school (first or second) as "made up of" this or that group of people. The second section reads in detail the massive self-study done by the department in 1951–52, investigating the verbatim construction of a vision for sociology. In many ways this was the period and even the very conversation that formalized the image of the first Chicago school.

Chapters 3 through 6 consider the first one hundred years of the *American Journal of Sociology*. Here the focus is less on the department than on one of its institutions. One important aim here is to excavate the deep history of scholarly publication; most work on scholarly journals is intolerably presentist. Moreover, the *AJS* is both part of and separate from the department. So I investigate the *AJS* in part to show the networked character of the Chicago school, the way it arises in the relations between the department and its discipline, relations in which the *AJS* has long played the central mediating role. I should emphasize that the very nature of the *AJS* has changed over the past century in ways that its continuity of name conceals. It began as a completely personal affair but became in its middle years a truly departmental journal. In later years it became a disciplinary institution largely beyond departmental control. But the discipline also was transformed, as we shall see, for it was in its early days very nearly dominated by the journal and its publisher, only to develop autonomously and then eventually to force the *AJS* to its own terms. Not only did the relations between a set of social institutions change, the institutions themselves underwent fundamental rearrangements. To understand the *AJS*'s history is to see this changing balance of department, journal, and discipline, and indeed to look beyond those three to the world of sociological ideas on the one hand and the larger environment of universities and scholarly publication on the other. Again, I focus on how an institution like the *AJS* exists as a lineage through time, not as a fixed entity.

One cannot contemplate the recent history of the *AJS* without thinking prescriptively about the future of journals. My study of the present state of sociological journalism takes me from description and theory to a prescriptive meditation on where our publishing ought to be headed. Continuing this prescriptive turn, the final chapter contains my own polemical reading of the Chicago tradition. As the reader will by then realize, such polemical readings are in fact the foundation of the tradition itself. To be a self-conscious writer in the Chicago tradition is to undertake such a reading. Moreover, the Chicago tradition—like the Marxist one in its different way—has always argued for a unity of thought and action. Prescription is to flow from intellectual judgment. I argue, then, that the fundamental insight of the Chicago tradition has been to take the location of social facts seriously, to see all social life as situated in time and place. This insight, I hold, can redirect and rebuild sociological inquiry.

There will be times when the reader will wonder what has become of the general themes I have stated here: the reconceptualization of social reality and the analysis of institutions as traditions. There will be thickets of detail, copses of complexity, and virtual forests of fact. But the social world is made by activity in structure, and we must therefore begin with action and detail, with social activity in its immediate contexts of social time and place. The sustaining themes will always remain, a road through the complexity to what I hope is a new, yet also a very old, view of the social world.

1 The Historiography of the Chicago School

The Chicago school of sociology has become big news. A swelling stream of books and articles has profiled its leaders and discussed its work. It has been taken to exemplify the very concept of "school."

This interest is recent; the 1960s saw a total of four articles on the Chicago school. But since 1970 has come a steadily increasing flow of work.[1] Urban sociologists, social psychologists, and ethnographers have all tried their hands at annexing the Chicago tradition even while Marxists and feminists have worked equally hard to debunk it. Surprisingly, much of the interest has come from Europe. From France Manuel Castells's 1968 article "Y a-t-il une sociologie urbaine?" launched a reconsideration of Chicago's urban studies. From Sweden Ulf Hannerz's 1980 book *Exploring the City* appropriated the Chicago tradition for anthropology. From England Martin Bulmer provided in 1984 the first fully archival treatment of the Chicago school, and Dennis Smith in 1988 published what remains its most radical reinterpretation. By the 1990s, there were original summary works on the Chicago school in Polish, Italian, French, Japanese, and Spanish.

Historical writing on Chicago is of two kinds. There is of course explicit historical analysis, aiming to delimit and examine the strategies, methods,

---

1. This chapter is based on a complete listing of all articles in First Search containing the phrase "Chicago school." I have also reviewed the *Social Sciences Index* and its predecessors from 1963 (where First Search coverage of *Sociological Abstracts* picks up) back to the 1930s. In addition, I have augmented the database with searches on particular Chicago faculty members as well as through nonautomated bibliographical chaining (tracing major references in order to pick up material on the Chicago school that is not keyword indexed as such; e.g., Hannerz's *Exploring the City*). Undoubtedly there are still omissions, for which I apologize. I have in a few cases referred the reader to material whose abstracts made it seem particularly important but that I am unable to read for want of language skills. My French is fine, but my German and Italian are rudimentary, and my Dutch nonexistent.

I should note that Routledge has just published a four-volume collection containing forty articles on the Chicago school from various periods, with an introduction by Ken Plummer (1997). It contains a fair amount of interesting material. Plummer's introduction is a basic discussion of the school's history, although it does not review historiographical problems and controversies. Kurtz's (1984) effort remains the most comprehensive bibliographical introduction to the writings of the Chicago school and its inheritors.

or people thought to make up the Chicago school. Writers of such works pursue their analysis from the point of view of the school—for itself, in its time, as it thought it was. But there is also much work chronicling the Chicago school in the process of invoking it in current substantive and methodological arguments, sometimes for its intellectual content, sometimes for its halo of legitimacy, sometimes for its utility as a target. These invocations may take the form of imagining a second and even a third Chicago school along with the original, inventing and rearranging various lines of intellectual descent.

The myths produced by these implicit characterizations have often overshadowed more explicit historical analysis, with the result that the underlying history is somewhat obscure. I therefore begin this chapter with a very brief sketch of the conventional history of the original Chicago school. I then move on to explicit historical interpretations and finally to the broader stream of implicit characterizations and lesser historical works.

My principal substantive object here is to review historical writing about Chicago. But I have also two subsidiary, theoretical aims. First, I want to reflect on the combination of solidity and fluidity that characterizes cultural objects like "the Chicago school." While I shall consider this topic more extensively in chapter 2, here I wish to show how the Chicago school was one thing to those who participated in it, another thing to its immediate inheritors at Chicago, and various other things to later writers. I want thereby to consider the relation between a set of events and people's constructions of them, both at the time and later. And at the same time I want to consider whether those events in fact made up a social entity with some obligatory character, either structural or causal. Was the Chicago school anything more than a list of events to be interpreted in any fashion desired?

My second theoretical aim is simpler. I wish to propose a natural history of traditions of historical writing, a characteristic pattern in which such traditions unfold. Obviously this aim is speculative. I have only one case at hand. But there is a pattern in this case that seems to generalize to many others.

I begin, then, with a brief discussion of the conventional understanding of the Chicago school.

The Chicago School as History and as Label

The customary view is that the Chicago school comprises a period, a set of professors, a set of students, and a body of work. The period is roughly the interwar years, about 1915 to 1935. The core faculty were Robert Park (on the faculty 1914–34) and Ernest Burgess (1916–52). To

Robert Park   1915 - 1935
Ernest Burgess

these might be added their contemporary Ellsworth Faris (1920–40), as well as W. I. Thomas (1895–1918) for the earlier period and Louis Wirth (1931–52) and Herbert Blumer (1931–52) for the later one. The students involved, most of whom wrote dissertations under Park and Burgess, included Wirth and Blumer as well as Charles Johnson, Everett Hughes, Nels Anderson, Ruth Cavan, Lyford Edwards, R. E. L. Faris, Harvey Zorbaugh, Paul Cressey, Walter Reckless, E. Franklin Frazier, Ernst Mowrer, Clifford Shaw, and many others.

The work these people produced falls under no simple characterization or single paradigm. There is, however, a typical stance to it, one that sets it apart from other sociological work at the time—for example, from the work inspired by Franklin Giddings at Columbia. It is often about the city and, if so, nearly always about Chicago. It is processual—examining organization and disorganization, conflict and accommodation, social movements and cultural change. It imagines society in terms of groups and interaction rather than in terms of independent individuals with varying characteristics. Methodologically it is quite diverse, but it always has a certain empirical, even observational flavor, whether it is counting psychotics in neighborhoods, reading immigrants' letters to the old country, or watching the languid luxuries of the taxi-dance hall. Even when the Chicagoans counted, they counted real people rather than disembodied ones.

In retrospect, the work can be seen to have some clear emphases. Some of these were conceptual, like the tradition's interest in the link between individual and group "minds," the problem it called "social psychology." Others were empirical, like the intensive focus on the city. Still others were theoretical, like the idea of ecology. But none of these emphases was absolute. It was rather the stance of investigation, the intensity of commitment, and the structural and processual vision—if anything—that made the Chicago school a "real" cultural unit.

However, since conceptual foci have been among the organizing principles of the debates about the school, it is useful to sketch them in a little more detail. There were three more or less self-conscious foci for departmental work. (By 1950 these were the three central examination areas.) The first was social psychology. The central progenitor of this concern was Thomas, with his concepts of attitudes and wishes. But also important—to a degree that has been much debated since—were the psychological ideas of the pragmatists James, Dewey, and Mead, as well as those of their colleague Charles Horton Cooley and their student Ellsworth Faris.

The second focus was what came to be called "social organization." This too had its roots in Thomas's writings. But it was also the animating concern of much of the work of Park, Burgess, and their students, particularly their work on Chicago. In later incarnations, the concern with social organization became identified with the fieldwork supervised by Hughes and his colleague Lloyd Warner.[2]

The third conceptual focus was ecology. Again, this was an animating theme of Park and Burgess's work, from the celebrated concentric zone theory to the list of community areas that still names the Chicago neighborhoods seventy years later. The ecological tradition had diverse roots and connections, which have been explored by Gaziano (1996). In a sense it made a twin with social organization; for while social organization studied the location of social events in time and process, social ecology studied their location in space and social structure.

In mentioning the Hughes-Warner epoch I have gone beyond the traditionally accepted waning of the Chicago school in the mid-1930s. But since the later history of the school has become a topic for many of the historical writers considered below, it is useful to sketch that history quickly. The departure of Park in 1934 is usually taken to mean the end of the school. But former student Hughes and anthropologist Warner arrived in the late 1930s to revivify many of the traditional Chicago concerns. After the war, the department saw an extraordinary generation of students, many of whom followed the traditional Chicago credo, even while others took up various newer sociologies. Those who followed in the old tradition—particularly the students of Blumer, Hughes, and Warner—are sometimes referred to as a second Chicago school. But it is important to recognize that they were not necessarily dominant in the department at the time and, indeed, that distinguished work of all kinds was being done at Chicago in the postwar period. (Chapter 2 considers this period in detail.)

The postwar glow was brief. By the mid-1950s the department was tearing itself apart. However, one student of the immediate postwar period—Morris Janowitz—returned to Chicago in the 1960s and tried to rebuild some of the older structures and concerns. His students are sometimes called a third Chicago school, but his efforts were clearly only one among many attempts to appropriate the older tradition. They simply happened to take place at Chicago, while others took place elsewhere.

The idea of a Chicago school is usually attributed to Luther L. Bernard's

2. Although the fieldwork tradition had a direct lineage back to Park, it also derived from anthropology via Warner (an anthropologist) and through the disciplinarily ambiguous figure of Robert Redfield, who was a graduate of the anthropology track of the Sociology Department itself (hence a peer of Wirth, Blumer, and Hughes in graduate school) and, more to the point, who was Robert Park's son-in-law.

1930 paper "Schools of Sociology." In the course of that paper Bernard did use the phrase "Chicago school" in something like its modern sense. But Bernard's other "schools" were not the "Columbia school" or other such sociologies. Beginning with the Greeks, his paper moved through the "Social Contract school" (Locke) and the "Ethic-Philosophical school" (Hutcheson) to the "Philosophy of History school" (Vico) and various nineteenth-century "Practical and Applied" schools. Bernard's concept of school thus seems flexible indeed.

But he did see Chicago as an identifiable collectivity. He mentioned human ecology, making it a subsegment of "behaviorist sociology" (the school to which he himself vowed allegiance) and called it a mere derivation of "the old anthropogeography" (1930, 129). In a similar swipe, he disposed of Park and Burgess's sociology text in a footnote. When he did mention a Chicago school by name (in another footnote, 131 n. 83), he spoke of it as the "chief representative in this country" of the "somewhat metaphysical viewpoint" of Durkheim! Bernard also spoke of a "personal school" of Robert Park, comparing it to Durkheim's personal school but invoking the comparison only to dismiss all such schools as unscientific personality cults (133).[3]

Bernard's glancing mention of Chicago apparently bespoke a broader consciousness. Maurice Halbwachs, writing in 1932 on "Chicago, expérience ethnique," wrote: "If there exists, at the University of Chicago, an original school of sociology, this is not unrelated to the fact that these scholars do not have to look very far for a subject of study" (1932, 17, my translation). Halbwachs's matter-of-fact locution suggests that Chicago was already generally seen as a unity of some sort by the beginning of the 1930s.

The first really substantial labeling of a Chicago school was, however, in Milla Alihan's book-length and largely negative analysis of what she called the "ecological school." Alihan's attack on the Chicago paradigm, published in 1938, clearly identified a school of work, a group of adherents, a style of analysis, and a body of theory. Although she too defined the Chicago school as a personal one (of Park), she saw much better than Bernard its coherence as a larger social structure, however much she doubted its worth as an intellectual enterprise.[4]

3. Of course Bernard had a personal agenda. He hated Chicago for passing him over when they replaced W. I. Thomas with Ellsworth Faris. He hated Faris both personally and as a representative of Meadean social psychology. In fact in 1931 he was about to lead a putsch against Chicago in the American Sociological Society, and it is little wonder that he labeled a Chicago school only in order to vilify it.

4. Alihan was a philosophy student at Columbia. I do not know of evidence suggesting that her book reflected institutional rivalry, although among her advisers was at least one prominent figure in Columbia social science, Robert MacIver.

Despite Alihan's clear identification, the actual label "Chicago school" does not seem to have been a staple of sociological discourse in the 1940s or even the 1950s. Shils's 1948 review of sociology did not mention the Chicago school by name, although it devoted many pages to decrying the atheoreticality of Chicago writings even while praising their documentary richness. The *International Index* (the precursor of the *Social Science Index*) and its imitator *Sociological Abstracts* (from 1963) have no entries for a "Chicago school of sociology" before 1964. Textbooks of the 1950s make minimal mention even of Park, much less of the Chicago school. Robert Nisbet's influential theory text *The Sociological Tradition* (1966) did not mention Chicago at all.

The situation changed somewhat by the late 1960s. David Matza's *Becoming Deviant*—a central book in late 1960s sociology—was constructed as a dialogue with the Chicago school, which it explicitly named. And Lewis Coser—a former teacher in the College of the University of Chicago—did include Robert Park, George Herbert Mead, and later W. I. Thomas and Florian Znaniecki in his widely read *Masters of Sociological Thought* (1971, 2d ed. 1977). But the general textbooks of the 1970s and 1980s still gave the Chicago school only a paragraph or two in the chapter on urban analysis. If the text came from the softer side of sociology, Chicago might also be mentioned in the discussion of interaction and symbols. This level of representation has remained stable virtually to the present. (For a review of texts see Brunt 1993.)

The relative invisibility of Chicago in the broader discipline has a number of obvious sources. From the 1940s onward much of sociology came to think of itself as a science, uninterested in what it defined as a prescientific past.[5] Moreover, the quantitative party that led this change was strongly associated with another department (Columbia). But the invisibility also reflected the manufacture, by Talcott Parsons particularly, of a Weber-Durkheim genealogy for sociology, a genealogy that would remain unmodified until a later generation insisted on adding Marx to the pantheon in the 1970s. Old Chicago was thus very much the sociology against which both the new quantitative studies and the new East Coast theory wanted to define themselves. It was neither highly statistical on the one hand nor European on the other.

But as chapter 2 shows, the idea of a Chicago school was not really clear even in the heads of the Chicagoans themselves until the early 1950s, when the waning of the phenomenon seemed to require its votaries to conceptualize it objectively. Both internal weakness (the squabbling between

---

5. Ironically, the same charge of scientific elitism has been leveled against the Chicago school itself. See Bulmer 1984 and Deegan 1988.

Blumer, Wirth, and Hughes) and external threats (the dominance of Harvard and Columbia) finally made a cohesive ideology important.

The Major Historiography

Historical writing about Chicago sociology falls roughly into three major periods. The first period condensed the image of the thing to be studied. The second brought comprehensive historical interpretations. The third brought both revisionism and complexification. Obviously these periods are only roughly delimitable, but they are a useful guide for analysis.

The early period comprises the 1960s and 1970s. R. E. L. Faris's *Chicago Sociology, 1920–1932* (first published in 1967) and James Carey's *Sociology and Public Affairs* (1975) were the anchor works. Faris had been a student during the first Chicago school years, and Carey (also a Chicago Ph.D.) had collected extensive interviews with the students of that period. Faris's book argued strongly that there *was* such a thing as a Chicago school. It identified major figures within the school—Park, Thomas, Burgess, and Faris—and insisted that the tradition had three parts: social ecology, urban studies, and social psychology.[6] Carey's interpretation emphasized the strong connections between the Chicago school sociologists and various groups outside sociology: reformers, professionals, city bureaucrats, and others. Much of Chicago's strength, Carey argued, stemmed from its extraordinary involvement in public affairs. Carey also traced in detail the background and experience of the students and faculty of the first Chicago school.

Both of these works, like most early works in the historiography of intellectual movements, emphasized personalities. Robert Park was absolutely central to both accounts, but Thomas, Wirth, Blumer, and even department founder Albion Small figured strongly as well, not just as administratively central organizers, but also as idiosyncratic personal forces. This personality theme would be continued in another work of this early stage, Winifred Raushenbush's fond biography of her former employer Robert Park, which appeared in 1979.

Another formative work of this first period, solicited by Morris Janowitz for his new series, the Heritage of Sociology, was James Short's collection *The Social Fabric of the Metropolis*. A graduate student from the

---

6. This view came directly from the department's own self-conception, as was illustrated by the debates in the early 1950s, discussed in chapter 2. But it would be repeatedly questioned as would-be heirs fought over Robert Park's legacy. The book's naming of Faris as a central faculty member is not merely due to filial piety. Although he published little, Faris was an influential teacher.

second Chicago school era, Short pulled together a set of short classic pieces that embodied the style of the original Chicago school.

As I noted above, during these early stages of its historical description the Chicago school also figured to some extent in collections on the theories and history of sociology. Even the new radical writers of the 1970s confronted the Chicago school, a fact that testifies to its rising importance in disciplinary consciousness. In *The Coming Crisis of Western Sociology*, Alvin Gouldner largely bypassed the Chicago school in order to train his heavy artillery on Parsons, but Herman and Julia Schwendinger (in *The Sociologists of the Chair* [1974]) spent considerable time branding the Chicago school as a lackey of capitalism.[7] As Dennis Smith later remarked in *The Chicago School*, the Schwendingers sounded "faintly reminiscent of Wisconsin or Kansas in the 1880s or 1890s" (1988, 15–16). They had a difficult time cramming the Chicago writers into their boxes, being forced to gainsay Albion Small's open-mouthed admiration of Marx and to portray the unrelentingly social psychology of Mead and Thomas as psychologically reductionist. Park and Burgess they called technocrats, working at "the most absurd heights of obscurantist abstraction."[8] The radical critique of the Chicago school continues fitfully into the present (e.g., Satzewich 1991).

These positive and negative works established "the Chicago school" firmly as a historiographical object. By 1980 the time, the place, the people, and the ideas were framed and sketched in. The late 1970s and early 1980s brought maturity and clarity to studies of the Chicago school. The major new interpretations came from Fred Matthews, Paul Rock, David Lewis and Richard Smith, and Martin Bulmer. Matthews, an intellectual historian, published in 1977 a large and subtle study of Robert Park. Park, he felt, was infinitely more complex than the traditional myths had made him. The complexities of his family life, the intensity of his commitments, his cu-

---

7. The Schwendinger analysis thus looked toward Kolko, Weinstein, and the other theorists of "corporate liberalism," a term that had begun to pass from the scene even as the Schwendingers wrote, being replaced by the more sophisticated and microlevel Marxist concepts of the new labor historians and others.

8. This labeling was all the more arresting because Chicago had, since the 1950s, been loosely identified with opposition to the mainstream politics of the ASA, in part through Chicago's alignment with the Society for the Study of Social Problems. As of the 1960s, the Chicago tradition was loosely defined as oppositional, radical. It is true that C. Wright Mills in his 1943 essay "The Professional Ideology of the Social Pathologists" had seen a considerable number of Chicago-influenced writers as conservative in their love for rural values and their unwillingness to theorize structural problems in society. But Mills's essay did not mention Chicago by name and indeed considered numerous writers who had no connection with Chicago. I discuss this issue in more detail at the end of chapter 2.

rious mixture of success and failure made a heady mix. For Matthews, however, the ultimate heart of Park was not his ideas per se, but a certain stance toward investigation, an attitude toward the work of sociology.

In the Lewis and Smith interpretation, by contrast, Park disappeared from the story. Focused completely on issues of social psychology, Lewis and Smith simply ignored ecology and urban studies, the other two legs of the Chicago tripod. Their principal aim was to show that Mead had not in fact been central to the Chicago tradition. They began by defining that tradition as comprising only symbolic interactionism, which they identified as the Dewey-Thomas-Cooley-Blumer social psychology, anchored on the concept of a social self developed and sustained in interaction. Mead, they countered, belonged to the "social realist" strand of pragmatism and hence was opposed to the "nominalist" social psychology of symbolic interactionism. Lewis and Smith's central aim was to attack what they saw as the selective rereading of the Meadean heritage by Blumer and later writers like Meltzer, Petras, and Reynolds (1975).[9]

Paul Rock (1979) stood between Matthews and Lewis and Smith. For him symbolic interactionism was the core of Chicago, but Park played an important role in shaping that core through his articulation of the formalism of Georg Simmel with immediate studies of social life. Indeed, even in his interpretation of the role of pragmatism in symbolic interaction, Rock was concerned to trace the influence of Continental philosophy (Kant through Simmel and Park, Hegel through Cooley, Dewey, and Mead) on symbolic interactionism. Rock was at pains to emphasize the oral and fragmentary nature of symbolic interactionism, a sociological paradigm that, in his eyes, seemed to practice what it preached: fluidity, process, change. These qualities, in Rock's view, played a central role in exposing symbolic interactionism to attacks from more systematic sociologies worked out in architectonic rigor.

In contrast to all these writers, Martin Bulmer focused on the institutional structures of the Chicago school. For him the essential matters were neither persons nor ideas but rather the structure of funding, the organization of the Social Science Division and the Local Community Research Committee, and the ability of Burgess in particular to hold the diverse methods and investigations of the Chicagoans together within a loose framework cobbled together out of the theoretical apparatus provided by Thomas and Park. In emphasizing diversity, Bulmer was attempting to redress what seemed to him an overemphasis on qualitative methods in most

---

9. In the Lewis and Smith account, Park was simply another symbolic interactionist! (Lewis and Smith 1980, 5).

interpretations of Chicago. (He had Lewis and Smith explicitly in mind.) In Bulmer, too, we find for the first time specific attention to the "making of a moment," the questioning of how Chicago sociology could have bloomed so quickly, produced so much, and faded so rapidly.

By the mid-1980s, then, there had emerged in the major historical interpretations a much clearer image of the Chicago school, but one that seemed quite divided. In the Rock and the Lewis and Smith interpretations, the Chicago school was most strongly identified with social psychology. The interactionist pragmatism underlying Thomas's and Mead's psychologies was not traced into other areas. In the Matthews and Bulmer interpretations, by contrast, the heart of the Chicago school was the fieldwork and ecological tradition, although both writers saw the combination of this with social psychology, particularly in Thomas. The divided image in part echoed a split within the tradition itself, for as chapter 2 shows, the opposition between the social psychology and social organization camps had become marked in the department by the early 1950s, the heyday of the second Chicago school.

But it was also true, as Lyn Lofland has pointed out in a fine essay, that "the 'Chicago School' is a kind of projective device; descriptions of it seem to reveal as much about those doing the describing as about the phenomenon itself" (1983, 491). The increasingly clear image of the historians did not percolate into the general consciousness, which continued to use the Chicago tradition as it saw fit, for current intellectual purposes. The most sustained of these current-purpose interpretations was offered by Berenice Fisher and Anselm Strauss, who in a sequence of articles and chapters (Fisher and Strauss 1978a,b, 1979a,b) explored and emphasized the interactionist and processual character of the *entire* Chicago tradition from Thomas forward. Unlike most retrospective writers, Fisher and Strauss emphasized the diversity of the tradition, but unlike many of the historians they believed that diversity masked an underlying intellectual coherence.

The late 1970s and early 1980s also saw a new emergence of the Chicago school on the European scene. In 1979 Yves Grafmeyer and Isaac Joseph published French translations of the crucial theoretical essays from Park, Burgess, and McKenzie's *The City,* along with related essays by Simmel and Wirth's famous "Urbanism as a Way of Life," prefacing them all with an interpretive essay. More important, Swedish anthropologist Ulf Hannerz wrote extensively on the Chicago school in his *Exploring the City* (1980), an attempt to establish and enclose a territory for urban anthropology. The polemical purpose of appropriating for anthropology the ethnographic study of the city sometimes overwhelmed Hannerz's historical interpretation of sociological writers. But the chapter on Chicago ethnographers did cover several major works in detail; another chapter was devoted to Erving Goffman (defined, as Goffman often defined himself, as "really an anthropologist"); and Wirth's "Urbanism" essay was the touchstone of yet another chapter. Indeed, Wirth's essay had already commanded European attention, for by 1970 Manuel Castells's Marxist attack on it (1968) had already begun to assume the status of a classic.

The late 1980s brought the first waves of revisionism, which reached full flood by the 1990s. The first revision came in Lee Harvey's (1987a) debunking of the various "myths" of the Chicago school. Harvey's book contained extraordinary administrative detail on the department and its members, but its main aim (in which it was largely successful) was to show that Chicago had not been dominated by social reform, had not been antitheoretical, had not been dogmatically qualitative, and had not been predominantly Meadean. Harvey went on to argue that the history of the department after 1935 was not a falling away, but rather a restriction and ossification of the original vision. Originally eclectic, by the 1950s the Chicago tradition had become what the myths projected back into the glory days: Meadean, dogmatically qualitative, and perhaps even dogmatically ethnographic. The "myths" were thus the realities of a later present, in fact that of the second Chicago school.

Much more sweeping were the works of Mary Jo Deegan, Dennis Smith, and Rolf Lindner, all published at the end of the decade. All three took the form of reembedding the Chicago school in larger traditions. For Deegan, this was the tradition of social reform and involvement symbolized by Jane Addams. Delving into the archives, Deegan (1988) emphasized the close and reciprocal relation between pre-Park figures at Chicago (Small, Mead, and Thomas) and the social reform movement, a connection that was broken by the advent of Park and his attempt to make social investigation "scientific."

Deegan's polemical agenda—to establish female origins for ideas associated with the Chicago school and to delineate the school's neglect of women—led her to a strategy of close analysis of personal relations. But the general relationship between the Chicago school and the social reformers is a larger historical question that has only begun to be explored. Bulmer too had spent many pages on the relation between the Chicago school and the social survey movement, the name given to the type of nonacademic empirical investigation produced by the reformers. He more or less accepted the Chicago school's own diagnosis of its difference from that movement—its

increasingly theoretical and "scientific" cast.[10] Bulmer and others have
subsequently investigated the social survey movement at length (Bulmer,
Bales, and Sklar 1991), while yet others have studied its greatest single effort, the Pittsburgh Survey (Greenwald and Anderson 1996). These works
make it clear that methodologically the Chicago school owed much indeed
to the survey tradition and was undoubtedly its most direct inheritor. Platt
(1994) has made much the same point.

Dennis Smith's volume on the Chicago school, published in the same
year as Deegan's (1988), placed it in quite a different context, that of general social critique. Smith's book responded to the radical critique of the
Chicago school begun by the Schwendingers. For Smith, the Chicago
school comprised liberal critiques of capitalism: serious critiques, to be
sure, but critiques accepting the basic framework of American democracy.
This interpretation meant that Smith saw the first Chicago school as merely
part of a larger Chicago sociological tradition stretching from Albion Small
through Thomas and Park to Wirth and William Ogburn and ultimately on
to Janowitz. Although the symbolic interactionists had for years been arguing for a Chicago tradition evolving over a long time rather than bounded
in a brief interval, this was the first identification of another such "long
strand" to the tradition.[11]

The third of the major revisionist works of this period was Rolf Lindner's *The Reportage of Urban Culture,* first published in German in 1990.
(The book was published in English translation in 1996.) Unlike Deegan
with her emplotment of the Chicago school within the survey and reform
tradition and Smith with his colligation of a longer tradition of theoretical
social critique, Lindner took Park as the central embodiment of the
Chicago school and located him squarely in the tradition of turn of the century newspaper reporting. Although recognizing an alternative lineage of
Park as a descendant of the Malinowskian fieldwork tradition, Lindner
found stronger links with the habitus of journalism.[12] But he also offered a

10. It is an interesting comment on gradualism in social science that Hannerz, like many
others before him, had attacked the Chicago school for exactly the reverse—atheoreticality.

11. The urbanist neo-Chicagoans, who formed into a group of "Chicago irregulars" and
founded the journal *Urban Life* in 1969 (see Thomas 1983a), often regarded the Chicago tradition as insufficiently critical. This argument would become stronger with the inevitable arrival of "critical ethnography," begotten by radicalism out of the old ethnography (see
Thomas 1983b).

12. This lineage is being reinforced by more recent German scholars who have unearthed
an important set of journalistic reports on Berlin that bear an uncanny resemblance to the
[later] products of the Chicago school. See Jazbinsek and Thies 1997 and also Smith 1979.

subtle reading of the Chicago school's relation to the reformist tradition, from which he felt it had only half emancipated itself. Indeed, he argued that "the Chicago sociology of the 1920s forms a point of intersection between two different cultural currents, the archetypes of which are the *reformer,* on the one hand, and the *reporter,* on the other" (1996, 199; his emphasis).

Thus all the revisionist work of the late 1980s took the form of reinserting the Chicago school into the flows of larger histories. For Smith, this took the simple form of arguing that the Chicago school of the interwar period was actually part of a much larger and continuous Chicago tradition that itself was part of liberal critiques of capitalism. For Deegan, Platt, and others who studied the survey/reform tradition, the first Chicago school needed to be embedded in the larger turn to formal study of society, a turn that grew out of reformism in the late nineteenth and early twentieth centuries. Chicago sociology seemed much less revolutionary in such a context, since urban ethnography and surveys had a long prior history. A similar argument, but tracing a different ancestry, was Lindner's attribution of Park's stance to the traditions of journalism. This linking of the Chicago school with writing and letters was echoed in a line of papers tracing links between the Chicago school and literary fiction—Lindner (1993) on James T. Farrell and Cote (1996) comparing Blumer and Steinbeck, for example.

Although these various revisionisms did represent a turning point in Chicago school historiography, none of them made an argument that was entirely new. Smith's idea of a Chicago tradition extending across several epochs had been foreshadowed by Fisher and Strauss's concept of a long interactionist tradition. Similarly, the school's reformist connections had long provided its only appearances in the general historical literature. The literary argument had a distinguished ancestor in Richard Wright's impassioned introduction to *Black Metropolis* (1945):

> I felt those extremes of possibility death and hope, while I lived half hungry and afraid in a city to which I had fled with the dumb yearning to write, to tell my story. But I did not know what my story was, and it was not until I stumbled upon science that I discovered some of the meanings of the environment that battered and taunted me. . . . The huge mountains of fact piled up by the Department of Sociology at the University of Chicago gave me my first concrete vision of the forces that molded the urban Negro's body and soul. . . . If in reading my novel, *Native Son,* you doubted the real-

ity of Bigger Thomas, then examine the delinquency rates cited in this book. (1945, xvii–xviii)

I should close this section with a discussion of histories of particular topics within the intellectual interests of the Chicago school. These range from specific reviews of theory and methods to such remarkable works as Reynolds's (1995) quixotic rereading of the history of criminology through a study of the career of Chicago school student John Landesco.

The interactionist-pragmatist lineage has been the most explicit object of attempts to codify an aspect of Chicago's theoretical heritage. (I shall consider this lineage below because of its highly presentist nature.) But there have also been historical interpretations of other scattered aspects of Chicago's intellectual history: Blake (1978) on Park's theorizing of collective behavior, Laperrière (1982) on the second Chicago school, Jaworski (1995) on Simmel's impact on Small, Park, and Hughes and (1996) on Park's and Hughes's impacts on Goffman, and Burns (1996) on the Chicago school and positivism.

There has been less work specifically on the methods of the Chicago school. Oberschall's (1972) brief early study was the lone specifically methodological history until the mid-1980s. There has been some work on ethnography (e.g., Jackson 1985 and Adler, Adler, and Rochford 1986), as well as Bodemann's (1978) interesting positive reading of the Chicago school's "engaged ethnography." In more recent years, writing about ethnography has become more textual/critical than historical. Denzin (1995) has provided the inevitable rereading of a Chicago classic from a textual point of view.[13]

Other methodological areas are less studied. Hammersley (1989) presents a useful summary of Blumer's lifelong and quite complicated reflection about sociological methodology. Verhoeven's 1980 interview with Goffman, published in 1993, recorded a famous insider's view of methods in the second Chicago school. Platt's general analysis of methods in the second school (1995) is detailed and magnificent. But Bulmer's book remains the main source on methods in the first Chicago school. (Platt's general history of sociological methods [1996] is, however, important as a reference.) Surprisingly, there is almost no work on ecology. Although there are some

13. I should also note Boelen et al. 1992, a retrospective on William Foote Whyte's *Street Corner Society*. Although Whyte had drafted the book before arriving to do graduate work, it did become a Chicago dissertation and, indeed, is the Press's biggest-selling sociological monograph of all time. Referring to Whyte and Warner, Platt (1996, 265 n. 16) raises the possibility of a "Harvard school" of ethnography.

single appreciations, (e.g., Burns 1980; Helmes-Hayes 1987), there is no sustained examination of the history of ecology as a method. On its theoretical history, see Gaziano (1996) and Maines, Bridges, and Ulmer (1996).

These particular topical histories do not challenge, but rather augment, the general interpretations given earlier. The major historiography of the Chicago school has a fairly simple trajectory. After spending thirty to forty years as a fond but somewhat unstructured recollection, the Chicago school received its first formal historical presentation about 1970. It was at this point that a particular period and particular people became firmly fixed as *the* Chicago school. In the subsequent decade, writers gradually gave substance to this image with a wide assortment of work, much of it biographical. By the early 1980s, the image was clear enough that there could be serious summary works and comprehensive studies of the school, as well as some controversial works contesting what were coming to be seen as standard interpretations. By the late 1980s these controversies had brought forth full revisionism. Writers like Deegan, Smith, and Lindner sought to reinsert the Chicago school into larger streams of inquiry and reform, seeing it less as an isolated moment and more as an instantiation of ongoing themes.

Other Genres, Other Visions

These explicitly historical studies of the Chicago school have been complemented by a host of other works. Some of these concern the Chicago school as a social phenomenon. Others focus primarily on its intellectual contributions. Works of substance, these invoke the Chicago school for present purposes, in current debates.

The first genre in the "social phenomenon" style comprises work that celebrates the Chicago tradition. Its simplest form is what we may call the "manufacturing Chicago" genre, work deliberately aiming to create a particular vision of Chicago's past. A peculiar fact about Chicago historiography is that such manufacture continues in the present. While intellectual traditions often receive their first formulations from hagiographic insiders, one expects historians to take over the past of a discipline as that past becomes less important to the forefront. Yet sociologists still regularly proclaim themselves the heirs of Robert Park or Herbert Blumer or Everett Hughes.

Undoubtedly the most industrious retrospective creator of the first Chicago school was Morris Janowitz. Himself a postwar graduate of Chicago, Janowitz returned to Chicago in 1962, a self-appointed prophet of the past. There he started the Heritage of Sociology series, which, despite its inclusive title, began as a republication of Chicago faculty and students: Small, Wirth, Park, Burgess, Ogburn, Frazier, Thomas. Also included in the series were the Park and Burgess text of 1921, James Short's (1971) collection of brief Chicago classics, and R. E. L. Faris's discussion of the department in the 1920s (republished in 1970 after an initial issue elsewhere). Bulmer's 1984 historical study would also be a Heritage volume, as would Lester Kurtz's more than comprehensive bibliography (1984) with its lengthy introduction.[14]

Janowitz himself wrote little about the Chicago school, his main contributions being introductions to the Park and Burgess text and to the collection of Thomas's writings in the Heritage of Sociology series. Rather, he tried to give the past reality by remaking it in the present. First, he saw to the hiring of Gerald Suttles, who became the core ethnographic teacher of a new generation. (Janowitz got people into the field but did not supervise them there.) Second, despite or sometimes because of his abrasive personality, Janowitz inspired a generation of students: William Kornblum, Albert Hunter, Charles Bosk, Ruth Horowitz, Thomas Guterbock, James Jacobs, Robert Bursik, and others. In doing so he rebuilt the mixture of ethnography, ecology, and commonsense theorizing that seemed to him the core of the Chicago tradition.[15]

But if Janowitz was the most industrious creator of Chicago's past, he was by no means alone. Gary Fine's 1995 edited volume, *A Second Chicago School?* also exemplifies the "manufacturing Chicago" genre. In area after area, the book traces a common pattern of thought, rooted in the traditional concerns of social psychology, fieldwork, and human ecology. Its vision is one of diaspora. For it the second Chicago school comprises the great

14. It is striking that early volumes also included Continental thinkers who had influenced the Chicago school but who had been omitted from the Parsons canon, the obvious example being Simmel. Kurtz was a Janowitz student and chair of the Chicago graduate student association, the Society for Social Research. It is likely that Janowitz's efforts played a large part in forwarding the historiography of the Chicago school. Certainly no other group of American sociologists has been the subject of so loud and energetic a tradition. The salad days of Columbia in the 1950s are remembered, but not as embodying a school. And there are neofunctionalists, to be sure, but other than a subtle invocation via the "neo" tag, the fabulous Harvard postwar generation remains unlabeled. Were there no other criterion for "schoolness" than self-consciousness, Chicago still would pass the test.

15. As I noted above, Janowitz's epoch is occasionally spoken of as a third Chicago school. But it was an echo of an echo, a relatively minor affair in a department bestrode by the mainstream quantitative work of James Coleman, Leo Goodman, and others. In fact, even the second school was only a part of the department's story at the time, for it lived alongside strong programs in substantive demography and survey analysis, as well as a variety of historical and other work. The separation of these traditions is largely retrospective. Dudley Duncan, for example, thought himself a student of both Ogburn and Blumer.

students of the period 1945–55, who took their ideas with them when they left to teach in the rapidly expanding American university system. To most of Fine's authors, themselves students of that postwar Chicago generation (and hence the would-be intellectual grandchildren of the first Chicago school), Chicago itself seemed seized by mainstream quantitative sociology in the late 1950s, and the Chicago school stance had to move on with the alumni to other departments.[16]

Beyond simple manufacturing of tradition lies a broader range of celebratory work whose impulse is to remind readers of figures and ideas from the Chicago tradition without making the analytic effort involved in reinterpreting that tradition. Often such celebration is organized around memoirs from old-timers. A major exemplar was the issue of *Urban Life* (11, no. 4) that in 1983 celebrated "The Chicago School: The Tradition and the Legacy." Here Nels Anderson and Ruth Cavan reminisced about the 1920s, Jon Snodgrass interviewed the now elderly jackroller, Martin Bulmer wrote about the Society for Social Research (an alumni association in the 1920s, later the department's graduate student association), and Albert Hunter, James Thomas, and Lyn Lofland reflected on the impact of the Chicago tradition on the present. Not surprisingly, given the venue, the Chicago tradition was defined by these writers overwhelmingly in terms of urban ethnography. But the social psychological accent was at least recognized, and the department's devotion to Mead (violently denied by Lewis and Smith three years earlier) was mentioned. The quantitative side of the department, however, indeed even the ecological and spatial tradition, disappeared almost completely.

Sociological Perspectives produced such an issue in 1988. For the first school period, there were memoirs from Kimball Young, riddled with factual errors but containing important nuggets of personal reminiscence. For the second school period, there were memoirs from Ralph Turner and Bernard Farber. Jonathan Turner contributed a strange argument blaming Chicago for contemporary sociology's distrust of general theory as well as

16. The concept of a second Chicago school is quite old; see LaPerrière 1982. Like most images of the first school, the image of the second school in the Fine volume (1995) elides the history in many ways. The great postwar generation at Chicago included Dudley Duncan, Albert Reiss, and Reinhard Bendix as much as it did Howard S. Becker, Ralph Turner, and Arnold Rose. Moreover, both Harvard and Columbia produced equally extraordinary and equally diverse cohorts in the immediate postwar years. It was the pent-up supply of talent, not some local magic, that produced the great postwar generations. What really made the second Chicago school different from those Harvard and Columbia groups was largely its concern about and, indeed, its retrospective objectification of, the first. See chapter 2. I should also mention, among "creations" of old Chicago, David Maines's industrious rehabilitation of Blumer.

for its excessive reliance on firsthand empirical research and quantitative analysis. In this collection the image of Chicago was more vague, admitting the eclectic mix of ethnography and quantitative work.[17]

A related genre is the "descendant departments" literature, tracing the diaspora to CUNY (Kornblum and Boggs 1986), to Arizona State (Ohm 1988), to Kansas (Van Delinder 1991), to Brandeis (Reinharz 1995), and so on. Nearly all such papers lament the 1950s turn of Chicago away from its roots, a turn that was both accidental and limited, as chapter 2 will show.

A final genre taking the Chicago school as a social phenomenon is less concerned with imagining or celebrating it than with considering it as an exemplary case of "schoolness." The core paper in this tradition was Tiryakian's "The Significance of Schools in the Development of Sociology" (1979). Tiryakian deprecated histories of social science in terms of great men, of pure ideas, or of general historical contexts. Central to sociology, he felt, were schools—groups of scholars in personal connection, with a charismatic leader, sharing a particular paradigm of empirical reality and a set of assumptions about how to investigate it. Tiryakian portrayed the charismatic leader as a man of big ideas, typically unable to translate his innovative view of the world into ordinary language. Epigones and auxiliaries actually spread the message.

Tiryakian based his model on the schools of Durkheim and Parsons (1979, 232 n. 8). The Chicago school was apparently forced on him by the logic of his argument. But his article spawned a host of follow-up work, a surprising amount of it focusing on the Chicago school. Faught (1980) interpreted Hughes's career in the light of Tiryakian's argument. Bulmer (1985) revisited the same empirical territory as Tiryakian and came to similar theoretical conclusions; a central figure, local support, and an open intellectual environment were essential. The same conclusion was reiterated by Cortese (1995). By contrast, Camic (1995) underscored the importance of local contingencies in shaping particular departments, although in the process accepting the outlines of the Bulmer-Tiryakian account of Chicago. Harvey (1987b), on the other hand, questioned Tiryakian's analysis as largely dictated by convenience.

All these genres of work, then, concern the Chicago school as a social phenomenon, a social and cultural structure with particular ancestors and

17. I am by no means sure I have found all the published "reminiscences" of Chicago. See also "Reminiscences of Classic Chicago," a transcript of a public conversation between Blumer and Hughes in 1969, published in Lofland 1980. The best quote in it is Hughes's "I don't like the idea of talking about a Chicago School or any other kind of school . . . go ahead and be a Chicago School if you like." Marx wasn't a Marxist, either.

descendants. They thus paralleled the more formal historical analysis of Chicago, providing an important reinforcement for the manufacture of a Chicago tradition. But a much larger literature invokes substantive ideas of the Chicago school in the context of current debates: urban studies, race and ethnic studies, and so on. These works are of less immediate interest here, but they do contain some useful historical work and are quite consequential because they have considerably wider readership than do the explicitly historical materials. It is their histories of Chicago that in fact define the public image of the school.

Some of this work has been inward looking, in particular the extensive literature on Chicago's theoretical heritage within the interactionist community. Such writing often takes the form of tracing the pragmatist roots of the school, an approach followed by Lewis and Smith (1980) as well as by Matthews (1985) in reviewing them. Feffer's 1993 book emphasized the reformism of pragmatism, as did Deegan's 1988 book and her comment (1996) on "feminist pragmatism." Joas's *Pragmatism and Social Theory* (1993) was a more theoretical account. In response to Joas, Denzin (1996) reread old pragmatism as a failure, urging a "poststructural" pragmatism based on the work of Nancy Fraser. A related (and quite tangled) literature has attempted to provide a core definition of symbolic interactionism, usually relying on some form of historical argument. See Meltzer, Petras, and Reynolds 1975, for an example. Rock's book (1979) is by far the most subtle of these. Another example, but off the usual track, is Lincourt and Hare's (1973) search for the influence of Chauncey Wright, Charles Sanders Peirce, and Josiah Royce on interactionism.

Nearly all of this work gives one the feeling that the details of history are far less important than its implications for who is "right" about symbolic interactionism today. But indeed most work on the ideas of the Chicago school is openly presentist, explicitly setting those ideas in the immediate context of current debates.

By far the majority of such substantive work concerns the Chicago school's view of the city. Over a quarter of the references retrieved for this review concerned urban studies in some degree. An extraordinary amount of this work (about a third of it) was not in English. Overwhelmingly, foreign attention to the Chicago school has been to its work on the city. (There are only relatively scattered foreign works on the Chicago version of social psychology, for example, a scarcity that contrasts with the profusion of American literature on this topic.)

Most work invoking the Chicago school's view of the city takes it as foundational in current debates. The typical article discusses the ways the

Chicago school both inaugurated the formal study of the city and provided a conception (ecological and successional) that has been challenged only in the past twenty-five years. Much work has been concerned with the criticism of the ecological view of the city by a variety of political economy perspectives after 1970. Lebas (1982) reviews this literature at length. More recent work on the city inevitably contains more or less extended study of the Chicago school's ideas.

Unlike the interactionists, the urbanists do not care who today has the relics and the writ. Usually the Chicago school figures as a tradition to be transcended or an orthodoxy to be overthrown. As a result, very little writing about the Chicago school's views of the city is explicitly historical; Chicago work is still part of the present. Miller's study of Wirth (1992) and Kuklick's notes on planning (1980) are the only exceptions. Miller notes a gradual change in Wirth's views, a shift away from the relatively standard Chicago-style passive assimilationism of *The Ghetto* to a belief in more explicitly driven individualism and democratization of social group relations. Kuklick's analysis notes the influence of Chicago school ideas in transforming federal housing policy, in particular the impact of successional ideas in focusing federal mortgage ratings on the race of borrowers. The central figure in that tangled story was, however, not a sociologist, but rather economics graduate student Homer Hoyt, whose monumental study of land values (1933) served as the foundation for emerging federal policies. (Hoyt was, however, strongly influenced by Robert Park. For a detailed discussion based on manuscript evidence, see Jackson 1985.)

By contrast with the urban literature, where the Chicago school still struts the stage as an active player and hence commands little "historical" attention, in the race and ethnicity literature the Chicago school's views are today seeing an extensive historical reevaluation after years of eclipse. The current profusion of studies of ethnicity and identity has led many writers down the diverse roads leading back to Robert Park. Park's theories of race relations profoundly shaped American conceptions of race, both directly and through their effects on major African American writers like Frazier, Johnson, Cayton, and Drake (see, e.g., Young 1994; Farber 1995). Park also wrote foundational work on relations between whites and Asians on the West Coast and began a flow of Asian American and Asian graduate students into Chicago that continues to this day, as Yu (1995) notes. The work of other Chicago figures has been less thoroughly examined. Warner's role in producing *Black Metropolis,* Wirth's as editor of the American edition of *An American Dilemma* (Salerno 1987, 25), and Janowitz's sponsoring of the conference-related Heritage of Sociology volume on black sociologists (Blackwell and Janowitz 1974) have not been studied. Frazier's work has of course seen considerable analysis, but as Platt (1992) has argued, the Chicago school was only one part of Frazier's story.

Work on Chicago studies of race and ethnicity has followed a slightly different history than work on the Chicago school in general. The 1960s saw numerous attacks on Park's theories, growing out of the continuing influence of Myrdal's *American Dilemma,* with its relatively psychologistic account of prejudice. At the same time, there was much work aiming to discredit Frazier, disliked by liberals because of the use (not in reality very extensive) made of his work in the Moynihan Report. By 1983 Fred Wacker published a response to this whole line of argument, replacing Park in his context by showing his radical break with the hereditarian and racist thought that had preceded him. But the opposition of Park to Myrdal has continued to fascinate many (e.g., Henry 1995). Views of Frazier have been revised by several writers, Platt the most important of them.

The two general works on ethnicity and the Chicago school are those of Stow Persons and Barbara Lal. Lal's *Romance of Culture in an Urban Setting* is a revisionist account, pointing to the similarities between Park's analysis and emerging themes within the study of urban minorities. (Lal's work, begun as a dissertation, first appeared in print as articles in the early 1980s and culminated in a 1990 book.) Lal emphasized the subjective, culturalist side of Park. Although she criticized Park for his inattention to larger structures of material determination, she underscored his anticipation of the many positive interpretations currently placed on minority subcultures. A similar view, extending the analysis to Hughes, Wirth, and later Chicago writers on race and ethnicity, is taken by Wacker (1995).

Persons's *Ethnic Studies at Chicago* is both more comprehensive and more dispassionate than Lal's book. It covers Chicago theorists from Small to Hughes and explicitly studies how they responded to and reshaped the larger context of racial and ethnic attitudes of their time. Persons makes Thomas, rather than Park, the central thinker in Chicago racial and ethnic writing. He focuses on the ways in which the concept of assimilation became reified into a universal directional process, undone only when Hughes reinserted racial and ethnic groups into the ecological framework emphasized by Burgess. In addition to his detailed discussions of Park and Thomas, Persons also examines Edward Reuter and E. Franklin Frazier as examples of workers in the Park tradition.

While the urban and race-ethnicity literatures have had a profound encounter with Chicago's history, the feminist literature has not. Aside from a handful studies of single individuals (Fish 1981 on Annie Marion MacLean and Kurent 1982 on Frances Donovan), Mary Jo Deegan's writings (e.g., 1988, 1995, 1996) constitute nearly the entire corpus of work on women and the Chicago school. Deegan's interpretation is part of her larger attempt to establish the existence of an alternative "feminist sociology" that grew in what she calls the "Chicago network." In her 1988 book Deegan was mainly preoccupied with demonstrating the Chicago school's derivative nature on the one hand and its deliberate exclusion of women from positions of professional eminence on the other. She paid less attention to delineating specifically masculine aspects of the theoretical stance of the school. The same can be said for Deegan's rather unflattering analysis (in Fine 1995) of the women of the second Chicago school, whose expectedly strong reply appears as Lopata's postscript in the same volume.

Deegan's work can also be seen as part of the feminist rediscovery of the centrality of women in American welfare politics and activity, a centrality that prior students of that area had never managed to get other historians to recognize. Another study relating reformist women and the Chicago school is Jennifer Platt's short article (1992) on Ethel Dummer, a Chicago philanthropist who, in addition to the sociological roles emphasized by Platt, was the dominant force behind William Healy and Augusta Bronner's formative work on juvenile delinquency. After their departure for Boston, Healy and Bronner's approach was institutionalized in the Institute for Juvenile Research, within which Chicago school research on delinquency (e.g., the work of Thrasher and Shaw) was based.

A specific concern of many European (particularly German) writers has been the Chicago school's role in biographical analysis. The method of corporate biography exemplified in *The Polish Peasant in Europe and America* never caught on in America, although Clifford Shaw and John Landesco applied it in studies of crime. Herbert Blumer's celebrated attack on the *Polish Peasant* in 1939 helped bury life history analysis as a sociological method, not to be resurrected until the work of Glen Elder in the 1960s and 1970s. But Europeans—particularly German sociologists—have recently become excited about Thomas's methods. Michael Harscheidt published a summary of this European tradition in 1989, commenting on the rise of computer-aided biographical analysis. (See also Niemeyer 1989; Pennef 1990; and Chanfrault-Duchet 1995.)

The topic of biographical analysis makes a useful link to the final literature I wish to note, biographical writing on the Chicago school itself. Writing on the Chicago school has often focused on individuals and personalities, and it is therefore not surprising that there is a substantial biographical literature about the school's leaders.

All the major Chicago figures have seen short biographical sketches. The Heritage of Sociology volumes always begin with short biographies of their subjects, and all the major Chicago faculty up to the 1950s are now covered by that series. But aside from the two biographies of Park there are no full-length biographical studies of Chicago school faculty. In part this is for want of material. Blumer and Thomas systematically destroyed their papers, although for Blumer, at least, there remain enough manuscripts and letters (in other people's papers) to reconstruct a life.[18] Small's, Faris's, and Warner's papers disappeared in bureaucratic snafus.

These are great losses. On Small, there is only Dibble's Heritage volume (1975), Christakes's short book (1978), some analysis in Deegan (1988), and a subtle reading in Dorothy Ross's *The Origins of American Social Science* (1991). Yet Small was clearly a remarkable man. The correspondence reported in chapter 3 reveals someone far different from the dry-as-dust lecturer so many seem to remember. Faris too was an extraordinary man, who played important and not always constructive roles in the university well after his retirement. There is virtually no biographical writing about him.

Warner is perhaps the most tragic loss. Despite a brief appearance as a fictional character in J. P. Marquand's *Point of No Return* (1949), Warner remains an enigma who shaped not only sociology but also his country. The Chicago ethnographic heritage—perceived by most writers to descend directly from Park to Hughes to the second Chicago school—owes as much or more to Warner's anthropological training and experience. It was Warner whose market research firm invented the concept of "brand image" and employed dozens of second Chicago school students to explore the images of cars, beer, newspapers, and other consumer products (Karesh 1995). It was Warner who orchestrated the studies of Morris, Illinois, and Newburyport, Massachusetts, from which emerged a class analysis that dominated American self-perceptions for much of the postwar period. It is sad indeed that we lack the resources to understand his formation and impact.

Of the other Chicago school figures we know more, but there are still no comprehensive studies. Ogburn's fairly extensive material—particularly his diaries—has not yet produced a full-length examination, although one is in progress (by Barbara Laslett; see also the work on Ogburn in Bannister 1987). Ernest Burgess's papers, rich indeed for general departmental matters, contain few truly personal materials and materials on his early life.

18. In a private conversation, Chicago alumnus Leo Shapiro told me that Blumer did not want what happened to Mead (retrospective re-creation of his ideas by others) to happen to him.

Bogue's (1974) is the best existing life history. (Shils's [1991] is charming but often wide of the mark.) Hughes seems to have thrown away much of his early material on leaving Chicago in 1962, although enough survives to write a decent biography, and Hughes studies seem to be on the upswing. (Jean-Michel Chapoulie is just completing an extensive study of Hughes; see e.g., Chapoulie 1996.) There remains Wirth, whose massive materials have not yet seen full biographical study. Salerno's "biobibliography" (1987) is tantalizing but short. Salerno does make clear the conundrum of Wirth's life: intense and wide-ranging activism coupled with a surprisingly slight academic product, albeit one that contains, in "Urbanism as a Way of Life," one of the most influential single papers in the discipline's history.

Of later figures, Janowitz and Philip Hauser are obvious possibilities for biography, for their papers are extensive, their careers long and influential, and their personalities interesting to say the least. As with Thomas, the best current biography of Janowitz is in the relevant Heritage of Sociology volume. There is no current biography of Hauser.[19]

Among the major students of the first Chicago school years, only Frazier has seen a full-length biography. Anthony Platt's excellent book (1992) demonstrates clearly that Frazier was much more than a Park student and that he in no way deserves the reputation he seems to have acquired as the man whose work on African Americans needs to be rejected wholesale. A dissertation biography of Robert Redfield (a student in the 1920s, later a faculty member in sociology and in anthropology) has just been completed and will shortly see book publication (Wilcox 1997). Since Redfield was central to the creation of the Chicago ethnographic tradition through his relations with Park, Hughes, and Warner, that work should greatly improve our understanding of ethnography and the Chicago school. Finally, there are short intellectual biographies or autobiographies of a number of second Chicago school figures: Goffman (Winkin 1988), Anselm Strauss (1996), and Tamotsu Shibutani (Baldwin 1990). (There may well be other such biographies that I have missed.)

Biographical analysis is particularly important because it seems clear in retrospect that personal charisma was a central aspect of the Chicago tradition. Most of the great Chicago sociologists were men whose intellectual

---

19. It is unfortunate that the late Edward Shils, whose extensive papers might contain important materials related to departmental history from the 1930s to the 1980s, saw fit to seal the personal portion of those materials for fifty years after his death. Although Shils played a role largely tangential both to the Chicago school (he was a student of Wirth's) and to the department (of which he was a member from 1940 to 1947 and from 1957 till his death in 1995), he undoubtedly collected important documents. Needless to say, a biography of Shils will be interesting indeed when it arrives. It's a pity we'll all be dead.

and moral passions overflowed into their everyday lives. Hauser, Blumer, Wirth, Janowitz: these were men who made many people—including some of their colleagues—very uncomfortable. Sometimes irascible and contemptuous, always committed and brilliant, they had little time for those without their passions and talents, and very little inclination to hide that opinion.[20] Others were more courtly and gracious; this was the public character of such men as Small, Burgess, and Hughes. But in the first two, at least, the public persona covered a decisive self that shocked other people when its actions came to light, an iron fist in a velvet glove.[21]

Between these two personality styles was the central figure of Robert Park, the enigma and talisman of the department's history. Of great passion and far-flung interests, Park had a restless and probing mind, but like his students Blumer and Wirth he ended up writing surprisingly little. Yet like Janowitz and Hughes, he sparked dozens of students and colleagues, spurring the great ones to distinguished careers and the lesser ones to the production of at least one great work. A definitive voice in the American definition of race, he knew the secrets of early twentieth-century race politics like no other white man. At home, his family life was often chaotic, and his children grew up feeling deserted by a father who they felt loved anyone

20. Blumer's contempt, even for some colleagues (e.g., Hughes), is clear from his letters. The same is true of Hauser, whose sarcastic remarks live on in departmental memory. He once told a colleague, in a department meeting, "Give you a raise? I would have lowered your salary if they had let me." Janowitz's abrupt antisociality was equally notorious. As many remember, he never said "good-bye" at the end of a phone call but simply hung up when he decided the call was over.

To some extent, the abrasiveness was a surface phenomenon. Janowitz, for example, was a man of profound moral commitments—to inquiry, to city and country, to friends, and indeed even to his often browbeaten students. The abrasiveness seemed to arise from his incomprehension of those who lacked such commitments. In Blumer and Wirth, and perhaps Hauser, the contempt and anger may have arisen partly from disappointment with their own work, for all three produced a smaller quantity of definitive, influential writing than they and others expected. They had their influence more as spokesmen, impresarios, and personal mentors than as writers.

21. Small's blunt attacks on capitalism were a great shock to those who expected the quiet gentleman to be colorless. And I shall tell below of Burgess's ironclad behavior as ASA president in the 1930s. His extravagant admiration for the Soviet Union in the days before the show trials is also hardly a Milquetoast matter, any more than his blunt dismissal of the fulminations of the Broyles and other un-American activities committees that investigated him in the McCarthy era. Hughes, to be sure, was indeed a quiet intellectual and scholar, one who hated conflict and let his younger friends bear the heat of many a departmental fight. But he shared with Janowitz an extraordinary ability to motivate and inspire students. (Blumer may have been the fount of symbolic interactionism, but in practice few students dared work with him; see Strauss 1996.) It was Hughes, like Janowitz later, who organized the collective discussions of fieldwork that supported and sustained communities of ethnographic sociologists. It was again a matter of charismatic personality, just a different flavor of charisma.

who was "other" more than he loved them.[22] It was an extraordinary life—one of the great lives of twentieth-century social science—and despite three substantial studies, it still awaits a truly definitive biography.

Conclusion

The first of my three aims—reviewing historical writing on the Chicago school—is now complete. But this intensive and perhaps sometimes a little tedious review of an enormous historical tradition leaves us in an even deeper quandary than when we started. At the very beginning, I gave a quick historical sketch of the Chicago school to guide our reading of the historical material. Now, with the multiple and conflicting views of that history dinning in our ears, we must return to the question of just what the Chicago school was. It helps to begin by figuring out some purely formal patterns in the historiography.

As I have noted, there is a natural logical sequence to the historiography of the Chicago school; one is tempted to expect it in most such bodies of writing. The historiography began with naming the thing to be studied: delimiting its members, its methods, its provenance. The first period distinguished the Chicago school from other things—from sociology as a whole, from work in other academic departments, from the social welfare tradition, from pragmatism. The philosophers of history have a nice word for this setting apart; they call it colligation. To colligate a set of facts is to locate them in relation to one another as members of a larger whole, to assemble them into something that is capable of being the central subject of a narrative. The first stage of writing about the Chicago school, then, was one of colligation.

The second stage, as I noted above, produced the main interpretations. This, then, is a stage of consolidation. The earlier works—the books of Short, Faris, and Carey—all to some extent accepted the everyday sense of the phrase Chicago school. But Bulmer, Matthews, Rock, and Lewis and Smith set themselves the task of more rigorously defining the object of investigation, not so much as a preliminary to deeper analysis of its origins and consequences, but rather as a *product* of that analysis. There resulted two potential views of the school, not agreeing in all respects, but concur-

22. It is clear that there have been suppressions about Park. See Deegan 1988, 154. One wonders, for example, about the meaning of Park's remark to Everett Hughes that "the penis is the true organ of memory," mentioned by Hughes in a letter to David Riesman (12 August 1959), in the Hughes Collection at the University of Chicago's Special Collections Department, box 46, folder 1. Short biographical sketches of Park are common. There are a dozen or more short articles sketching his life and discussing his work in particular areas. An attempt to codify Park's work is Lengermann 1988.

ring about the crucial time period, about the potential lineages involved, and the problems to be addressed. In Matthews and Bulmer, in particular, one saw a single interpretation from two sides—the charismatic leader in Matthews and the institutional structure in Bulmer.

Confronted with these interpretations, the major works of the third stage all made the argument that the Chicago school was not really all that different from what had gone before, that it was really an outgrowth of reformism, or newspaper reporting, or anthropological fieldwork, or the American tradition of critical social theory. In the third phase of disciplinary historiography, that is, the colligation is undone. The object originally defined is returned to the flow of the historical process more generally. No school is an island, these works say, either in social space or in social time.

But if a three-stage history seems likely, it also seems clear that this pattern of setting apart and then rejoining will occur not once but many times, repeating itself in the historiography of the Chicago school as in that of any discipline or school. An argument will come to respond to Lindner, Deegan, and Smith by holding that Chicago in the interwar period really was something unique.[23] Thus there may be not a single sequence of colligation, interpretation, and revision, but rather a cyclical pattern in which "they were new" alternates with "they had many precursors."

But though no school is an island, the increasing interest in the Chicago school suggests that there was, in fact, something real behind the phrase. To theorize what that something was, we can begin from the current historiographical tradition. It tells us first that the Chicago school was a social, a cultural, and even a personal structure. We see the social structure in the elaborate research programs and arrangements described by Bulmer, in the pattern of careers common to graduates of the school, and in the department's publication program.[24] We see the cultural structure in the immense impact of the Park and Burgess text and in the consistent pattern of investigation across dozens of studies. We see the personal structure in the extraordinary succession of charismatic figures across the department's history,

23. That the length of the cycle is about twenty to thirty years reflects, no doubt, the exigencies of academic careers. Any individual requires a good five to ten years of work to mount a serious attack on a standard belief and to build up a new one. Nor can such a new view be established by one person in any but rare cases. It thus takes ten to fifteen years for a new view to establish itself, in the course of which it will, needless to say, elicit the responses that over the subsequent decade or so will bring it into question. This cycle of interpretations seems likely to be continuous unless interest in the topic flags, in which case the career necessity of novelty is less and the cycle will slow down.

24. It is interesting to note that the most common dates for the beginning and ending of the Chicago school accurately reflect the birth and death of the University of Chicago Sociological Series. Could the *real* determinant of our image of the Chicago school be its publications?

and indeed in the persisting attempts to analyze as well as to claim that charisma today.

For each of these structures, of course, we can see the antecedent lineage: reformism for survey methods, pragmatism for symbolic interactionism, newspaper reporting and anthropological ethnography for fieldwork, reformism and political economy for the varieties of social critique, and so on. And certainly the vast "manufacturing Chicago" industry and the many and diverse claims of Chicago descent make it clear that those various lineages survive into the present. But the lineages intersected at Chicago in a way that produced something more than an accidental conjuncture. To be sure, the many interpretations of the Chicago school testify to the multifarious things bound into it. But while analysts may wish to pursue one or another of these historical lineages, it is plain from the historiography as a whole that the intersecting of these lineages in a particular time and place did something to transform them all as they passed through.

What exactly was this transformation? This is not the place for a full theory of social entities. But it is useful to draw some conclusions—and some questions for reflection—from the history of the Chicago school. To say that the Chicago school was a social structure—a social entity—involves asserting that in some sense the arrangement of people and local institutions at Chicago in the interwar years had consequences that went beyond mere aggregation or addition. The most obvious evidence of this, noticed by many writers, is that in general those who wrote the great Ph.D. dissertations of those years did not produce further works of equal distinction. Although it has been common to attribute this career decline to alumni's physical removal from the charismatic influence of Park, it is clear that other faculty as well, and students, and indeed the whole arrangement of research at Chicago were responsible for this mutual fertilization.

The causal influence of the school is equally clear in its impact on the traditions bound up in it. The Chicago school played a central role in *separating* reformism and sociology and *turning* survey methods from advocacy to dispassion. It provided pragmatism with one of its refuges from the onslaught of European analytical philosophy. It helped turn ethnography from contemplating others to contemplating ourselves. It built a new, academic model for critical politics "within the system." In none of these endeavors was it alone, of course, but all these developments would have looked quite different without it. The school drastically changed those past lineages that were bound into it.

Thus we think of the Chicago school as a social thing because it had consequences that go beyond those implicit in the historical sequences that flowed into it, because it was an "efficient cause"—in Aristotle's term—of later events. We should be clear that these *social structural* consequences are relatively independent of the Chicago school as *cultural* object. The Chicago school was not a fully formed cultural object until after it had virtually completed its life as a social structure. Of course the school did have a cultural structure contemporaneous with its structural emergence; this was the symbolic system loosely implicit in the theoretical writing of Thomas, Park, Burgess, and the others. But overt cultural recognition and labeling of the school did not come until about 1930 and was not complete until about 1950, as chapter 2 will argue. There is, of course, no necessary reason why the social object should come first (pace William Ogburn's theory of cultural lag). Cultural labels often appear for social "structures" that in fact have no emergent consequences at all. But in the case of the Chicago school, the social thing came first.

That this is so makes it easier to work out a history of the (later) cultural object, for much of that history takes the form of arguing over the interpretation of past events, as we have seen throughout this chapter already and shall see further in the next. But the history of the social structural object itself is harder to envision. For it concerns not labels but effects, and these are not really knowable without employing either comparisons across cases or counterfactual reasoning. How were these effects produced? The difficulty of this question tells why the standard recourse has been to fall back on the individual charisma of Robert Park. Only Martin Bulmer, in his insistence on the crosscutting and interwoven character of everyday department experience, has any other microlevel account for why those who worked and studied at Chicago should have had such remarkable experiences and produced such remarkable work.

But it seems likely that at both the cultural and social levels, the Chicago school "emerged" as an entity because of what we should see as a complex process of mutual reinforcement. As in any social situation, each individual lineage entering the Chicago world in the interwar period had its own effects on the others. So the ideas of Thomas or Park contributed to the methodological thinking of students and colleagues, the problems selected for investigation by the reform traditions shaped the kinds of concepts employed, and the substantive focus on the city helped force an interaction of different methodological styles. The school emerged as a social entity when these various forces began to reflect around on one another in a circular manner, when they began to resonate systematically. This mutual reinforcement then magnified the effects of the individual relations. The whole structure gained a force that enabled it, for a time, to reproduce itself and to confer a new authority on its external effects. This account of "emergence" follows that for physical systems like lasers. Individually, the mirrors and light sources simply have diverse directional effects. But when they come into certain alignments they produce extraordinary new forces. What is different about social entities is that those new forces may facilitate the emergent entity's attempts at reproduction.[25]

It is this facilitation that separates emergent social patterns from mere accidents. Many patterns in social life arise as mere standing waves. They happen because forces and constraints around them continually reproduce them. But sometimes such patterns end up remaining even when the supporting forces are taken away. It is then that we speak of the emergence of a social thing.[26] Indeed, in this sense the retrospective creation of the Chicago school during the second Chicago school period is perhaps the best evidence that there really was a first Chicago school.[27] To that creation I now turn.

25. Note that I am not making a "multilevel account" of emergence in which structures are made out of people. The elements that go into the social structure are not whole persons, but parts of them, as well as preexisting social and cultural structures. Personalities and social structures are fundamentally entities of the same type. See Abbott 1995a.

26. There is a story in one of Edgar Rice Burroughs's science fiction novels that captures the situation nicely. In *Thuvia, Maid of Mars* (1920), the hero and heroine at one point witness a battle in a long-hidden valley. When the battle is over, they notice there are no dead bodies. It turns out that the soldiers are all telepathically created, and that there are in reality only ten or twenty people alive in the city that sent them forth. These people fight out their rivalries by pitting their imaginary legions against one another. Later in the book the lovers escape from the city, chased by more imaginary warriors. One of these "forgets" to go out of existence when the mind that animates him tells him to and remains a fixed character for the rest of the novel. Social thingness is equivalent to this forgetting to go out of existence when the external forces conducing to the existence of a state of affairs fall away.

27. An alternative interpretation of such "great moments" in cultural history is the view that such moments are made by the convergence of a number of "preadapted" ideas and symbols, which resonate with a peculiar urgency precisely because of the transient, irreproducible nature of their relation to one another. Patrick Cruttwell's magnificent *The Shakespearean Moment* (1960) is the most compelling exposition of this argument I have read.

2 Transition and Tradition in the Second Chicago School

With Emanuel Gaziano

In chapter 1 I investigated the first Chicago school by diving beneath its historiography to the loosely woven social "object" that it really was at the time. In the present chapter I turn to that object's *cultural* identification by a later generation. It is one thing to say that the Chicagoans of the postwar period were the cultural inventors of the first Chicago school and quite another to show that invention taking place. Luckily, Louis Wirth produced and Ernest Burgess saved an extraordinary document that captures much of the cultural work involved. Therefore I turn here, with the collaboration of Emanuel Gaziano, to the primary materials that can produce such a history, both social structural and cultural.

We work at a very detailed level, for a particular theoretical reason. We wish to make the history of the faculty in this period so immediate as to de-objectify it, bringing the reader below the level of the commonly accepted "there was a steady move toward quantitative work" narrative. If we can make readers see this faculty as a group much like themselves, fighting all the usual academic battles with all the usual strange alliances, we can re-open the issue of what it means to speak of "a school." Once it is clear that no one faculty member stood for any absolutely consistent and unified position, we can begin to reflect on how coherent positions exist as collective relationships and emergent symbols *above* the bricolage of the individuals. That reflection then transforms the question of how a school or tradition gets created into the question of how a group of bricoleurs can through interaction produce and maintain an apparently coherent set of traditions to which none of them subscribes in toto. We take this last to be the central issue of analyzing a first or a second Chicago school.

We begin with an analysis of the faculty itself and of its university context. We then focus our discussion on a Ford Foundation–funded self-study of 1951–52, engineered by Wirth and chaired by Burgess. By a stroke of extraordinary good fortune, the four-hundred-page transcript survived in Burgess's papers. For a year, the department argued with itself about the nature and future of sociology and about its own role in that nature and future. Here we can see in detail the mind of the department in which the second Chicago school—and the first—took shape.

The Department and Its Environments

To the students in the University of Chicago Department of Sociology in the years 1945–60, the department's collective being must have seemed both immediate and remote. It was immediate because the department was small while students were many and because the faculty, then as now, engaged students directly in its research. At the same time it was remote because the principal faculty had known each other so well for so long. Burgess had been on the faculty since 1916, Ogburn since 1927, Wirth and Blumer since 1931, Warner since 1935, Hughes since 1938. Four of these—Burgess, Blumer, Wirth, and Hughes—had been Chicago students before becoming faculty. Some of the "new faculty" were old faces too. Although Hauser had been in Washington for a decade before his own return in 1947, he too had been an instructor and a graduate student in the 1930s.[1]

In 1951–52 the core of this tight group disappeared. Ogburn and Burgess retired (although circumstances forced Burgess to remain another year).[2] Blumer went to Berkeley. Wirth died. Only Hughes, Warner, and Hauser remained. There were some new faculty. In 1950 Leo Good-

---

1. Before reading these notes, the reader should consult the sources and acknowledgments section following the epilogue. Dates of faculty service are notoriously difficult to specify, partly because the long-standing practice of hiring internally meant that many people oozed into faculty status gradually. Also, positions were often retrospectively redefined (because someone completed a Ph.D., for example). There is therefore room for reasonable disagreement. These dates cannot be exactly specified without reading the faculty personnel files for the period, which remain sealed (if they remain at all—we are not sure where they are). The lists given by Harvey (1987a) in his book on Chicago, while roughly accurate about dates of service, are often mistaken about rank. David Riesman, for example, was tenured throughout his official service in the department in the 1950s, Donald Bogue was tenured before Harvey thinks he was, D. G. Moore was never a full professor, and so on.

2. Much pressure was put on Ogburn to stay, pressure that he respected but withstood. "I think I had better withdraw from the university. I am writing now so that you can be making other plans and cease your efforts to have me stay. I do appreciate more than I can say the wish that the department would have me stay on" (Ogburn to Wirth, 21 March 1950, LW 62:7). Both Burgess and Ogburn spent an extra year in the department, ostensibly to reap the benefits of certain Social Security provisions (Burgess to Blumer, 13 November 1950, EWB 3:1; Wirth to Blumer, 14 December 1950, LW 1:8). In fact, Burgess remained to chair the department while the administration made up its own mind who should be chair in the long run.

Note that relations among the tight core group were extremely close. Burgess's many letters to Wirth and Blumer are clearly affectionate, and his letters to Ogburn are warmly collegial (e.g., Burgess to Ogburn, 17 April 1947, EWB 16:10). The Wirth-Blumer correspondence (in LW 1:8) makes it clear that Wirth was Blumer's best friend in the department, both of them

man had been recruited by Wirth and Hauser from Princeton. Demographer Donald Bogue moved onto the regular faculty from his replacement teaching job midway through the 1950s. (These two were the only faculty members recruited in the period who would end up seeing long Chicago service.) Other than these few, however, the working faculty throughout the postwar period comprised mainly assistant professors. Often these were locals who stayed briefly before departing—Edward Shils (1945–47, returning [as professor] in 1957), William Foote Whyte (1945–48), Harold Wilensky (1952–53).[3] A few remained longer—Herbert Goldhamer (1947–51), Albert Reiss (1948–52), Otis Dudley Duncan (1951–57), D. G. Moore (1951–55), and Anselm Strauss (1952–58). And a few short-service professors came from outside the Chicago orbit—Assistant (later Associate) Professor Donald Horton (1951–57) and Assistant Professor Nelson Foote (1952–56).[4] David Riesman came into the department from the university's College faculty in 1954 but left in 1958. Associate Professor William Bradbury (1952–58) was another college-related appointment. There also began in 1954 a string of recruitments of recent Columbia Ph.D.'s; Peter Blau (1954–63), Elihu Katz (1955–70), Peter Rossi (1956–67), Allan Barton (1957), and James Coleman (1957–59, returning in 1973). Of these, Rossi, Katz, and Blau stayed for significant periods. In terms of faculty present, then, the years 1945–60 included the last

sharing a coolness toward Hughes, about which Blumer was the more outspoken. The only negative relationship in this core of four was the apparently intense dislike between Blumer and Ogburn, about which considerable ink has been spilled. Even Blumer and Hauser had a past. Blumer had been Hauser's M.A. adviser, and in 1934 they had published a book on the results (*Movies, Delinquency, and Crime*). Subsequent events were to prove them intellectually closer than anyone might imagine, as we note below. For the material on Hauser's M.A., see Hauser to Gideonse, 26 March 1932, and also Hauser's warm letter to Blumer of 14 February 1934, both in PMH 14:6. Hauser did not correspond with Blumer during his recruitment after the war, perhaps because Blumer was in Pittsburgh much of the time. Their relationship may also have cooled somewhat.

3. There were many more locals who held the rank of instructor for a few years in the late 1940s—Tomatsu Shibutani, Buford Junker, and Donald Roy, for example. After 1951 the rank of instructor seems to have disappeared. The practice of extensive local hiring was a source of friction with the administration, as we note below.

4. Some of these are less familiar names in the Chicago roster. Goldhamer was a social psychologist hired in 1946 to participate in "our new general course in the social sciences at the divisional level . . . . it was a general intro to the social sciences, run at the third year for the move into 'majors,' which of course don't yet exist" (Wirth to Harry Gideonse, 2 September 1946, LW 4:2). (The remark about majors reflects the lack of electives in the Hutchins College.) Goldhamer left in 1950 because he was refused promotion and had better offers elsewhere (Ogburn to Goldhamer, 6 February 1950, 20 March 1950; Ogburn to Burgess, 10 March 1950, all in EWB 16:10). Horton was a Yale anthropology Ph.D. (1943) and a collaborator of Ogburn's. He would later attach himself to Warner. He moved into regular faculty status from research associate status in 1951–52.

five years of the old faculty regime and a somewhat longer period of transition.

During these years, the University of Chicago was best known not for its graduate schools, however, but for its charismatic chancellor, Robert Maynard Hutchins, and the revolutionary College he had created. By this time the "Hutchins College" had a curriculum of four years of required courses. It allowed few electives, and those only in the last two years. It admitted students directly from the tenth grade on the basis of an examination. Its education was largely aimed at great books and great ideas.

This extraordinary experimental college had its own faculty. Hutchins had abolished the universitywide Faculty of Arts and Sciences and assembled departments into Humanities and Social, Physical, and Biological Sciences Divisions. The College faculty itself constituted such a separate division, and thus many faculty pursuing what was elsewhere called sociology were located not in the department but in the College. David Riesman was best known of these, but in the late 1940s his coinstructors in "Soc 2" (the second of the three year-long, required social science sequences) included Daniel Bell, Lewis Coser, Murray Wax, Howard Becker, Joel Seidman, Mark Benney, Phillip Rieff, Benjamin Nelson, Joseph Gusfield, and Reuel Denney (MacAloon 1992). Other sociologists, both faculty (Wirth) and students (Janowitz) taught in other Social Science core courses. Hiring in the College had little to do with academic credentials; most of these people had no degree, although some—Gusfield, Wax, Becker, and Janowitz, for example—were local graduate students. (Of the departmental faculty only three, Shils, Bradbury, and Riesman, had actual joint appointments in the College.)

The College "sociologists" shared with their College colleagues an intense but general intellectual commitment, something that for Hutchins was explicitly opposed to routine academic work. Hutchins's love of high thoughts and classic texts made him distinctly hostile to empirical science. His repugnance for empirical social science in particular was unconcealed. As a result, the Division of Social Sciences, and with it the Department of Sociology, did not fare well during the Hutchins years (Bulmer 1984, 202–5).

In January 1951 Hutchins, then only fifty-one, unexpectedly resigned. His replacement was Lawrence Kimpton, a philosopher who had become a career administrator (Ashmore 1989). Although Kimpton did not immediately destroy the Hutchins College, by 1955 it was clear that he would ultimately do so (McNeill 1991). Free-floating intellectuals who had been purely College faculty began needing homes elsewhere. Such considerations brought David Riesman into the Sociology Department, with the support of Hughes (then chair) and Social Science Dean Morton Grodzins, but in the face of sustained opposition from Philip Hauser (Riesman 1990).

The animus between department and College that developed in the Hutchins years had a long-standing effect on the department; it guaranteed that the department would not make a distinguished record in general sociological theory, precisely the kind of work represented by Riesman, Shils, and Bell in the Hutchins College. Although department members disagreed about many things, the various factions united in their antipathy to Hutchins's views. Even the diplomatic Ernest Burgess resented Hutchins's attitudes, as did Lloyd Warner and Philip Hauser (Farber 1988, 349–50).

Shils's career illustrates the results of this feud. Originally appointed jointly in Sociology and the College, Shils moved out of both into the Committee on Social Thought in 1947. Social Thought was one of Hutchins's pet creations: a collection of great intellectuals free to browse at will in social knowledge, but aimed against "narrow specialism." To Hutchins, theoretical and empirical work on society were intellectually and departmentally separate affairs. To be sure, Shils eventually reentered the Department of Sociology (in 1957), and Donald Levine, another theorist, was hired in 1962 (after a period of fieldwork had made him acceptably empirical). But both were marginalized. (At a graduate student party in 1955, Hauser had publicly announced his opposition to Levine's thesis proposal.) Yet in these very years Riesman and Bell (inter alia) built the "theoretical" careers that eventually made them central members of the Harvard Social Relations pantheon. At the same time, Shils was collaborating with Parsons at Harvard in the Carnegie Foundation–sponsored work on the "general theory of action." "Theory" was thus an active area in sociology. But most of the department wanted none of it. Nor was this antitheory prejudice a matter of quantitative researchers only; Warner and Hughes also opposed the concept of dissertations in theory.[5]

The College was not the only external university force shaping the department during this era. The university's small size and interdisciplinary character meant that faculty had important extradepartmental commitments. The National Opinion Research Corporation (NORC), a nonprofit survey house founded in 1941, was one of these. NORC moved to Chicago from Colorado in 1947, a move sociologist Clyde Hart required as a condition of his taking the job as its director. Hart, who like Warner had only a

5. On Social Thought, see Nef's founding memo, "The Committee on Social Thought of the University of Chicago" (n.d.), PP52 150:6. Shils's trajectory can be traced in official university publications. The Levine story is from Levine himself (personal communication).

B.A., became a full professor of sociology. Under the Hart regime (till 1960), NORC principally housed researchers funding themselves on external grants. (The contract survey arm, which was to dominate NORC's funding in later years, matured only under Peter Rossi in the early 1960s.) All study directors at NORC during the Hart era were either recruited from, graduates of, or courtesy faculty in the sociology department, including Hart himself, Josephine Williams, Shirley Star, Eli Marks, Jack Elinson, Ethel Shanas, and Louis Kreisberg. At one point, late in the 1950s, sociology faculty feared block voting by the NORC contingent and moved to lessen the NORC presence.[6]

But other units drew faculty attention and commitment as well. The Committee on Human Development (HD), for example, was another of Hutchins's interdisciplinary centers for reflective, qualitative social science, dating from the early 1940s. Burgess, Hughes, and above all Warner put much of their time and effort into HD, whose offices were then in Judd Hall, two blocks from the sociology department. The central figure in HD was Ralph Tyler, professor of education, who became dean of the division in 1946 and remained so until 1953. Tyler, an aggressive power broker centrally located in university politics, played a determining role in Sociology during this period.[7]

Another external tie was with the Industrial Relations Center, whose affiliates included Wilensky, Moore, and Blumer, the latter capitalizing on his experience in mediation. There was also the Committee on Education, Teaching, and Research in Race Relations, an interdisciplinary study center of which Wirth was chair (and over which he had fought with Hughes [Turner 1988, 317]). There was the Family Studies Center, for which Burgess had raised the money and of which Foote was the first director.[8]

Yet another research center was the Chicago Community Inventory, a

6. A useful source on the history of NORC in this period, and the source of our information about money and work flows is Rebecca Adams (1977). The coalition supporting NORC was an interesting one. Wirth, for example, saw great prospects for it (Wirth memo appended to memo of Burgess to the faculty, 24 August 1949, LW 62:6). This vision was hardly disinterested; Hart had been a graduate student of Wirth's in the early 1930s. Wirth undoubtedly played a central role in NORC's choice of Chicago.

7. Another central figure in HD was Robert Havighurst, a specialist in education. Although HD was particularly the home of Lloyd Warner, Warner also had a contract survey research firm downtown (Survey Research Incorporated) in which students like Lee Rainwater were active. The firm specialized in a kind of qualitative market research tied to Warner's class analysis. See Karesh 1995.

8. The Industrial Relations Center drew students like Donald Roy. Inside and outside the race relations committee, the relationship of Wirth and Hughes was very complex. The two collaborated on a large research project on racial discrimination in the Chicago public

mile away in NORC's building at 4901 South Ellis. Run by Hauser, the CCI was a center for his students and protégés. The money for CCI had originally been raised by Wirth and Burgess, but the whole operation was gladly given to Hauser on his return in 1947. As director of studies of Chicago communities, Hauser was explicitly the heir of the Chicago school in the eyes of Burgess and Wirth, whatever retrospective judgment makes of the matter.[9]

The research centers were the centers of department activity, particularly for the younger faculty. Daily life was spent less in the Social Science building itself than in whatever quarters one's research center occupied. (Hence the invisibility of any particular faculty member to students not located in that member's center. Recall that most faculty did not teach undergraduates.) Moreover, much time was spent hustling for research money, and much effort spent eking out what money was found. A fundamental faculty schism emerged in this period to divide the hustlers—both the wealthy and the would-be wealthy—from the nonhustlers. Paralleling this was a distinction between bureaucratic and artisanal research. Only a few—Hughes is a conspicuous example—had feet in both camps. Wirth and Blumer tended to work alone, while Duncan and others were collaborators and Hauser, increasingly, was a large-scale bureaucrat.

Department and Administration

But the College and the external centers played less of a role in shaping the department than did the administration. For the documents leave little doubt that in the eyes of the university administration the department was more or less "in receivership" from 1950 to 1957. If we take as a working definition of receivership the breaching of a department's control over its appointments, the receivership period probably runs from 1950 to 1953. The only way to understand the detailed history of the faculty between 1945 and 1960 is to work carefully through the department's relation to the administrations: chancellors Hutchins (to 1951) and Kimp-

---

schools, Wirth working on gerrymandering of districts and Hughes on issues with teachers. But Hughes tended to define race relations more broadly than Wirth did, focusing less on American issues.

9. For the NORC location, see R. Likert to Hart, 25 March 1948, PMH 14:10. CCI was at this location until 1955, when it moved to 935 East 60th Street. NORC moved to 5711 South Woodlawn in 1954. On the funding of CCI and the Burgess-Wirth view of it, see Burgess to Hauser, 27 September 1946, and Wirth to Hauser, 12 February 1947, both in PMH 14:9. Hauser collaborated widely, at one point seeking Warner's aid in interesting St. Clair Drake in a CCI project on Chicago's black population (Hughes to Riesman, 18 March 1954, ECH 45:16).

ton (after 1951) and deans Ralph Tyler (1946–53), Morton Grodzins (1954), and Chauncy Harris (1954–60).

The central theme of administrative discontent was insularity. In a letter to Hutchins, Tyler contemptuously described Ogburn's research proposals of 1950 as hopelessly out of date. Seven years later, Hauser would still be justifying his personnel policies to a new dean by crowing about how few Chicago graduates the department was now hiring.[10]

The sources of this attitude are obscure. It is possible that Tyler was influenced by Hutchins's own long-standing dislike of Louis Wirth, one of the department's central figures. And certainly concerns about insularity would not have been allayed by the recruitment of old Chicagoan Hauser from the Census. But overall, it seems more likely that worries about Chicago insularity reflected the realities of disciplinary change. Harvard was emerging as a prime force in theory, as Columbia was in empirical research. As the administration heard about these fads—and administrations do hear about them whether departments like it or not—it may have begun to worry that the middle generation of Wirth, Hauser, Hughes, Warner, and Blumer (four of the five being local Ph.D.'s) was not of the same disciplinary eminence as the senior generation of Burgess and Ogburn. Thus it was the administration that first saw Chicago as something less than the whole of the discipline, a specific (and dated) paradigm.

In a curious way, the department's position was inevitable. Nationwide, university enrollments soared after the war, never to stop soaring until the late 1970s. The consequent seller's market for academic talent put the department in an unexpectedly weak position precisely as it needed to rebuild for a coming generation. One can read the changes here discussed as simply the department's desperate response to this changed structural condition. Of course the obverse of the department's weak hiring position was a strong placement position. It may well be that the great distinction of the postwar generation of students *after* they left Chicago, by contrast with the relative weakness of the first Chicago school students after *they* left, derives from precisely this seller's market. More of the second school students found employment at good universities.

The administration's already antagonistic attitude toward Sociology began to worsen after the war. Shils, one of Hutchins's favorites, left the department for the Committee on Social Thought in 1947, giving as his reason a Hutchinsonian desire to think broadly about society. At the same

10. Tyler to Hutchins, 6 December 1950, PP52 148:1. Hauser to Harris (8 December 1958, SSV). One commenter noted that when Tyler later went to the Palo Alto center, he showed the same taste.

time, Hauser was returning as heir apparent to the Burgess-Wirth wing of empirical sociology. It undoubtedly did not help that Hauser and Wirth were close friends—Wirth found Hauser his Chicago house—nor that Hauser, who had taken a substantial pay cut to come to Chicago, immediately became active in the faculty's attempt to overturn the "4E regulations" that effectively forbade faculty consulting.[11]

It was clear to all that the department was about to face a major turning point. The retirements of Ogburn and Burgess were expected, and the university did not continue even the most eminent of faculty beyond age sixty-five. Moreover, the administration's fears of departmental insularity were not unfounded. In thinking about replacement, Burgess thought first of locals: "In considering personnel for the department, it seems to me that we should take account of our own PhD's." The department did do just that, for Dudley Duncan was recruited to return to Chicago, after brief sojourns at Penn State and Wisconsin, in the spring of 1951.[12]

But the first clear indication that the transition would be problematic was the department's curious inability to replace Herbert Goldhamer. When he found out that Goldhamer would not be returning from his year's leave in Washington, D.C., Ogburn (acting chair for Burgess) considered continuing Tamotsu Shibutani (a recent Blumer Ph.D. then teaching on a three-year appointment), getting Ellsworth Faris to come back and teach with Shibutani (Faris was seventy-six at this point), or "bring[ing] Robert Faris here for a quarter or so from Seattle if his father isn't considered a possibility." That the latter two expedients were considered suggests both insularity and a kind of desperation. Meanwhile the department tried, and failed, to secure a substantial teaching commitment from Josephine Williams, a recent Chicago Ph.D. who turned them down to go full-time at NORC.[13]

11. The Hauser and Wirth houses were connected by a private electronic telephone arrangement (Hauser to Glass, 11 January 1957, PMH 4:2). On the Hauser recruitment, see the extensive correspondence between Hauser, Wirth, and Burgess in PMH 14:9. Hauser's initial strong status was shown by Wirth's ability to install him as secretary of the Social Science Research Council, the internal grant-giving agency that oversaw divisional research funding (Tyler to Wirth, 21 October 1947, PMH 14:10). Hauser's worries about money are evident in his negotiations (in the same files), and the 4E episode is evident both in the draft protest document (18 May 1950, PMH 14:10) and in letters to Hughes and Horton (then acting chair) of 18 May 1953 during the affair of his Berkeley offer (PMH 14:11).

12. See Burgess to department, 25 November 1949, PMH 14:10, with a list of 115 graduates!

13. Ogburn's diaries indicate that, unlike Burgess, he had folded his tents in anticipation of retirement (WFO 46:4). Therefore the futility of these expedients may be more a reflection of Ogburn's state of mind than anything else. In any event, Ogburn wrote Burgess (who was on leave in California, leaving Ogburn as acting chair) on 10 March 1950 (EWB 16:10) saying that Goldhamer was probably leaving (he had already been on leave in Washington for a year). That

Yet the list of candidates for positions in late 1950 suggests either that the department was in fact looking outside or that it had already succumbed to administration pressure to do so. In a letter of 30 October (to Blumer, EWB 3:1), Burgess lists those under consideration for tenured appointments in social psychology: Theodore Newcomb, John Dollard, and Goldhamer (to be reprieved and promoted). Outside social psychology, the potential hires were Frederick Stephan, Conrad Taeuber, and Hans Speier. Potential untenured hires, seen by Burgess as fallbacks, included Jack Seeley, Herbert Hyman, Arnold Rose, Philip Selznick, and Otis Dudley Duncan. Some of these were Chicago graduates, some were not.

But matters were moving above the department level as well. In 1950 there was a concerted attempt, not mentioned in Burgess's letter, to entice Robert Merton and Paul Lazarsfeld to Chicago. Merton was impressed. He had always admired both university and department. Lazarsfeld was less interested, perhaps because of his market research client base in New York, perhaps for family reasons. The two had agreed to act together, so Lazarsfeld's ultimate unwillingness meant that both remained in New York. The administration was again to attempt Merton and Lazarsfeld (separately) later in the decade.[14]

---

the various expedients were raised with Blumer still on the faculty might be thought to suggest strongly that his departure was expected even at this point, two years before his actual resignation, although the stated reason for hiring was the end of Shibutani's appointment as an instructor (Burgess to Blumer, 19 December 1950, EWB 3:1). But in fact Blumer's was the primary voice against Goldhamer's promotion, and that it was taken seriously enough to deny promotion implies that Blumer was expected to stay. Moreover, Ogburn's letter to Burgess four days later (14 March 1950, EWB 16:10) clearly takes Blumer's continued presence for granted. And Burgess himself, writing to Blumer later that year (30 October 1950, EWB 3:1), while Blumer was on a leave in Hawaii, discusses social psychology hires at length in a way that suggests that he, at least, had no inkling of Blumer's (possible) intentions.

14. Professor Merton was kind enough to tell me this story from his point of view. For the University of Chicago side, see Wirth to Blumer, 27 October 1950, LW 1:8. A central problem was that salaries were frozen, part of the financial debacle left by Hutchins and cleaned up, over the course of a decade, by his successor Lawrence Kimpton (McNeill 1991). The administration was also trying to cut down on tenured appointments; see Burgess to Blumer, 30 October 1950, EWB 3:1. Wirth's opinion was that the offer was *not* joint, and that Lazarsfeld was making it look as if he were the real target. According to Wirth, the offers were turned down not both at once, but seriatim (Wirth to Blumer, 14 December 1950, LW 1:8). Incidentally, Wirth's bitterness may have reflected a feeling of friendship spurned: Wirth had maintained cordial professional relations with Lazarsfeld since the mid-1930s, when he had invited Lazarsfeld to Chicago to meet the Seminar on Racial and Cultural Contacts. The later offers were separate—Merton in 1954 and Lazarsfeld in 1958 (Hauser to Harris, 10 September 1958, SSV). It is noteworthy that the administration conducted the 1954 negotiations with Merton itself, although with the department's authorization: "If the situation warrants [we will] have Everett Hughes join us at one stage or another of our discussion" (Grodzins to Merton, 15 February 1954, PP52 148:2).

Another departmental strategy for handling the transition was seeking long-run active status for the retiring Burgess and Ogburn. Both refused. In Ogburn's case the refusal was heartfelt. "For four or five years I have been taking less and less interest in University affairs, its committees, in thinking and planning for the Department of Sociology and the University. It might indeed be said that I have, in view of my impending retirement, been neglecting this phase of my work." By contrast, Burgess was still advising the occasional student in the mid-1950s. It may have been very consequential for the department that Ogburn gave so little help in the transition.[15]

At this very time, late in 1950, the department sent forward to Dean Tyler the name of Louis Wirth as chair to succeed the retiring Burgess. Wirth had certainly waited his turn; he had been on the faculty for twenty years. He was without question the central figure in the department. Close to Burgess, he was also best friend in the department of both Hauser and Blumer, as well as an old acquaintance of Clyde Hart. To be sure, his relations with Hughes were less close (although they collaborated on the Chicago school desegregation study), and he got along badly with Warner (but Warner was to some extent marginalized in HD). But overall Wirth was probably the central actor in the active department at this point. Unfortunately he was detested by the administration, largely because of his outspoken criticism of the university's position in the community. Tyler turned Wirth down, requiring the department to think again. Meanwhile Burgess remained chair, a situation that persisted off and on for nearly two years after his retirement.[16]

15. The correspondence on retirement is Wirth to Burgess, 28 February 1950; Burgess to Wirth, 5 March 1950; Ogburn to Wirth, 21 March 1950; all in LW 62:7. The quote from Ogburn is from the diaries, WFO 46:4, entry for 20 March 1951. This attitude explains, by the way, why Ogburn absented himself from the faculty seminar of 1951–52 and why he played so little role in the department's struggles to survive.

16. We are very lucky that Blumer was on leave in Hawaii during this episode, for other department members—particularly Burgess and Wirth—wrote him long letters about it. For Wirth's private views about the administration, see Wirth to Harry Gideonse, a close friend who had left the Chicago faculty (2 September 1946, LW 4:2): "I read the clipping about the new world constitution with great interest. The boys are certainly hiding their light under a bushel. I am afraid if the world is going to be dependent on their solution to its problems, it is going to have to wait for a millennium or two." His own version of the administration turndown was, "I was informed by [Dean Ralph] Tyler that I was not acceptable because I had for twenty-five years consistently disagreed with the Administration accept [*sic*] on the issue of academic freedom. I do not regret having done so and have no passion to be Chairman as you well know, but it leaves us in the air for the time being" (Wirth to Blumer, 14 December 1950, LW 1:8).

Blumer wrote to Wirth (21 December 1950, LW 1:8) saying, "I am sorry the Administration would not accept the recommendation of the Department concerning your appointment as chairman. The Administration is running true to form. I fear that the compromise result of

By 1951 the department was forced to heed the administration message a little more effectively. The department agreed to meet and discuss "the likely trends in the different fields of sociology and what the department of sociology at the University of Chicago could do in regard to this development." Burgess's annual report of 1951 shows that the department's one (failed) senior recruitment was external, and of the junior recruitments, one was internal (Duncan), one mixed (Horton had worked with Ogburn for four years), and one external (Foote, who nonetheless was directly tied to Chicago through his mentor Leonard Cottrell). Burgess viewed the planned "faculty seminar" (the Ford Foundation self-study discussed below) as an attempt to fight off the administration's claim that the department lacked intellectual depth. The annual report itself was the first such document, part of a planned effort to increase information to both administration and faculty.[17]

Burgess's drafts for an undated "departmental aims" document of 1951 show what the various faculty then had in mind. He recorded his conver-

---

the impasse will be the ultimate selection of Everett as Chairman, something very unfortunate in my judgment, since he is not qualified by ability, scholarship, or student respect to fill the position" (LW 1:8). This and other letters show Blumer's extremely close relationship with Wirth. For Burgess's view of the chair fiasco of 1950, see Burgess to Blumer, 19 December 1950, EWB 3:1. Many other faculty, of course, shared Wirth's dislike of Hutchins. Hauser wrote Blumer about a conference during his stint in Washington with the Federal Emergency Relief Administration: "I hope [the conference] will be more interesting than listening to Mortimer Adler. St. Thomas does seem so far away" (14 February 1934, PMH 14:6).

Although or perhaps because Hutchins had largely ignored the problem of the community, it had become a matter of burning importance. Hyde Park had been gradually declining for years, and the sudden changes following from the Supreme Court's 1947 decision on restrictive covenants had rapidly brought the situation to a crisis level. Wirth spoke to this issue often and incurred Hutchins's implacable opposition for doing so. One commenter said that the true reason for Hutchins's detestation of Wirth was that Wirth had uncovered information that the university had bankrolled supposed "community" organizations that were supporting restrictive covenants and that he provided extensive material to the lawyers arguing to strike those covenants down. We have not found documentary confirmation of this story, but it would account for the heat of Hutchins's relationship with Wirth.

A characteristic Wirth-Hutchins encounter is a memo from Wirth to Hutchins (25 January 1946, PP45 35:4): "Some of my friends here tell me that at a recent dinner party on the North Side they heard you say that the IQ of the Sociology Department was very low. It is interesting to know what you think of us, but I doubt whether you will improve the Department or advance the interests of the University by such public proclamations." Hutchins replied: "Sorry—I have no recollection of this alleged conversation."

17. The minutes quote is from 5 March 1951, LW 62:8. Burgess's annual report is 27 August 1951, EWB 33:2. The projected annual report is discussed in "Steps in Achieving Objectives," n.d., EWB 33:2. Other "steps" were strengthening faculty at senior and junior levels, getting more fellowships, and funding student research. Also listed in steps are two pages of "interdisciplinary efforts," which translate into leveraging the faculty with outsiders in order to extend instruction and research.

sations with each. Duncan talked at length about his mentor William Sewell.[18] Hart, not surprisingly, wanted better integration with NORC. Wirth told Burgess to play to departmental strengths and to avoid the new grand theory. "The problems we wish to deal with are actual problems existing in the world and not conjured up problems. There is a clamor for theory with contemplation; we should study social life and not abstract from it." Hughes, too, toed the Chicago line; he told Burgess of the tradition of sending students into the city, of following problems where they lead, and of making use of the city.

The outsiders gave slightly different advice. Goodman told Burgess to get as many top-notch people as he could. He emphasized divergence of views. Horton, like Wirth, stressed playing to strengths, but he insisted that the new systematized theory had to be taken seriously. Warner's lengthy comments mainly concerned his own area of social organization.

The document that came out of these conversations was titled "Objectives and Program of the Department of Sociology." Like the discussions, it shows that the drift toward eclecticism was coupled with a very firm sense of and confidence in the local tradition. The department's objectives were to be as follows:

1. The development of a sound body of sociological theory interrelated with social life and empirical research.
2. Cooperation with the other social sciences.
3. The all-around training of our students.
4. The selection of those areas for research in which we can make the most significant contributions.
5. Emphasis on ideas rather than organization.
6. Revival of the publication program of the department.
7. A research program in:

   urban problems—CCI, Planning Department, NORC
   stratification/mass society—Duncan, Foote, Hauser, Horton, Hughes, Warner, Wirth
   intellectual life of the city—[what would now be called urban culture]
   social trends[19]

18. On the back of the Duncan notes is yet another list of candidates: Robin Williams, Franklin Edwards, Morris Janowitz, Guy E. Swanson, Natalie Rogoff, Josephine Williams, Kingsley Davis, Robert Merton, Paul Hatt, Samuel Stouffer, and Fred Strodtbeck; although Burgess was looking somewhat to the non-Chicago outside world by this point, the list is about 50 percent old graduates.

19. Apparently other faculty members were asked to contribute their own documents, so we have "On a Program for the Department of Sociology" by Reiss, also in EWB 33:2. The

This was in fact a profoundly conservative document. In its own eyes at least, the department saw the stratification area as the only seriously new area for departmental research, and Warner had already given that area a strong Chicago accent. Thus, while faculty were willing to think somewhat eclectically in terms of hiring strategy, most still had a pretty clear idea that Chicago stood, and should stand, for a particular approach to social science, enshrined in the justification for objective number 1, a sound body of sociological theory interrelated with social life and empirical research:

> This contribution is timely in view of the present trends in sociology and would counteract certain existing tendencies to develop sociological theory out of abstractions with little or no relation to social phenomena. By making this contribution, the Department would exercise a balancing and steadying influence in the sociological field.

There is little question who is the enemy. More important, the implicit argument here is not that "there are many sociologies and we do not desire to house certain versions of sociological inquiry," but rather that "sociology *is* what we do but some other 'sociologists' don't really understand what sociological inquiry is." The administration, ironically, took an empirical view of the discipline, in which the mere existence of Parsons as a sociologist at an eminent university (not to mention his flourishing program) meant that what he did was legitimate sociology. At root, this difference of views was the central difficulty between department and administration. Curiously, it was exacerbated by the fight between them, since much of the time the word "sociology" functioned as an indexical term meaning one thing to one side and another to the other.

Throughout the late 1940s and early 1950s, a crucial factor exacerbating internal problems and relations with students and with the administration was the lengthy absence of key department members. Blumer spent much of 1946 as full-time chair of the arbitration board solving a Pittsburgh steel strike. Hughes spent much of 1948 in Frankfurt, helping to get the university there going after the war. Wirth spent time on leave in Stanford, Paris, and Beirut. Perpetually on the move, Hauser had returned to Washington in 1949 as acting director of the Census, failing to get the per-

---

"Objectives" document is unsigned and unfinished. Internal evidence assures that Burgess either wrote it or rewrote it—there are near verbatim quotes from the discussions just referred to—but the document's organization and arguments exactly resemble those of Duncan's draft of department aims discussed in the last faculty seminar meeting. Probably Burgess asked Duncan to rewrite his draft, since Duncan and Foote were the most active of seminar participants.

manent directorship because he attempted to defend the Census against the Democratic patronage machine and was then faced with trumped-up loyalty charges. His return to Chicago was brief, for he immediately left on a fifteen-month sojourn to Burma as census adviser. Blumer too was absent on a long leave (at the University of Hawaii), in 1950. Hughes spent time at Columbia.[20]

The year 1951 did bring one piece of good news. This was the unexpected departure of departmental bugbear Hutchins at midyear. But still, few issues were resolved.

By the winter of 1952 the department was proposing two unacceptable candidates for chair instead of just one. There is no documentary evidence who these were, but it seems overwhelmingly likely that they were Blumer and Hauser.[21] Neither was acceptable to the administration, a fact communicated by Dean Ralph Tyler in late February. The department was bluntly ordered to think again. Nine months later, an administration press release announced Hughes as chair. A complex history intervened.[22]

A preliminary event was the disappearance of two crucial players from the scene. Wirth died quite unexpectedly in early May, and Blumer an-

20. For Blumer's various trips, see the Wirth-Blumer correspondence in LW 1:8. For Hughes, see Hughes to Burgess, 22 March 1948, EWB 9:3. Hughes went to Germany at the behest of the university administration and was quite worried that the resultant slowing of his research would impede his promotion. Hauser's trips are quite evident in his correspondence both within the university (PMH 14:6–11) and beyond it (PMH 3:1–13, 4:1–5). On the Census affair, see Hauser to Stuart Rice, 8 October 1954, PMH 3:12. For Wirth, see correspondence with Burgess in EWB 23:3. It is curious that in the department's great spread over the world landscape the administration could not see evidence of its continuing eminence.

21. Hughes was acceptable as chair nine months later and so is ruled out. Warner was at this time inactive in sociology and hence an unlikely candidate on internal grounds. That leaves Wirth, Hauser, and Blumer. We know Wirth was both an internal candidate and unacceptable, but he had just been unequivocally refused a year before. We know that Tyler found Hauser unacceptable (Sewell, personal communication) and that Hauser had the ambition to want, indeed to expect, to be director of the U.S. Census Bureau, a much bigger job than department chair. About Blumer much less is known, although his ambitions are evident in his acceptance of the chair at Berkeley on his resignation in July 1952. He too was a longtime local, and we know that Hauser, for one, considered him one of the ten most eminent sociologists in the country (Hauser to C. Mady, 2 March 1954, PMH 14:8).

22. Tyler made his views clear in his letter to full professors (Burgess, Blumer, Hart, Hauser, Hughes, Warner; for some reason Wirth's name was left off [EWB 33:5, 13 February 1952]). The issue of the chair was still open at this point, well over a year after Wirth was found unacceptable to the administration (which now meant Kimpton, Hutchins having resigned in the meantime). The announcement of Hughes's chairmanship was by press release (17 November 1952, PP52 151:1). Tyler, like Kimpton, was deeply worried about factions and personal disagreements in the department, although at the same time he worried that the great continuity of the department over the past twenty years meant that "new ideas and new directions are necessary." He chose to ignore that the department was already conducting the faculty seminar on the future of sociology.

nounced his resignation, equally unexpectedly, about the same time.[23] With these disgruntled locals off their hands, the new administration began looking outside for a chair. Chancellor Kimpton talked to senior sociologists around the country, both getting advice and trying to recruit. In the summer of 1952 he sought to bring Samuel Stouffer back, apparently without bothering to notify the department. At the same time, William Sewell (of Wisconsin, a Minnesota Ph.D.) was recruited as a potential chair. Sewell got the full treatment. Kimpton promised massive resources. Sewell's longtime acquaintance Ralph Tyler pressured him strongly. But Sewell didn't move to Chicago, for reasons that were plaguing the administration's general plan of overcoming insularity. Hyde Park had become "nearly unlivable." Moreover, as in the Merton-Lazarsfeld recruitment, the university's financial situation created difficulties, despite Kimpton's promises. Meanwhile, on its own the department was trying to get Kingsley Davis, though not as chair.[24]

When it became clear about midsummer that an internal chair was necessary, Donald Horton was acting chair. Horton himself had no desire for the office; it was early in his career, and he needed more time for research. At a faculty meeting he listed the various people who had refused to become chair, including Hughes. The only remaining possibility, he said, was Dun-

23. In general, Blumer's departure is hard to understand. His nemesis Ogburn was retiring. With his friends Wirth and Hauser, he was about to acquire dominance in the department. His dissatisfactions, although long-standing, had not prevented his remaining before. But there were crucial forces driving him out. Some were professional. An ambitious man—as his subsequent Berkeley chairmanship shows—he was (probably) denied the chair at Chicago and foresaw the ascension to that office of Hughes, of whom he thought little. But the crucial reason was personal. Blumer's wife required a milder climate for her health. This was undoubtedly the principal motivation for the move, as well as for the great local secrecy with which it was carried out. We do not know when Blumer began negotiating with Berkeley. He resigned 22 July 1952 (PP52 151:1), quite late in the year by contemporary standards, although the department knew he was leaving at least by 28 May 1952.

24. The "unlivable" quote is from Professor Sewell (personal communication). There is some unclarity in his mind about the date of the offer made to him and no documentary information on it. Summer 1952 best squares his own recollections with material for which we have documentary evidence. It is noteworthy that in Professor Sewell's recollection Everett Hughes wrote the original offer letter to him, not Burgess. This may mean the offer was later (summer 1953), but Sewell also recalled that Blumer was not yet gone. Most likely Hughes was acting for Burgess during one of his quarters out of residence. There is absolutely no indication in any department correspondence about the Sewell offer, so we may take it as administration induced. Oddly, Sewell's only close connection in the department was Duncan, whom he had known as a student when he was teaching at Oklahoma and mentored closely since. Sewell had arranged Duncan's appointments at Penn State and Wisconsin and indeed urged him to go to Chicago rather than stay at Wisconsin in 1950–51.

On Davis, see Foote to department, 20 February 1953, and Duncan to Hauser, 15 July 1952, both in PMH 14:11. The Kimpton-Stouffer letter, 10 July 1952, is in PP52 151:1.

can. Shortly thereafter Hughes, who disliked Duncan intensely, changed his mind and announced himself available.[25]

Hughes was acceptable to the administration for a number of reasons. There was a link through HD, in which both Tyler and Hughes were active. Indeed, it was in this year that Hughes (and Foote) moved onto the HD Executive Committee (Warner had already been on it for a decade). Perhaps, too, the administration may have felt that Hughes would be weak enough to allow them to dictate departmental policy. Or they may have simply been buying time while other expedients were tried.

Once Hughes became chair, the department quickly polarized. Coming after the expected losses of Burgess and Ogburn, the unexpected losses of Wirth and Blumer had turned a worrisome transition into an openly recognized rout. Therefore pressure for an instant solution was great. But the loss of Burgess and Wirth—probably the most central people in the department despite the latter's acerbity—meant an empty middle. Moreover, Blumer's and Wirth's departures removed the important constraints that these friends had placed on Hauser's often domineering behavior. Taken together, these various forces divided the department sharply.

Other forces reinforced that separation. Less visible now, but central at the time, were long-standing political differences. The Burgess-Wirth wing of the department was politically active and reformist. As a result, Burgess and Hauser had both been targets of national-level loyalty investigations, Burgess in connection with work for the Public Health Service and Hauser in connection with the Census directorship. Burgess, like Ogburn, had long-standing memberships in various American-Soviet friendship organizations, and the two of them, together with Wirth and other university faculty attached to various organizations on the attorney general's list, had been investigated in the Illinois "Red-ucators" hearings in 1949. Blumer's politics were aligned with his friends' activism and reformism, although he was not investigated. By contrast, Hughes and, particularly, his close friend Riesman to some extent felt themselves victims of a Left backlash against McCarthyism. Similarly, neither Hughes nor Warner was a reformer in the manner of Thomas or Wirth. As one commenter put it, "More than sociology divided Hughes and Warner from the rest."[26]

25. Although we lack documentary evidence for this story, several personal sources told conforming versions of it.

26. Burgess was investigated in 1949 (by Broyles in Illinois), in 1951 (by the FBI for the U.S. Public Health Service), and in 1953 by the Jenner subcommittee. Ogburn and Wirth were cotargets with Burgess (and nearly fifty other faculty members) in the Broyles affair, in which Hutchins used his talent for ridicule so effectively against the politicians (Ashmore 1989, 276). See materials in PP52 2:7 and PP45 4:1. On Riesman and Hughes, see particularly Riesman to

There was, too, a difference of style. Hughes was an aristocratic gentleman. Distant, witty, and gracious, he was forbearing to his enemies and quiet, even timid, in public meetings. (He could be hard on students, however.) His friend Riesman, although less retiring in public settings, was equally the gentleman, scion of an old Philadelphia Jewish family and proud of its heritage of learning and professionalism. The Riesman-Hughes correspondence often concerns private schools, English and Continental traditions, and detailed markings of social class. By contrast, Hauser was a brash, self-made child of poverty from Chicago's Jewish Far West Side. Duncan was a plainspoken second-generation sociologist from Oklahoma. While Wirth and Blumer remained this gap of style was not so great, for both of them, although brilliant and caustic, were longtime acquaintances of Hughes. But with them gone and Riesman arrived, the gap became an abyss.[27]

Over the three years of Hughes's chairmanship, these various forces worked themselves into an open war. To some extent this war worked itself out on the turf of "quantitative versus qualitative," but, as we shall see, these and many other intellectual issues were merely symbolic units manipulated in a competition driven by other things.

From the start things were difficult. Blumer's first act on going to Berkeley was to recruit Hauser at a formidable salary. Kimpton himself had to intervene to retain Hauser. Indeed, the administration had little confidence in the department's own personnel efforts. Kimpton admitted to alumni of the department that it was not as good as it ought to be, even while emeritus chair Ellsworth Faris, one of his important advisers, was telling him that Hughes's judgment could not be trusted and that there was serious doubt around the discipline about recent appointments.[28]

Hughes, 22 June 1953, ECH 45:16. The left group was carrying on the strong reformist heritage of the earlier Chicago school.

27. Hughes's style is evident in his correspondence with Riesman, warm but without Riesman's exuberant affection. His caution under fire was proverbial and is shown in the seminar examined later. Riesman's style is equally proverbial and equally clear in his correspondence with Hughes. For the depth of the abyss, see Riesman to Hughes on Duncan, 1 June 1955 (see note 34 regarding location).Undoubtedly the special heat between Riesman and Hauser had to do with their very different styles of Jewishness, on which see Riesman to Hughes, 15 May 1957, ECH 46:4.

28. Blumer also tried to hire Goodman and Duncan in the years immediately after leaving Chicago. So much for his image as purely qualitative. Faris retained a strong interest in the department. "I am, you can well imagine, greatly interested in the department and hope that its strength and preeminence will not be diminished" (Faris to Burgess, 12 July 1951, EWB 7:10). The Faris-Kimpton letter is 5 December 1952, PP52 151:1. Of department members, Faris had probably been closest to Wirth; see the letters in LW 3:7. (Wirth was of course dead by this point. Faris seems to have disliked Hauser intensely.) Blumer's recruitment of Hauser lasted

In the early stages, it was not clear which departmental faction the administration wanted to support. Kimpton seemed to genuinely regret the loss of Blumer yet found himself "in complete agreement with" the retiring Ogburn over Ogburn's anti-Blumer memorandum "Some Criteria for Appointment to the Department of Sociology." In part this administrative confusion simply reflected the mixed signals coming from the department itself; Burgess's last official message to the chancellor strongly praised the very appointments that emeritus chair Faris had attacked six months before. More important, however, the whole axis of departmental struggles was shifting. The division was no longer Hughes-Warner versus Blumer-Wirth, but it had not yet settled into the new alignment of Hughes-Riesman versus Hauser.[29]

No secret was made of the department's troubles. Hauser spoke with characteristic gusto of "our present position of mediocrity among the Departments of Sociology in the United States." Gradually, strategies emerged to deal with the situation. All of these aimed at an eclectic department. A cohesive core remained in the graduate curriculum areas and in the prelim examination, which dates in its modern form from the self-study discussed later. But the goal of eclecticism, originally the heart of administration policy, became by 1953 accepted by the department.[30]

Most faculty urged a variety of approaches to eclecticism. For example, Hauser urged three strategies: hiring major outsiders (like Kingsley Davis),

---

over two heavy years. For the first offer, see Hauser to Hughes and Hauser to Horton, both 18 May 1953, PMH 14:11. That the first offer was turned down we know from Burgess's letter to Kimpton (30 June 1953, PP52 151:1) thanking him for his intervention. Kimpton was having trouble keeping Tyler himself at this point, and so Tyler's opposition to Hauser may have mattered less. Blumer kept at it (Blumer to Hauser, 10 November 1953, PMH 3:6; Hauser to Hughes, 4 June 1954, PMH 3:11; Blumer to Hauser, 10 June 1954, PMH 3:11; Hauser to Hughes, 17 July 1954, PMH 14:11). Hauser finally said no in summer 1954. Blumer was also trying to hire Goodman (personal communication) and Duncan. He kept after Duncan for years (see department minutes, 4 October 1956). For Kimpton's public position on the department, see T. K. Noss to Kimpton, 25 April 1952, PP52 151:1: "You may recall that last Thursday night, you told me with a frankness I appreciated that the University of Chicago Department of Sociology is not quite what it used to be. Somewhat sadly I had to agree with you but with some reservations."

29. Kimpton to Blumer, 28 July 1952, PP52 151:1; Kimpton to Ogburn, 18 August 1952, PP52 151:1. The Ogburn memorandum is in fact an obvious attack on Blumer, with its glorification of quantity of academic production (Blumer's was relatively small), its attack on public service (Blumer's arbitration work), its explicit valuing of "IQ, imagination, and insight" over "brilliance, debating qualities, skill in dialectics, verbalism and exhibitionism," and its argument that "the role of theory as formerly held is due for some deflation." It is the third characteristic—verbal brilliance—that clearly targets Blumer, for the faculty seminar transcripts make it very clear that Blumer firmly enjoyed—and very much succeeded in—holding his own against all comers, whether his position was reasonable or not.

30. Hauser's quote is in a memo of 17 February 1953, PMH 14:11.

Once Hughes became chair, Riesman's role became more open, although he did not officially enter the department until fall 1954. Already in late 1952, just as Hughes's ascension was announced, Riesman was "scouting" for new faculty, in this case Lipset. In an early letter, he wrote that Hughes was the only true heir of Park, that he ought to break with Hauser and his party, and that he needed strong departmental allies (of whom Riesman, clearly, would be one).[35]

Riesman, however, was equally aware of attacks on his and Hughes's version of social science from the humanistic side. He had a low opinion of Hutchins's old favorite Richard McKeon and worried that the good (i.e., broad vision) social science of the Social Relations Department at Harvard was beleaguered by antiscientific humanists like Arthur Schlesinger Jr. Once in the department Riesman played a central role in recruiting, largely because he spent so much of his time on leave at other universities, traveling the lecture circuit, and vacationing in the East. He more than anyone else was the source of the connection with Columbia, for he was a great admirer of Lipset and the Bureau of Applied Sociological Research and a friend of Helen and Robert Lynd. Rossi and Katz both came to Chicago's attention through Riesman.[36]

Riesman's practical aims in these recruitments were twofold. First, he wanted young people to supervise the immense projects he and Hughes had begun, like the one in Kansas City. The pair had lost a major grant through Chicago's lack of such young project directors, and Riesman made their potential as study directors a central part of his judgments of possible hires like St. Clair Drake and Morris Janowitz. Wide-vision social science need not be small-scale social science; bureaucratic ethnography has a long pedi-

---

of Riesman's opinions. But nonetheless the overall pattern and tenor are unmistakable; despite his active recruiting of interesting young people, Riesman played a largely destructive role in departmental politics in the four years of his department membership. Unless otherwise noted, the correspondence is all in ECH 45:15–16 and 46:1–4, ordered chronologically. We cite it simply by date. On Riesman's reaction to Hughes's chairmanship, and to Burgess, Wirth, and Blumer, see Riesman to Hughes, 22 August 1952 and 27 August 1952. In particular, Riesman believed he had been stabbed in the back by Wirth for a job possibility at Haverford; see Riesman to Hughes, 9 March 1953.

35. On Lipset, see Hughes to Riesman (n.d., ca. October 1952). The cited letter of Hughes is 21 March 1953.

36. On McKeon (Riesman also disparaged Enrico Fermi and Sewall Wright in the same phrase) see 23 June 1953. On Harvard, see 31 August 1954. On BASR see, among many others, 29 June 1954, and on the Lynds, 22 August 1952. All letters in this note are Riesman to Hughes. Our aim here is to demolish the notion that divisions in departmental politics were dictated by or even distantly related to intellectual positions. *Both* Hauser and Riesman liked quantitative work or at least (in Riesman's case) admitted it was needed. But they wanted different versions of it. It was much more important that they hated each other.

gree reaching back through Middletown to the Pittsburgh Survey and Charles Booth.[37]

But Riesman also wanted votes. His ratings of prospective senior recruits were more in terms of their prospective departmental politics than in terms of their work, even after one makes due allowance for the intimacy of the letters. His attitude toward tenure candidates clarifies this feeling. When Riesman admired a candidate's work, he discussed the work in the letters. When he did not, he discussed the candidate's personal style and voting potential.[38]

Hughes clearly tried to keep Riesman at arm's length. His letters are learned and affectionate, but when Riesman needed reining in—he occasionally led people to think he was offering them jobs—Hughes was diplomatic but firm. More important, Hughes refused to become the grand leader Riesman wanted, opting to take a leave and return to full-time scholarship rather than continue his labors as chair.[39]

By 1955 departmental polarization was complete. The addition of Riesman, together with his close association with Hughes, Warner, Horton, and Foote in the new Center for Leisure Studies, meant a coherent focus for the "qualitative" party, centered on the close friendship of Hughes and Riesman. Nearly all of the Riesman party were also on the Executive Committee of HD. Moreover, Riesman had made a great impression on Marshall Field, a key member of the university's Visiting Committee, and had thus become an administration darling. He had also been on the cover of *Time*. Meanwhile, Hauser was increasingly identified with NORC. He had arranged, with new dean Chauncy Harris and NORC's Clyde Hart, a new relationship between the department and NORC. His personal power bases—the Population Research Center and the Chicago Community Inventory—were successful and well integrated with NORC. And Bogue was now tenured regular faculty, as was the meteoric Goodman.[40]

The first major issue that clarified the polarization was Foote's tenure. Foote was by this time securely within the Hughes-Riesman party. He had

37. On the lost grant see 5 May 1954, and on Drake and Janowitz, 22 July 1954, both Riesman to Hughes.

38. Votes were a perpetual concern to Riesman; see, e.g., Riesman to Hughes, 1 June 1955.

39. On the job issue, see Hughes to Riesman, 30 April 1954 and 8 May 1954. On Hughes's relief at quitting, see Hughes to Riesman, 3 August 1956.

40. Various letters through the PP52 series (151:1, 2, 2.1) show that Hauser in fact cultivated Kimpton considerably, sending him reprints, notices of his activities, and the like. On the Leisure Center, see Riesman to Hauser, 26 September 1955, PMH 14:11. On the Field affair, see W. B. Cannon to Riesman, 19 January 1955, PP52 148:4. On the new NORC see Norton Ginsburg to Hauser, 23 July 1955, PMH 14:11. Interestingly, it was Hauser, not chair Everett Hughes, who at this time made a major presentation to the trustees on the department. See the Riesman memo above. Riesman was on the cover of *Time* 27 September 1954.

underlined that position, and lost Hauser's original goodwill, by besting him in a public debate over "cumulation" in sociology sponsored by the Society for Social Research. An exponent of participant observation and an active researcher, Foote had, however, also offended Warner by siding with Duncan on the latter's critique of Warner's work. As a result, he had little chance for success. He moved to the private sector, where he became a major figure in applied sociology.

Matters came to open conflict in 1956, by which time local opinion agreed that Everett Hughes would not have a second term, which, in any case, he did not want. Hauser and Riesman were the candidates. (Apparently, looking for an external chair had been stopped.) The faculty was still about evenly split between quantitative and qualitative parties, although the balance inclined toward the qualitative. Warner, Hughes, Riesman, Foote, Horton, Blau, and Strauss were all qualitative in one way or another, although only Hughes and Strauss really represented old Chicago. Hauser, Goodman, Duncan, Bogue, and Katz were quantitative, although themselves divided between survey work and demography. Candidates Hauser and Riesman disliked each other intensely. Hauser was publicly contemptuous of Riesman's work, and Riesman had made it clear that he would leave the university if Hauser became chair.[41]

The affair was undecidable in the department, and the Riesman party somewhat cynically approached Leo Goodman as a compromise candidate. Goodman was a methodologist's methodologist and hence necessarily acceptable to the quantitative faction. Goodman was willing, but Dean Harris would not accept him. After interviewing each tenured department member individually, Harris decided to ask Hauser to chair the department for one year, at the end of which the situation would be reviewed. But the chancellor overruled him. Kimpton felt the department ought to have a firm decision, and he made Hauser chair for three years. Kimpton's feelings for Hauser seem always to have been strong, and it seems likely that he saw in Hauser the strong hand necessary to rebuild the department. After all, for Kimpton this particular academic headache was now six years old.[42]

41. The men were also absolutely different as people, as we have noted above. Riesman's position paper on the future of the department survives, 8 March 1956, in ECH 46:2. It contains various olive branches offered to the other side but is not really a centrist document. In it Riesman discusses in cold war metaphors Hauser's attack on a Hughes-Riesman student at a dissertation hearing and goes on to discuss the two camps in considerable detail. His statement makes it clear that Warner was the only person who really tried to reconcile the two sides. On the public nature of Riesman's position, see Riesman to Hughes, 19 May 1957, which tells of Grodzins's warnings to Kimpton about Riesman's probable departure.

42. Hauser had extensive prior administrative experience both in Washington and in Chicago. He been associate dean of social sciences under Ralph Tyler in the late 1940s before

Yet his motives in this choice were by no means unmixed. In responding to media star Riesman, who at once moved ahead on an offer from Harvard, Kimpton seems affectionate and deeply regretful. "You would desolate the University if you accepted the Harvard offer. . . . I do hope you remain and hope I could help to make your life about here a happier one." On the other hand, his enthusiasm for Hauser was great, and they were sufficiently close that Hauser apparently raised with Kimpton the delicate issue of the department's tenure vote on Duncan. It seems clear that Kimpton, like Tyler and Harris, regarded the "youngsters" with their "techniques of modern social research" as the future of the department.[43]

The immediate effects of polarization continued to be felt largely by the junior faculty. In 1955 it had been Foote's turn. Now came Duncan's. Like Foote, Duncan had another job waiting—in his case an open tenure offer from Blumer at Berkeley. Like Foote, Duncan got the easily predicted mixed vote. Unlike Foote, however, Duncan stayed, entering full-time research status after 1957. (He reentered the department briefly in 1960–62 before eventually leaving for Michigan.) Some thought him happy with the result—his research flourished—but others were not so sure.[44]

In 1957 the last victim became Anselm Strauss, who like Duncan was on his way to a career shaping whole subfields of the discipline. Although there were some new faces (Rossi had been promoted and Fred Strodtbeck brought in from the Law School), the result was the same.[45]

Thus the brief Hughes epoch closed with the reduction and isolation of the qualitative wing of the department. True to his promise, Riesman left within

---

he burned his bridges in the 4E episode. Sources for the Goodman twist of the "chair affair" are Leo Goodman and then dean Chauncy Harris. Harris is our only source on Kimpton's role. Kimpton left no personal records about it.

43. Kimpton to Riesman, 1 May 1957, PP52 151:2.1. Hauser to Kimpton, 16 January 1959, same location. The "youngsters" quote is from Harris to Board of Trustees, 13 November 1959, SSV.

44. The Duncan decision, like the chair debacle, was simply an outcome of prior politics, although Duncan had mortally offended Warner, one of the swing voters, before he arrived. In 1950 the *ASR* had published Duncan's characteristically sharp and effective attack on Warner's entire oeuvre in social stratification (Pfautz and Duncan 1950). Interestingly enough, it was a Chicago attack; the theoretical justifications invoked the names of Park, Burgess, Wirth, and Simmel. Warner, Duncan said, was being misled by the anthropologists. (Duncan himself attributes the theoretical parts of the paper to his coauthor Harold Pfautz.) In hindsight, it is easy to read Duncan's article as a white paper for the *American Occupational Structure* (Blau and Duncan 1967). The university finally admitted its error on this particular decision. In 1979 Duncan was given an honorary degree.

45. On the Strauss tenure decision, see Riesman to Hughes, 24 October 1957. Riesman accused the other side of favoring sociology with large divisions of labor, rather curious given his and Hughes's Kansas City project.

a year. Foote was gone, Strauss going. Warner and Hughes held on, although Warner left four years before retirement when the administration refused him a distinguished service professorship in 1959. Unlike Riesman, Hughes was not bitter, indeed cautioning Riesman against bitter talk in public.[46]

Even after Hauser assumed control, the Kimpton administration never seems to have lost its sense that the department was in crisis. In mid-1957 Vice President R. W. Harrison wrote Kimpton that "Hauser is not through with building of tenure-covered aspects of Sociology and is thinking of three or four more spots" and made it clear, apropos of the potential tenuring of Peter Rossi, that the administration might regard that tenure as foreclosing other perhaps more desirable possibilities. This was clearly still a department on probation.[47]

In his chair's report of 1958 Hauser notes "a sharp break from adherence to identification with the 'Chicago School' of Sociology." He proudly lists the origins of current teaching faculty, notes that only four of thirteen are Chicago graduates, and speaks of "some grumbling on the part of some Chicago graduates that we have gone to far in the avoidance of placing Chicago men on the faculty." He speaks of "the complete disappearance of the earlier bipolar division of departmental interests." (Riesman was gone by this point.) But at the same time he is worried about managing the transition impending through Warner's and Hughes's departures. There is an immense amount of material about NORC in the report, indicating that NORC's relation to the department had become a major problem. Finally, Hauser regrets the "serious loss" of James Coleman.[48]

A year later, Hauser was less sure. "I would say we are still in a state of transition." He mentioned Warner's loss, about which he in fact cared little, but began to worry about the potential loss of Goodman, who was planning to take a leave at Columbia in his hometown of New York City. Hauser rated the department as well rounded, which he clearly now viewed as a virtue. He saw social psychology as rescued by Strodtbeck, who could draw in Katz, Rossi, and Jim Davis. Rossi and Duncan MacRae (a joint appointment with political science) would make up a program in political sociology. On the weakness side, he noted the social disorganization field but hoped the appointment of James Short would at least shore it up. And he

---

46. On the Warner affair, see Hauser to Kimpton, 16 January 1959. In keeping with his "take no prisoners" attitude, Hauser opposed Warner's promotion. Warner had of course been a central force against Duncan, Hauser's most important protégé. On Hughes's cautions to Riesman, see Hughes to Riesman, 15 May 1957.

47. Harrison to Kimpton, 24 June 1957, PP52 151:1.

48. Hauser to Harris, 8 December 1958, SSV.

was pleased with the strength of theory (Shils was jointly appointed in the department, and Vernon Dibble had been appointed), which sounds surprising given his widely publicized views.[49]

That Hauser was publicly pleased to be stronger in theory indicates how far Chicago's distrust of "theory"—and it was strong both in the quantitative camp and in parts of the qualitative, as we have seen—had finally bowed to administration pressure for eclecticism. Also, it is noteworthy that joint appointments were crucial to the new department. That much of the Hughes strategy Hauser continued with verve.

A number of things contributed to Hauser's ability to create a stable moment for the department. The most obvious was the removal of his adversary Riesman. The second was administration cooperation, extended for the first time in six years. But third was Hauser's own ability as a judge of academic horseflesh. His ratings of his staff (present in the sources but unquoted here) were nearly unerring, both at the time and in terms of later careers. Yet that judgment extended only within those realms he himself knew and liked. It may be true that Hauser recognized at once the extraordinary potential of Harrison White, then a postdoctoral student retraining himself in sociology and only two years past his physics Ph.D. But on the other hand he worked hard to get rid of Foote and Strauss, and in his insistence on ignoring locals he ignored department graduates who were achieving disciplinary eminence—Goffman, Becker, and others.[50]

Despite Hauser's apparent hostility to the old Chicago tradition after 1957, he eventually helped rebuild it. Since the early 1950s he had been pushing Morris Janowitz on the department, and in 1962 Janowitz was finally secured. Once in Chicago, Janowitz energetically rebuilt the tradition—insisting that the Press reissue the old departmental classics, inserting those classics on the prelim examination list, sending students into the field, backing appointments of scholars like Gerald Suttles and David Street. This was essentially the program of the "Departmental Objectives" document of ten years before. A generation of students flooded back to the field, from William Kornblum to Ruth Horowitz, Charles Bosk, and Michael Burawoy.[51]

49. Hauser to Harris, 3 November 1959, SSV.

50. On White, see Hauser to Harris, 3 November 1959, SSV.

51. Janowitz was actually someone Hauser and Riesman agreed on, although Riesman like many others found Janowitz's personal style distasteful in the extreme. See Riesman to Hughes, 22 July 1954. In studying this history one cannot avoid the conclusion that Hauser's take no prisoners attitude grew, like Riesman's, out of their almost visceral dislike for each other. Whether a third party of sufficient force could have controlled the two is matter for speculation; certainly Hughes did not have the fortitude.

Thus the postwar department did not, as is commonly assumed, move inexorably toward a quantitative stance. And to the extent that such a stance emerged, it was not the department but rather the chancellor who made the final decision. In the department most evidence controverts a strict quantitative/qualitative interpretation for this period. Hauser and Wirth were intimate friends, but Wirth disliked Warner. Blumer did not have a very high opinion of Hughes, but he thought enough of Hauser to try to lure him to Berkeley and, in return, was highly regarded by Hauser himself. Riesman took the lead in the recruitment of Alice and Peter Rossi. Goodman was willing to be a qualitative party's candidate for chair.[52]

Rather, the department in this period revolved around a number of strong relationships. During the years 1945–51 the whole group was held together both by the immense weight of their common memories and by two central figures—Burgess in the older generation and Wirth in the younger. All this was changed by Burgess's retirement, Wirth's death, and the departure of Blumer. With their disappearance and Hughes's attempt to strengthen his hand by absorbing Riesman, the rifts opened wider. The disappearance of Wirth and Blumer also removed the strong personal forces wedding Hauser to Chicago-style thinking; as his vita shows, he became more of a demographer in the strict sense. (He also became, in many ways, more an impresario than a researcher.)

As this rift opened, younger people without the depth of memories allied with the powerful personalities of the middle generation, and squabbling became more open. Tyler's opposition to the abrasive, dominant Hauser left the department in the hands of Hughes, who had been something of a departmental outsider for a long time. It was this—and the presence of Riesman with his strong views—that produced the relatively brief period of open factional conflict, conflict that cost the department, in Foote, Duncan, and Strauss, three figures who would be central to the discipline over the next three decades.

In cutting this Gordian knot, Kimpton's decision for one side had the effect of eviscerating the other, at least temporarily, but did not bring the department long-run peace. But the Kimpton decision did establish the turf on which peace would be made. For if Riesman had become chair, Hauser might very easily have accepted Berkeley's continuing blandishments, and Riesman could have led the department toward the combination of grand theory and qualitative empirical work that had come to mark the Ivy League departments other than Columbia. For the department itself, then,

52. On Wirth and Warner, see Farber 1988, 342. Riesman's claims about the Rossis are in Riesman 1990.

the crucial transition years were from the administration's refusal of Wirth in 1950 to its designation of Hauser in 1956.[53]

The faculty's history from 1945 to 1960 thus falls into three periods: the gradual emergence of the split between Wirth-Blumer and Hughes-Warner, the polarization between Hauser and Riesman, and the Hauser hegemony. These periods are separated by two turning points: the seminar debates of 1951–52 and the chairmanship battle of 1956.

As one watches the web of alliances and battles unfold, it becomes clear that no one individual maintained a constant position throughout. Hauser could attack theory in one breath and pursue Neil Smelser in the next. Hughes could feel unappreciated at one point and defend the department that had rejected him at another. The Riesman party could damn Hauser's work as "industrial" and yet mount projects that dwarfed most of the quantitative research. As we said earlier, we cannot find the "Chicago school" at the level of individuals. Enmeshed in the constant ebb and flow of interaction—the deals over hiring, the proposals for grants, the challenges of students—individual faculty make use of ideas at hand, imposing on them a style that, while perhaps modeled on a tradition, is uniquely personal.

The Department That Viewed Itself

The Chicago school is therefore something that exists between individuals. It is not above them, for that would imply a nesting of individuals within groups, and as Mead argued, self and society both emerge from one process. Thus it was in the process of faculty interactions that there emerged and solidified the tradition that would later be called the Chicago school. Fortunately, we can see this emergence in detail in the faculty seminar of 1951–52.[54] This year-long fight over who really wore the mantle of

53. Riesman saw Parsons's Social Relations Department as a social science ideal, but under threat. That he felt this at a time when Parsons's flow of turgid tomes was well under way— *The Social System, Economy and Society,* and *Toward a General Theory of Action* were all in print by this point—indicates his complete failure to grasp what the Chicago tradition was about. Hughes had profound insight into Riesman, who, he saw, was actually much more interested in undergraduate teaching than anything else. See Hughes to Riesman, 15 May 1957, on the latter's resignation.

54. In 1950 the Ford Foundation gave grants of $300,000 apiece to seven institutions for the expansion of social science (Foote to Seminar, 12 May 1952, EWB 33:4). At Chicago the funds were auctioned by the Social Science Research Council, a divisional committee of which Wirth was the chair. The department used its funds to support and transcribe a seminar. It seems likely that the seminar was Wirth's idea. He made the application for the money (seminar minutes, 11 October 1951), he set the agenda with a long fall memorandum (undated, but eventually distributed 10 December 1951), and he often dominated discussion. Moreover, Wirth's opening presentation makes it clear that his interlocutors had only hazy ideas of what

Robert Park shows how the loose tangle of maxims and practices that had sustained the department in its glory years could come to be molded, in the minds of those who argued about it, into an independent object, a thing capable of reproducing itself through their later work. Not that those maxims and practices were not taught in various graduate programs throughout the country, nor that they would not have lasted without the seminar. Rather, this kind of argument forced the participants to bundle together all the various strands, to objectify them in the person and the heritage of Park, and to thereby make in their own minds a cultural object that would attract to itself, and claim parentage of, many sorts of activities throughout diverse areas of sociology. The very looseness of the seminar reflected this task of assemblage. Every time one more thing was crammed into the concept of "sociology" (which here meant "Chicago sociology"), something else would fall out on the other side. The sticks piled on the heap would not stay there until they began to be woven together enough to provide a restraining framework.

The seminar debates are thus about the creation not of the second Chicago school but of the first. As its era closed, the survivors tried to define it for themselves. In so doing they (and others having similar conversations) transformed the dying subject into a living object. That object survived the partisan squabbles of the 1950s and was available for Janowitz to husband, as it was available to Hughes for transplantation to Brandeis.

The seminar ended in a moment of despair. It was late May 1952. Louis Wirth was dead. The department had just been suddenly told that an "objectives" document was immediately needed by the chancellor. Yet before they put the objectives into final form, Nelson Foote proposed that they should "hear a few 'last words' and ask a few questions of those who won't be here next year." Reiss, Blumer, Williams, Burgess, and Ogburn (who was not present) were leaving.

Blumer led off with a ringing valediction:

> Mr. Blumer: . . . I have the belief that much of the eminence of this department for over half a century has stemmed from the fact that the leaders in the Department have been quite concerned with try-

---

was planned. In his annual report to Dean Tyler (27 August 1951, EWB 33:2), Burgess platitudinizes the seminar as dealing with research and training. But in opening the seminar on 11 October 1951, he simply turned it over to Wirth. All documents relevant to this seminar are located, in roughly chronological order, in EWB 33:2–4. All primary material referenced in these sections is in those folders, so we have provided no direct citation, but only dates. We have dated some of the undated documents by inspecting the vouchers for reproducing them, which are in SSV.

ing to develop, not an assemblage of discrete facts, but something in the nature of a coherent body of knowledge of human group life as such. We can certainly note that in the case of Dr. Small; we see it most forcefully in the instance of Dr. Park, who combined with his very vigorous research interests a very pronounced and steady concern with trying to weld together a picture of human group life as such. I think, from my own point of view, based on my familiarity with the work of Dr. Thomas, that he likewise was concerned with the effort to develop something in the form of a coherent scheme for the study of human group life. I think the loss of that sort of interest would be most unfortunate in the Department.

After Blumer finished, Burgess turned to Reiss:

> *Mr. Burgess:* Mr. Reiss, you're leaving us—a fact which qualifies you for the status of wise man.
> *Mr. Reiss:* I think that I agree thoroughly with Mr. Blumer, when one looks at what is happening to sociology today. I find myself in the position, very often, of kind of going along with the stream. It doesn't quite square up with the views of society which characterize what has come to be known as the Chicago school of sociology and which I learned as a student in the Department.
> *Mr. Burgess:* Why did you deviate?
> *Mr. Blumer (to Burgess):* Why did *you?*

Here, in Social Science 106 on the evening of 28 May 1952, was the end of the road: the young generation gently confessing a loss of faith, the middle generation accusing even its elders of forgetting. Was Blumer right that only he had the true relics of Chicago? Or did the discussion rather signify that the relics taken separately were so much worthless wood? Or was it that in squabbling over their inheritance the children of the 1920s manufactured the relics within themselves?[55]

55. The group that sat down to this discussion in October included Burgess but not Ogburn, who had dropped out of departmental affairs by this point. Of the next generation, Hauser was out of town for the entire year, but Wirth, Blumer, Hughes, and Warner were present. All were in their early fifties. Nearly all the rest of the group were thirty or less. Duncan, Goodman, Reiss, Josephine Williams, and Shirley Star were all very recent Ph.D.'s. Foote, Harold Wilensky, and D. G. Moore were graduate students. Only Donald Horton, an anthropologist collaborating with Warner, and Buford Junker, a graduate student who was Warner's chief fieldworker, were between these two groups in age. Neither was very active, so the meetings took the interactional form of senior professors arguing among themselves or with much younger people.

The discussions were—as the administration would have predicted—untainted by knowledge of non-Chicago sociology. Of ten Ph.D.'s in regular attendance, eight were from

The twelve seminar sessions covered a variety of topics. They began with two full sessions on agenda setting. These led to a decision to consider the "syllabi," or annotated reading lists, on which the new foundational exams were based.[56] There were then three sessions each on the syllabi for Social Psychology and Social Organization, respectively, with one brief interpolated meeting on the shortened, *Announcements* texts for all six syllabi. The last three sessions include two about very particular matters— Nelson Foote's report of a project on participant observation and a Psychology Department proposal to found an "Institute of Behavioral Sciences" at Chicago. The final session, although designed to help Dudley Duncan redraft the department's "objectives" document, in fact turned into a wake for the Chicago school.[57]

The seminar began with a murky discussion about what to do and how to do it. Burgess asked Wirth to set out "what ideas have occurred to him." In Wirth's elaborate scheme, there are three main topics—the discipline's subject, its relation to other social sciences, and its subfields—from which four subsidiary topics flowed. (The subsidiaries were the actual content of teaching, the discipline's presuppositions, understudied topics, and actual research problems.) In the discussion, Blumer strongly urged consideration of "the fundamental logical problems of our discipline." Against him, Foote urged empirical study of work in other departments, particularly Harvard and Columbia, more successful because of their study of the

---

Chicago. Of four graduate students, three were at Chicago. Nelson Foote, a Cornell graduate student, was the only voice persistently representing "other versions" of sociology in the discussion. Attendance at the seminars was very regular, with eleven of sixteen attendees making at least nine of twelve sessions. The irregulars included Warner, who attended only five meetings, and the NORC group of Clyde Hart, Star, and Williams.

56. There were syllabi for each of the six major areas (Social Organization, Social Disorganization and Change, Social Psychology and Collective Behavior, Population and Human Ecology, Theory, and Methods). These were large documents (typically thirty pages) of citations and notes, to be mastered by graduate students desiring to specialize in the field. The current form of the documents was new, but the areas (other than theory and methods) were over twenty years old at Chicago. Short versions of the syllabi were published in the *Announcements* and formed the basis of discussion at session 8. At the time of the seminar, only two of the syllabi were complete, as a remark of Foote's at the second meeting makes clear. That is why only two were discussed.

57. There may have been meetings whose minutes somehow did not make it into Burgess's files. But internal evidence suggests strongly that these twelve were the only ones held. Thus the only lengthy conversations concerned social psychology, which was Blumer's chief responsibility, and social organization, which was that of Warner and Hughes. We thus have searching examinations of two major strands of the Chicago school, Blumerian symbolic interactionism and Hughesian, anthropological study of social organization. Missing is the third leg of the stool—human ecology. Its syllabus unfinished, it was present only in its comments on the others.

"more timely" problems of large organizations as opposed to Chicago's studies of "social problems." Warner too urged an empirical approach, suggesting that they proceed at once by studying the subject syllabi themselves. When Burgess agreed with him, a clear opposition emerged between Warner and Burgess on the one hand and Wirth and Blumer on the other. Hughes and Hart then reconciled the two, suggesting that at the next meeting the department continue with general issues but thereafter turn to consideration of the syllabi. Both also raised the issue of methods, which they felt Wirth had obscured.

In this first meeting arise a number of themes that recur continuously: the contrast between Blumer's insistent abstraction and others' desire for an empirical understanding of the discipline, the multicornered worry about the justification of method, the comparison with Harvard and Columbia. But this first meeting also shows the amorphousness of the major participants' positions before the exigencies of discussion formalized them. Here Hughes was the broker between Blumer and Burgess. Never again.

At the end of this meeting, each department member pledged to write "a statement of what he would like to see done," as Hart put it. Most wrote a short paragraph or page. Hughes and Warner each wrote a few pages. But Wirth wrote four thousand words on his own three central questions—the field, its interrelations, and its subdivisions. For him the seminar was an *apologia pro vita sua*, a chance to set forth verbally and in print the credo of the Chicago school as he understood it.

No such aim or urgency informs the writing of Hughes or Warner. For them the day of unity is past. There is no one Chicago school; there is rather a department of "several smaller nuclei of interest and enterprise, constituted each of one or more individuals," in Hughes's kind phrase. Warner is more blunt. "For purposes of maintaining outward peace among us, each and all of us pretend to ourselves that our relations are such that we are inwardly as well as outwardly harmonious and that there is general consensus among us. I do not believe that [this] is true in fact." Both Warner and Hughes favor an archipelagic definition of sociology. It is a "way of viewing problems of social behavior and organization that arise in all areas of life" (Hughes) or "the study of the organization of human behavior, in its persistence" (Warner).

Wirth, by contrast, thinks that sociology really is something. He starts with what it is not: study of society, of group life, of social institutions, even of social interaction. Nor is it simply what sociologists do, by which judgment he denies Foote, Hughes, and Warner. He settles on "sociology is concerned with what is true about man by virtue of the fact that he leads a group life." He recognizes the ill definedness of "group" but says that "the group factor refers to the universal fact that men live in association with others, that they interact with others, or are affected by and affect others."

After noting that groups of humans differ from groups of other things, he moves on to state that sociology should be a science: public, verification-ist, predictive, cumulative. He then emphasizes that

> our data are the real-life situations in which human beings find themselves and not some artificial problems we might concoct in our imagination. We will have a science of sociology to the extent that we address ourselves to the actual life situations in which people are involved.

Finally, he urges a very cautious approach to universal propositions.

> We should, I believe, not attempt to arrive at universality for the sake of universality, if as a result we distort our picture of social re-ality to a point where it is no longer recognizable or meaningful and if the abstractions at which we arrive are so abstract that they can no longer be referred back to concrete instances or empirical situations.

Wirth never improved on this statement, which was in fact a staple part of all his courses. He was not a systematic thinker, although an inspired polemicist and a leader of his colleagues. No more than Park—his prede-cessor as leader of the Chicago school—could he articulate the core of the school as other than a series of maxims. But here they were. Find the group-ness of groups, which lies in how people and groups affect other people and groups. Aim at science, but not so much that you lose the reality. Talk about real people and real problems. Beyond that, Wirth's position was simply a list of vague axioms.[58]

The second session (25 October 1951) settled on the procedure of con-sidering the two existing syllabi (social psychology and social organization) in terms of the questions Wirth had set forth at the first meeting. The group unanimously rejected the idea of spending the Ford money on planning an actual training program, as had been done at several other departments; it

58. Wirth does in fact note the specific connection of sociology with certain particular ar-eas of inquiry—family, criminality, community. He knows that these give rise to the archipel-agic impression. But for him the other quality, of "sociology as a general social science," is more important. Unlike Hughes and Warner, for whom recognition of sociology's general character allows one to get on with the business of discussing its local subdivisions, Wirth feels we must define the heart of sociology itself as a general point of view. He and Parsons agreed on that, though on nothing else. Joseph Gusfield tells a story of Parsons's coming to give an im-portant lecture at Chicago. Wirth sat in the front row opening and reading his mail.

was premature to train people if you could not specify what you were training them for. (There was an overt condemnation of Harvard and Columbia here.) But again Warner intervened to make it clear that for him, not doing what Harvard was doing meant precisely "learning how to disagree." "It could be assumed that, just as Harvard has in effect tried to work out a basic, over-all doctrine, we ought to develop our 'line.' We all know that we aren't the kind to do that." This position, which made the extraordinary research freedom of the university into a general model for intellectual life, explicitly forbade the search for a Chicago core that was central to Wirth and, in his own way, to Blumer.

The agenda-setting meetings thus pushed the major departmental figures into two groups. On one level this was surprising, for Blumer, Wirth, and Hughes each believed himself individually to be the heir of Robert Park. But there were deep differences between the pairs. Hughes and Warner were productive scholars with numerous large projects under way or being planned. Blumer was a perfectionist who refused to publish manuscripts others would have regarded as long since finished. Wirth had actually published very little in the past decade, although he too was sitting on a book-length study. As this contrast implies, Warner and Hughes were far more enmeshed in empirical social investigation than were Blumer and Wirth. There was a contrast in students, too. By this time Hughes was beginning to attract many of the best students in the department, as he previously had not. Blumer and Wirth, with their extraordinary verbal performances, often frightened students away.

The first two meetings thus established a chiasmic irony. Wirth, representing the party of abstraction, codified the Parkian practices. Yet his codification denied itself: Don't abstract, it said, don't lose sight of real people and problems. And Hughes, despite his appearance of concreteness and laxity, knew exactly what he meant when he called sociology "a way of viewing problems of social behavior and organization." Although his archipelago model seemed to imply live and let live, his later seminar performance shows him to have a very clear conception of Parkian research: its core was precisely that militant openness to experience that Wirth here urges in abstract terms.

Charged with the Social Psychology syllabus, Blumer held that field against all comers for next three meetings. Throughout, the same ironic connections began to establish themselves between his and the others' positions.

Blumer begins by saying that unknown to itself social psychology is more confused now than it was when he wrote his own thesis twenty years before. For there is a delusion of nonconfusion, induced by mistaking techniques and methodological standards (those of then current survey-based attitude research) for answers to basic problems. He then throws the floor open. Hughes poses some harmless questions ("Why do you consider social psychology a field?" "Do you like the term 'social psychology'?"), to which Blumer responds with a basic position:

> If one is going to study [the things that happen to the child in interaction] the important thing is to study them through the use of orientations, schemes of approach, and bodies of ideas, the content of which is congruent with what one can observe. This might seem to be a very simple statement not worth making. I make it because—and I could defend this—the overwhelming majority of the approaches today ignore this point.

Hart disagrees bluntly with the latter assertion, and they spar for a few minutes about stimulus-response theory, which Blumer condemns out of hand. He claims that "field investigators" (survey workers) fail to use the knowledge that a person always "acts on the basis of how things appear to *him*." But Hart retorts that survey workers are continuously rethinking the interview situation from the interviewee's standpoint.

Hughes begins to gently chide Blumer for demanding so much. "Maybe the number of people should be very small, and social psychology an exceedingly select field." Blumer rejects him with anger. "I would be the first to disown any allegation that before people could make observations [all] theoretical confusion has to be eliminated. That would be idiotic." He then specifically attacks Hughesian research: "Students sent out on field investigations may go astray at a number of points by virtue of the fact that they have a schema of objects which derives either from the culture of their group or from a particular doctrine." Foote replies for the empiricists: "You seem to advocate a lingering intellectual hypochondria in which we dwell upon all the dire things which may go wrong if we do attempt research."[59]

The fact, however, is that they all believe in the same thing. Hart thinks he is being interpretive enough by wondering what respondents make of interviews. Hughes couldn't possibly live with NORC-type interviews but

---

59. It is painfully clear from this discussion that, as his letters suggest, Blumer thought Hughes a very second-rate mind. On the other hand, they agreed that both had had the experience of finding their work and their students confined over the past decade. Blumer raised the point specifically, late in this meeting, and Burgess demurred. (Ogburn was obviously the culprit; all faculty voted on M.A. and Ph.D. proposals, and he clearly had carried out his prejudices.) But Hughes jumped in to defend Blumer.

thinks he is being interpretive enough by sending students directly into the field. But for Blumer that too fails to adequately reach the realm of the "other." All three agree on the nature of the Parkian standard itself: Be reflective and stay close to reality. They simply disagree about its empirical content. Thus tradition begins to emerge in the form of a maxim that, in one set of words, can mean radically different but "similarly shaped" things to different people.

Burgess then reset Blumer the task of stating the foundations of social psychology. After holding that social psychology must embrace universal propositions on the one hand and historical interpretations (accounts) on the other, Blumer lists five problem fields calling for universal propositions: "the nature of original nature, the nature of group life, of interaction, of the formative process of the individual, and of the kinds of association that the individual may develop." Thus, for Blumer social psychology was the master social science; the last item embraced all of social organization, as the first did all of pure psychology. In between lay group life, interaction, and the formation of individuals. A quick glance verifies that this is, in more or less the same order but with slightly different emphases, the outline of the Park and Burgess textbook of 1921. Blumer is claiming, as he was always to claim, that social psychology—under its later label of symbolic interactionism—was the proper name for the entire Chicago tradition.[60]

Indeed, in these contradictory claims and counterclaims the central themes of the Chicago tradition begin to be heaped into a coherent woodpile. Blumer and Wirth want to set forth a Chicago vision of social life, while Warner and Hughes think one cannot and should not do so. Blumer believes that the heart of sociology is the intellectual problem of how individual and group reciprocally affect one another. Wirth believes that the heart of sociology is a set of maxims: theory grows out of research, and so on. Neither Warner nor Hughes cares what the others think is the heart of sociology. They just want to get on with doing it, which for them takes the form of research following Wirth's maxims and animated by Blumer's problem. One side practices what the other preaches, while attacking the preaching because it doesn't practice and itself being attacked because its practice doesn't quite live up to the preaching. Of such bound-up contradictions are symbols made. For either side would defend the other against

60. The meeting closed with a discussion on particulars and universals that got Blumer, and everyone else, into a complete mess. It was relieved only by Blumer's hilarious travesty of Merton's then recent phrase "middle-range theory" as "middle-class generalizations," of which, of course, Blumer disapproved as being illegitimate hybrids of the universal and the particular.

any outside conception of preaching or practice, be it Parsons or Lazars-feld. The argument is all about what Chicago sociological practice really meant.

The later meetings on social psychology fill out many of these same top-ics. Blumer is unwilling to admit that any research is good, yet also unwil-ling to openly deny the possibility of good research. Indeed, the second social psychology meeting—in which others propose dozens of research strategies and Blumer rejects them all—persuades one that Blumer's real fear is of seeing Mead's insights become simply a "model" to be tested, on the same level as stimulus-response, or psychoanalysis, or (his new bane) cybernetics. He fears lest the Chicago heritage be mangled by the cogs of Ogburnian verification.

Blumer was right that the fate of subtle ideas in little minds is often bru-tal, but in his fear for his ideas, he hid them. His dilemma captures precisely the problem of willed transmission of tradition. He feared to write his ideas out lest they become mere objects; indeed, his most influential single work—the article collection of 1969—was dragged out of him against his will. But by keeping them within he objectified his ideas in another way; he was scandalized when (outside the seminar) Becker told him that students memorized a set of eight student-generated "Blumerian theorems" in order to pass the social psychology section of the prelim (Becker, personal com-munication). Yet only by letting his ideas out into use—by handing them over to others as subjects—could he avoid this dreaded routinism.

The same issue arose in the third meeting, in which there was a long dis-cussion of motivation. Blumer says motivation "represents one of the most confused and ill-understood conceptions that you can find in the litera-ture." The whole literature can be condensed to "you have motive and then behavior." (For Blumer, of course, interpretation and construction of be-havior came in between.) But Foote catches him out. "That is only one scheme." "Do you agree with me that that is the most common one? State another one," retorts Blumer. Foote calmly lists three, then tells Blumer he has just written a review of motivational theories placing forty of them un-der six heads. Here again is the problem of being one among many. For Blumer, social psychology is not just another model, a way of figuring out a problem. It is a whole approach to thinking about social life, a framework, a stance. He backs off, in real confusion for once, and Burgess saves him by changing the topic to the relation of social psychology to psychology more broadly.

This is the exact moment of transmission. For every learner makes of his elder's theories an object, objectifying even the most subjective and intentional aspects of a master's approach. But then in the work itself, if the student is up to it, the subjective transformation occurs. In Blumer's case the clearest and oddest example of this was Duncan, who had gotten A's in all of Blumer's courses. Here in the seminar, Blumer's position of high and absolutist scientism was shared throughout by Duncan alone, who also advertised his Blumerism by circulating to everyone, just before the second meeting, a highly constructivist document titled "Confessions of a Confused Young Sociologist and Aphorisms for a Proper Relativist Sociology." Duncan went on to a distinguished career of what many took to be the epitome of empiricist, objectivist positivism. Yet late in his career Duncan began to show his true colors, colors that many of his later admirers found appalling indeed. *Notes on Social Measurement* (1984) betrays a disappointment with empirical sociology as great as Blumer's in 1951. Duncan had broken some of Blumer's eggs, to be sure, but he was still trying to make a Blumerian omelet.[61]

This third meeting touched another aspect of the Chicago tradition—ecology. Here too was the curious phenomenon of denial by Blumer's abstractions of something that in fact was central to his own ideas. Reiss raises the issue of how social psychology relates to ecology, defining ecology as "the study of human aggregates in time and space." Blumer attacks at once, saying that time and space are just part of the setting for interaction, the later being what really matters. And others belittle time and space as simply two among many facts conditioning a certain social relation. Duncan tries to defend his colleague but is unsuccessful. So in a quick few minutes a central aspect of the Chicago tradition seems to be set aside. But in fact to Wirth, as to Burgess, and in the last analysis to Blumer, it was location in time and space, certainly social time and social space, that was the heart of what they had tried for two decades to defend against Ogburn. Exactly what the new sociology of variables did was take social facts out of their contexts. Context was what Wirth had in mind when he spoke of not losing touch with social reality. Thus we can only conclude that Blumer belittles Reiss's position because, once again, of his pathological fear of objectification.

In summary, throughout these discussions Blumer and Wirth effectively make of "sociology" a pure form of subjectivity. Every attempt to assign it a content is denied. Every attempt to pin it down to a given practice is

---

61. This episode suggests a two-stage loss model for a tradition. Blumer had the central commitments but did little research. To the Duncan generation, he and others passed on those commitments. But in *their* teaching, that next generation somehow trained a lot of people who mistook the methods for the commitments that animated them. In their hands the methods became the dead machinery Duncan rails against in *Notes*.

throttled. This issue came to a head at the close of the third social psychology meeting, in a brilliant analysis by Nelson Foote of what we would now call paradigms. He argues against

> slicing up the field of social science into a series of orderly pastures, with such-and-such interrelations. I feel that there is something terribly unreal about discussing the relationship between social psychology and other fields of knowledge, as if you were negotiating a cartel arrangement.

No, he says, the relation between fields is actually different. They are all imperialists. They all claim all of social life. He, as it happens, is an adherent of one of these views, social psychology. Social psychology, he says,

> is a very elaborate world-view and is quite self-consistent. . . . As a world-view it contains or provides its own conceptions of history, of causation, of institutions and human nature. A comprehensive philosophy regulates the types of problems it presents itself, the way in which these problems are formulated, and even the nature of the evidence regarded as proof.

Blumer—who has been nothing if not imperialistic throughout the last three meetings—is scandalized by this relativism (which he calls "vitalism with a vengeance") and wants no part of it. For him, social psychology is simply the right view. It makes the appeal to real data. When Foote chides him that "real" is just what he, Blumer, thinks is real, he puffs up:

> I just can't understand what your thinking is, in suggesting that this area of test has no status other than to answer to my personal whims. To the contrary, it is the area of common human experience—open to anyone who is willing to view it with discernment. It doesn't require a lot of queer and, accordingly, discardable instruments.

When Blumer finally figures out what Foote means—that even the "area of common human experience" is simply Blumer's own assertion—he is scandalized and at once raises the extreme example of Nazi social psychology. Would force make that true? "I don't care to have truth determined by power," he says.[62]

62. Note that the shape of this argument is exactly the current one. Foote's statements might have been copied verbatim by Thomas Kuhn ten years later, although Foote himself says his position was inspired by J. B. Conant. Blumer's position, oddly enough, is the position of contemporary empirical sociology, defending itself against the extreme positions of postmodernism. And the final argument for the existence of "real truth," as always, is that most relativists agree with Blumer's desire to have truth determined by something other than power.

Both men are right. On the one hand, Chicago sociology was a profound, existential commitment, as Blumer argued, not just another "perspective" or model to be tested. On the other, to avow such a commitment was to stand above the rhetoric of science Blumer so admired, and ultimately above the world of empirical reality toward which that commitment was in fact made. It is in the unstatable gap between these two positions that the Chicago position lived, just as it was in having the argument about the two sides that that unstatable gap could be stated and transmitted to another generation.

The meetings on social organization have little of this fire. From the start, things are different. For one thing, there is a group—Hughes and Warner—who with their assistants Donald Horton and Buford Junker have already discussed how they are going to present the social organization syllabus. The presentation (by Hughes) sets forth a basic theme for the next two meetings, which is that the social organization group has essentially become at one with the Anthropology Department. Robert Redfield of that department was involved in writing the syllabus. There are joint courses. There are joint researches.

The existence of a group, with external allies, is not the only difference. Unlike Blumer, the social organization group has a body of routine research practices—field methods. It has worked out its own answers to a group of difficult questions distilled (by the ever rigorous Duncan) out of prior discussions: questions about reflexivity, about universal statements, about models, about fidelity to reality. And the group has a basic concept—"the interacting man, the man who is in varying degrees sensitive to the actions and gestures of others"—that is straight out of the Chicago lexicon.

The first social organization meeting sees Blumer in a characteristic mode. Warner takes a pragmatic stand, saying that ideas in social organization are tested by how much further insight they produce. Blumer asks how that judgment can be made. Again, he plays the scientific absolutist. (The attack is indeed reminiscent of Duncan's published attack on Warner.) Here again, while believing deeply in the Chicago-style unity of theory and research, Blumer derives such high standards from his theoretical rules that research becomes, in practice, impossible. This result was precisely the reverse from Duncan's, who believed in the same unity but founded his equally impossible standards on methodological rigor and, later, on the substantive validity of measurement. Again it was a case of understanding the same pile of sticks from different sides.

The second social organization meeting questioned the real relation of the social organization field to anthropology. There was long and fierce argument. Wirth regarded the two fields as fundamentally different. Anthropology was focused on small, self-contained, preliterate societies. It knew nothing of sampling or method. It emphasized different institutions. Its master concept was culture. Sociology studied large, differentiated, modern societies. It had sophisticated methods of various kinds. Its master concept was society. Hughes patiently pointed out a hundred evidences against differentiation—borrowing of concepts, trespassing on each other's types of societies, the use of "society" and "culture" in both fields. But Wirth was not convinced and went on to point to what he felt were serious holes in the social organization syllabus—lack of material on politics and power, on conflicting groups, on change and dynamics. Hughes gently conceded all of this, even going along with a discussion suggesting that separating the social organization and social change syllabi conduced to the appearance of stasis in the social organization syllabus. His handling of his group's syllabus has all the quiet confidence that Blumer's lacks. Whether this reflected the actual coherence of his own views or simply a willingness to admit incoherence in a way that Blumer would not is not really clear.[63]

But the emotional commitment of Hughes to his position becomes clear in his "Morning-After Fantasy on Night-Before Reality, with Counterpoint on Two Themes, 'Sociology begins at home' and 'let us not be static in our view,'" which was sent to seminar members the next day. This is a satirical retelling of the history of the department in which Hughes shows that his views had just as fine a Chicago pedigree as anyone else's and that credentials as "sociologists" matter little, the great figures of the department having been a Baptist economist (Small), an English professor (Thomas), a philosopher turned newspaperman (Park), and a psychologist (Faris). All had gone far beyond the bounds set by Wirth and Blumer in their discussion of sociology, as Hughes shows again and again. The document is written as

63. The syllabi tended to be identified with the old major courses. The social change syllabus derived from Ogburn's course of the same name. Duncan was particularly concerned, both in discussion and in a special memo of 4 February 1952, that the Ogburnian perspective on overall social change in complex societies not be lost. "The Department is losing, by retirement, a man who was able to make a distinctive synthesis of views and approaches of sufficient cogency and appeal to render his name virtually synonymous—in American sociology, not only at the University of Chicago—with the idea of 'social change.'"

It is hard, in retrospect, to imagine the emotions riding on the Park lineage. In this respect too the anthropology issue was emotionally charged, for anthropologist Robert Redfield—who had so much influenced Hughes and Warner and had collaborated with them on the social organization syllabus—was not only another Park student but also Park's son-in-law. The Redfield and Hughes families were close. Other aspects of the Park heritage, however, had gone elsewhere; Blumer, for example, got Park's office. One should recall that Wirth, Blumer, and Hughes all received degrees from the department when it still included the university's anthropologists (in their time, Fay Cooper-Cole and Edward Sapir).

a hilarious parody ("any sociologist who leaves the country except to attend conventions or to advise the lesser breeds is obviously a traitor who wears an anthropology pin on his undershirt") and is filled with insider jokes ("And when Thomas had to go elsewhere to pursue his new experiences he left behind to Mr. Faris, a psychologist by training . . . "). It must have been a real slap in the face indeed to Wirth and Blumer. For underneath its satire is the bold assertion that Hughes himself was the real inheritor of Robert Park.

The story of the seminar is, then, the story of Social Psychology and Social Organization, of Blumer versus Hughes and more broadly of Wirth and Blumer versus Warner and Hughes. It is a story in which the pragmatists became romantics. Nothing would satisfy Blumer but that he vanquish whatever failed to meet his perfect standards. Yet he had not himself the heart, nor the wit, nor in reality the inclination to create the synthetic social psychology that would have met his own standards. And it is a story in which the romantics became pragmatists and thereby built practical foundations for the survival of the insights they all valued so much. Hughes indeed had Park's "romantic temper"—a love of the new and interesting social fact—but he organized routine research practices to find such facts.

In the context of these great debates, the later meetings of the seminar—discussing the Behavioral Sciences Institute and Foote's "Participant Experimentation" document—add little. And so we come again to the final meeting of 28 May 1952.

After the wonderful byplay about deviation quoted above, Reiss confesses his fall from Chicago standards and leaves with a valediction: "It seems to me that the Department ought to try to implement what has come to be known as the 'Chicago point of view'—the emphasis upon the group as an interactive system, viewed in terms of change and process." He predicts, with unerring accuracy, that structural-functionalism will last about fifteen years. He fears the loss of the middle of the discipline, a manifold tying together of real theory and real research.

> While I have these reservations about the way the science is going, I have equal, if not greater, reservations about another trend in sociology, which is in the direction of a sort of literary sociology. . . . I'm thinking of a kind of literary treatise of which I think you find quite a number in the field.

True to his origins, Riess was saying no to Parsons, and to much of survey research, and perhaps even to David Riesman.

While the older generation battled over Park's inheritance, the younger generation had gotten the point. Reiss knew well what was in the gap between Wirth's maxims, Blumer's abstractions, and Hughes's research practices. In that gap was the intense subjectivity that was to animate him, Duncan, Strauss, and dozens of their peer students of this period, a desire to follow all three imperatives with a certain neurotic intensity. This was what he meant by "the Chicago point of view." Covering that intense subjectivity was the heap of maxims and abstractions and practices—the object now defined as the first Chicago school. But Reiss, like all the rest, knew that the heart of the matter was not the ideas and the techniques, but the attitude and the emotion.

It is Blumer who turns the discussion toward closure. "Mr. Burgess, we certainly want to hear what you have got to say." Burgess replies: "I heard Mr. Blumer remark that he regarded me as a deviationist. I don't think I am." There is laughter and joking. The group encourages Burgess to redo the Park and Burgess textbook. (In fact he did not. As I noted in chapter 1, Morris Janowitz got it reissued in 1970.) Then a few of them return to the issue of the great "sociologists" who were not sociologists. Foote, who admires them profusely, lists E. H. Carr, Peter Drucker, David Riesman, Daniel Bell, and William H. Whyte. There is much discussion and debate about whether any academic could play such a bridging role—are Veblen and Schumpeter examples? The discussion flickers toward Durkheim (Did he study the big picture or just little things like most sociologists?) and gradually extinguishes itself on the issue of the memorandum for the chancellor. "What of this document? Are we ready for it to go to the Administration?" asks Burgess. There are some comments, some caveats. Closing the seminar, Duncan speaks for them all in denying this one last request to trap the Chicago subjectivity in an object: "I would feel rather ill-equipped to write a statement of what sociology is all about and how it stacks up with other disciplines." Thus ended and thus was born the original Chicago school.

Envoi: The Discipline

The death and life of the Chicago school came in a period marked by distinct changes for sociology as a discipline. These have been well studied by Stephen Turner and Jonathan Turner in *The Impossible Science* (1990). The maturing of market research and the demonstrated efficacy of social research in the war combined to create a substantial market for applied social survey work. Continuous opinion polling dates from this period, as does serious government funding for empirical social research. Market power was thus one force strengthening the hand of the quantitative researchers at Chicago, for now in addition to the demographers' long-standing grip on the Census (through Hauser), there emerged a powerful foundation in survey work. NORC was of course central to this.

Intellectually, the period brought the rise not only of survey research, but also of the grand theory of Talcott Parsons and his colleagues at Harvard. Parsons's long dominance of the American Sociological Association, together with his position at a prominent university, gave him ideal resources for intellectual empire. A string of fine students spread the gospel from Cambridge. The Carnegie Foundation funded his project on "a general theory of action." However, Parsons's relation to the emerging empiricist tradition was largely arbitrary. He and Samuel Stouffer, a Chicago product (and former faculty member) who directed quantitative work at Harvard from 1944 to 1955, talked much together, but with little real effect. They were much further apart than Merton and Lazarsfeld at Columbia.

But there was an inevitable reaction to the rise of what C. Wright Mills (1959) was soon to call "grand theory" and "abstracted empiricism." It came first in the movement to found the Society for the Study of Social Problems, in which those who made up the second Chicago school were to play so strong a role. The SSSP emerged in exactly the period of the faculty seminar. It reflected a number of emerging splits in the discipline: Midwest versus East, radical versus establishment, activist versus scientist. The success of the SSSP proved that the revolution of the ASA against its Chicago tutelage—the movement that founded the *American Sociological Review* in 1936—was in fact a revolution from above, despite the use it made of discontent among the plebs (see chapter 4 and Lengermann 1979). Its result had been not a "more open" journal and society, but rather one dominated by Harvard and Columbia rather than by Chicago. Not surprisingly, Chicago became the leader of the opposition.[64]

Although the original impetus for the SSSP came from Brooklyn College and Alfred McClung Lee, it was not for symbolism and political alliance alone that Lee and the others turned to Chicago figures for three of its first four presidents (Burgess, Blumer, and Arnold Rose). For people from the old Chicago tradition figured prominently in the movement to found SSSP. Of twenty-one people at the SSSP organizational meeting, nine were Chicago Ph.D.'s and two (Burgess and Wirth) were current Chicago faculty. And the graduate students of the second Chicago school became a large part of the organization's backbone. Of fifty-three people who have

---

64. On the history of the SSSP, see the various papers in the twenty-fifth anniversary volume of *Social Problems*, particular Skura 1976 and Lauer 1976.

been either president, vice president, or editor of *Social Problems* (and whose Ph.D. department we can identify), fifteen have been Chicago Ph.D.'s. From the second Chicago school period studied here come Rose, Helena Lopata, Ray Gold, Louis Kriesberg, Joseph Gusfield, Howard Becker, Albert Reiss, Lee Rainwater, Joan Moore, and Murray Wax.

In the 1950s the SSSP was in fact the organizational home for the old Chicago style of empirical research on social problems. It was odd that of those remaining at Chicago, only outsider Donald Bogue really carried on the tradition of applied research on major social problems. As for the rest, they gradually scattered through the discipline. Blumer and Hughes left Chicago and flourished. Foote, Duncan, and Strauss—casualties of polarization—went elsewhere to transform the discipline. Riesman came and—never having really figured out the Chicago tradition—left. The Columbia group too came and went, although Coleman eventually saw Chicago as a worthy successor to Columbia and returned.

As for the idea of the Chicago school, it became an animating force in some people's minds, an obnoxious fiction in the eyes of others. The maxims and insights and practices that make up the objective face of the school were available in many other places as well. And the burning subjective experience of sociology as a commitment was felt in Cambridge and Morningside Heights and Bloomington as in Hyde Park. What made Chicago unique was the ritual rehearsal of these things through an obsession with the tradition itself.

As we have argued throughout this chapter, it was precisely the debates over the tradition that knotted that tradition together—in the debaters' minds—into a solid cultural object. I noted in closing chapter 1 that social structures achieve endurance when, like lasers, they acquire a certain internal resonance. Here we see a second process of entity making: the interplay of a set of social structures with cultural attempts to define it. Although the rivalry prevented any one man from claiming the full Chicago heritage, jostling and mutual criticism succeeded in aligning the mirrors and light sources into a powerful something indeed.

3 Albion Small's *AJS*

The seminar of 1951–52 celebrated and preserved and tried unsuccessfully to objectify the subjectivity of the Chicago sociology tradition. Other department activities perhaps succeeded better. If one were looking for a single object encapsulating sociology at Chicago, it would be hard to find anything more imposing than the century of squat little volumes that make up the *American Journal of Sociology*. What more obvious evidence of continuity, solidity, and tradition? Yet if the *AJS* is in some sense the physical condensate of a century of department life, its history shows better than anything else the many ways in which institutional change wears a false guise of continuity. A centennial generally leads us to stylized reflections: How did we arrive at today's golden age? How did we fall from heaven? Who are our famous men and our fathers that begat us? But these teleological tropes are false to the social process as lived. There is in fact little in common between Albion Small's vest pocketful of his friends' writings and the current arbiter of assistant professorial destiny other than the journal's title, the shape of its volumes, and the general area of intellectual concern. Internal change and external pressures have remade the *AJS* several times over its long life. Parts of what was the *AJS* have migrated elsewhere: both literally (the "News and Notes" section to the *American Sociological Review* and eventually to *Footnotes*) and figuratively (the reformist interest to *Social Problems, Social Service Review,* and other places). And new traditions have been woven into it, again both literally (double-blind reviewing) and figuratively (a central role in academic personnel procedures).

Moreover, the history of the *AJS* is not one history but many. For the *AJS*—like the Chicago school itself—lies at the intersection of many other social institutions. To write the history of the *AJS* is not just to discuss a journal. It is also to discuss the constitution of a department and beyond that of a discipline and of whole fields of discourse. It is to discuss the emergence of communication forms in science, the growth of refereeing and commentary. All these things happened through the doing of a particular set of human activities—finding articles, editing them, printing them—

everyday activities that have produced the thirty feet of periodicals embossed with one title and one colophon.

So again we find ourselves wondering about a social thing, in this case a journal, located at and produced by the intersection of a number of social and cultural forces. We shall see that, like the department, the *AJS* achieved even through its steady changing a certain social structural reality, generating the power to reshape and redirect the various lineages that constituted it—department and discipline and discourse. Parallel to but not identical with the department itself, the *AJS* was an institution in time.

The transition from studying an epiphany like the 1951–52 seminar to studying an enduring institution like the *AJS* may seem abrupt. But the opposition between them is merely apparent. In studying the *AJS,* we analyze not a thing but a long braid of moments, in which the various elements flowing into the *Journal* are knotted and rebraided and divided again and again. The social reality of the *AJS* changes constantly through this braiding, even as the physical shape of the volumes remains the same. In studying the seminar, we studied one particular act of braiding, one particular knot. Here there are many. The two analyses thus study different aspects of one social process.

I shall structure my investigation of the *AJS* around the three periods into which the *Journal*'s history naturally falls. The first period consists of the editorship of Albion Small, who relinquished the *AJS* when he retired in 1926. The second runs from 1926 until roughly 1955, a period during which the *Journal* was a principal outlet of a small, incipient profession. The third runs from about 1960 to the present. In that time the *AJS* has been a central part of the elaborate bureaucratic structure that makes up a modern academic discipline.

These periods reflect turning points in the history of the discipline as well as of the *Journal.* Until 1925, "sociology" meant a loose collection of people who believed—each in his or her own way—that it was useful to apply formalized knowledge to social problems. Sociologists proper were a group of perhaps one hundred to two hundred people who were attempting to precipitate, out of this diverse interest in social life and problems, a specialized academic discourse. These academics were a mere platoon in the battalions of the social survey movement, which themselves marched within the still larger brigades of the charity organization movement, the social gospel, and the emerging profession of social work. This little platoon of sociologists achieved one great feat; they established a permanent base by getting sociology enrolled as one of the basic liberal arts departments in universities.

After 1925, an increasingly sharp line between sociology and applied social problems work left the discipline free to develop this beachhead in academia. Quantitative, variables-based research helped build a new identity. Yet the discipline remained small. In 1950 senior faculty in sociology departments with graduate programs all knew each other in an immediate, personal way.

The 1950s and 1960s changed that. Not only did sociology seize the public imagination, it did so as new populations swelled the universities: veterans, baby boomers, women. The discipline more than doubled in the 1950s and then doubled again in the 1960s. By 1970, disciplinary institutions like the *AJS* had lost their face-to-face character forever. Since the transition period for the *AJS* lasted more than a decade, however, I have given the transition a separate chapter (chapter 5), turning to the modern journal, and issues of sociological journalism more broadly, in chapter 6.

The choice of a demographic periodization for the history of the *AJS* reflects not merely substantive concerns but also the more immediate fact that this disciplinary demography partly determined journal structure. Transformations in the *AJS*'s editorial procedures derived from changes in flows of manuscripts and in networks of referrals, changes that themselves arose in disciplinary demography.

This threefold periodization also reflects the nature of the sources available. There was for many years a locked safe in the *AJS* office; hopes were high that it contained the incunabula of *AJS* history—Albion Small's correspondence or Ellsworth Faris's handwritten notes. But the safe proved empty, and only the *AJS* volumes themselves, together with one year of Small's correspondence, bear witness to the period before 1925.

For the years from 1925 to 1960, there remain various items of *AJS*-related correspondence in the papers of some editors and faculty. Unfortunately Helen Hughes, managing editor of the journal from 1944 to 1961, was a resolute spring cleaner who once a year threw out the *AJS*'s own records. Herbert Blumer, editor in the 1940s, was similarly destructive, and little survives of his *AJS* work other than his correspondence with Louis Wirth, saved by the latter. Similarly, Everett Hughes destroyed most of his *AJS* material on leaving Chicago in 1961.[1]

1. Before reading these notes, the reader should consult the sources and acknowledgments section that follows the epilogue. In AJS1.12 are letters from Helen and Everett Hughes to then editor C. Arnold Anderson concerning the *AJS* papers, which they argue had disappeared by the 1940s. Everett Hughes writes, "When I moved into Burgess's office [Social Science 313], I found the most extraordinary pile of unclassified paper and correspondence. There were even a few checks from the 1920s sent in payment for subscriptions. Whether the poor devils ever got the journal I do not know. Nor do I know where the early correspondence concerning the

In both of these early periods, moreover, the nature of the materials bespeaks the substantive reality of the journal. No *formal* records survive because, in fact, there were none to survive. The informal records are sketchy precisely because the *AJS* was run informally. From 1965 onward, by contrast, the *AJS* archives are complete. They contain all manuscripts, reviews, and manuscript and editorial correspondence, as well as annual reports and similar special documents. This too underlines the validity of my periodization, not merely in the massive collection of submissions, but also in the precise bureaucracy of their handling.[2]

Discipline and Journal at Their Founding

Like many things at the University of Chicago, the *AJS* was the creation of the university's first president, William Rainey Harper. An old Chatauquan, President Harper was deeply committed to spreading knowledge beyond the university walls. Two of the university's three original "units"—press, university extension, research university—were purveyors, not originators, of knowledge. But while the university extension program proved a great success, the magazine intended to report that success was itself a failure (Storr 1966, 204). So Harper—who never let money go unspent and indeed often spent money that he didn't have—sent the money to sociology. Albion Small tells the story as follows:

> I was taken completely by surprise when, as I was about to leave his office after a consultation on routine business [Small was Head Professor in sociology] Dr. Harper abruptly remarked, "We have got to give up the *University Extension World*. It would be a pity

founding of the Journal might be" (12 January 1966). A letter from Helen Hughes the same day makes it clear that she routinely threw everything out once a year.

2. The materials from the last period of the *Journal* present problems of confidentiality. The Press currently has the *AJS* archives under full restriction, allowing access only for this particular history. I have wherever possible cited material from the modern period anonymously. Certain people—chiefly editors and editorial staff—are of course absolutely identifiable and have been treated as such. An interesting theoretical issue was raised by my copyeditor's suggestion that for consistency *Journal* not be used as an alternative short title for the *AJS* and that uses of it be changed to *AJS* or to "the journal." In reflecting about why I objected to that change so much, I came to realize that it undermined the very foundations of my argument. For my general aim here is to question the enduring "thingness" of the *AJS,* and through that to question the thingness of social entities more generally. But in that case the *AJS* was not an example of the class "scholarly periodical" but of the much larger class "social thing." Using the word "journal," however, made *AJS* an example of a scholarly periodical; it is the capitalized and italicized form—a proper name—that denominates a particular social thing. As a result, we compromised on the usage that when *AJS* in fact does represent scholarly periodicals, I use "journal" to refer to it. The far more numerous uses of *Journal* occur where I am thinking of the *AJS* as simply an entity.

for that subsidy to be transferred to anything but publication. Are you willing to be responsible for a journal of sociology?" The audacity of ignorance to which I confessed above . . . had never gone to the extreme of imagining our department commanded the necessary resources for such a venture. On the other hand, it was no time and place for men who would flinch at a challenge, and there was no room for doubt that Dr. Harper intended his suggestions as a "dare." After a brief consultation with my colleagues Henderson, Thomas, and Vincent, I reported to Dr. Harper that we believed there was a vocation for a journal of sociology, and that we were ready to undertake editorial charge of such a publication. When the announcement was made shortly after that the *University Extension World* was to become the *American Journal of Sociology,* the editors had not even promises of material enough to fill the first number. (Small 1916, 786 n. 1)

The language of this passage can easily mislead a modern reader. The protagonists in this conversation were not the senior, desiccated bureaucrats we might imagine. Harper was thirty-nine years old. He had received a doctorate from Yale at eighteen and had become the first president of the University of Chicago at thirty-four. Small was forty-one. Both men were profoundly religious. Small had trained for the ministry; Harper had been a professor of Old Testament studies. Indeed, Small's colleague Henderson was university chaplain as well as professor of sociology. The peculiar language of "vocation" in Small's account was thus not a quaint way of speaking; Small meant vocation in the literal religious sense of calling.[3]

That the *AJS* took shape within an environment of strong religious commitment is hardly surprising. So, in fact, did much of American academia. Until the founding of Johns Hopkins University and similar research institutions, most American colleges had been institutions for educating clergymen. As a consequence, clergy were by far the largest educated group in America; neither medicine nor law required a bachelor's degree. College teachers were very few, and it is thus not surprising that most faculty came from the clergy or clergy families.[4]

3. A decade later Small would be sitting by Harper's deathbed, comforting a man who feared that God would not forgive him for wasting his life founding a university when he should have remained a Bible scholar (Storr 1966, 365–67).

4. College teachers' numbers were about 6 percent those of the clergy in 1900. See *Historical Statistics* 1976, 1:140. The connection of sociology with religion is somewhat stronger than that of some fields, but the constant repetition of that fact has led most of those who write on the history of sociology to forget that education breeds education, that most educated heads of household in America were clergymen, and therefore that *all* academics in the early part of this century were disproportionately likely to come from clergy households.

But beyond this general religiousness of academics in the late nineteenth century, sociology had a particular affinity with religion, an affinity we see clearly in Small, who once remarked that social science was a "sacrament" (Dibble 1975, 4). The idea of sociology arose among those concerned with social welfare and social problems. This whole area of endeavor was dominated throughout the late nineteenth century by the clergy, who provided its theory (through the social gospel), much of its structure (through "institutional churches" and through public support of the settlement house movement), and much of its volunteer manpower.

When Small christened his journal the *American Journal of Sociology,* then, he meant by the word "sociology" neither an academic discipline nor a subject matter. For him "sociology" denoted a loose claim that formal theories of society were relevant to practical social reform, a claim that went beyond cognitive assertion to invoke specific moral and religious values. Sociology was simply the academic avatar of the ramshackle empire of social welfare.

The thirty years of Small's editorship span the transition of sociology from this loose set of claims about theory and practice in social welfare to a recognized unit of the academic division of labor, a standard department throughout leading universities. It is worth reviewing this "disciplinary structuration" because Small's journal, as we shall see, played an important and in some ways unexpected role in it.

Like all disciplines, sociology began small. As of 1894, Daniel Folkmar found "29 colleges having regular courses in sociology, using the term in the looser sense to include charities and corrections, while 24 have sociology proper, defining the term as the study of society" (quoted in Tolman 1902–3, pt. 2, 85). Ten years later Frank Tolman found that 185 colleges had some kind of instruction in sociology, and 45 had three or more courses in sociology. However, the reader should not be led to imagine sociology as a growing plant, unfolding inevitably toward its telos. These courses would be completely unrecognizable to the current sociology undergraduate; they included things like Anthropological Geography, History of English Cities and Towns, Modern Socialism, Organized Philanthropy, and Private Property Rights. In Tolman's list were ninety-six courses on general sociology, sixty on "social economics," fifty-six on social reform, forty on charities, thirty-nine on social philosophy, thirty on criminology, twenty-six on social ethics, twenty-two on the state, and twenty or fewer on the rural group, nationalities, social legislation, religion, education, art, democracy, comparative sociology, social history, primitive societies, social psychology, and history of social theory. Nor were these courses being taught by people with Ph.D.'s in sociology. There probably were not more than one hundred of those in the United States in 1905.

These various pieces of sociology coalesced into an association (the American Sociological Society, hereafter ASA) only after the *AJS* had been published for about a decade. Although the larger constituency of the new organization was composed of practical reformers, it was the professors who took the lead in founding it.[5] The ASA too began small. The December 1905 meeting was attended by 50 potential members. By the end of 1906 there were 115 members. The organization had about 300 members from 1909 to 1912, then climbed to about 800, where it stayed from 1916 to 1920, then rose to 1,100, where it remained from 1924 to 1928. This was *not* a history of steady, slow growth, however; there was enormous turnover. From 1910 to 1930 the median percentage of new members in any given year was about 25 percent. From 1910 to 1916, the only period for which we have detailed figures, the first-year survival rates for new members fell from 0.94 (1910's new members) to 0.62 (1915's). Two-year survival rates were below 0.5 by 1913. What this meant is that the inner core of founders was already in the organization by 1910 and was surrounded by a fast-changing penumbra that tried the organization and then quickly left. The early *AJS* was thus the journal not of a stable group—a sort of modern profession writ small—but rather of a tiny handful of people with a lot of fair-weather friends.

Who were these ASA members? L. L. Bernard surveyed sociology teaching in the United States in 1910 and found 55 full-time faculty at 40 institutions. There were 372 people teaching sociology part time at another 308 institutions. Since ASA membership was 335 in 1910, we can make the educated guess that the organization comprised all 55 full-time faculty, 50 to 100 part-time faculty, and 100 or so "practical" workers.[6]

---

5. I hereafter refer to the American Sociological Society by its modern acronym—ASA. (The organization's original name was changed for the obvious reason when acronyms came into fashion.) I shall also call it "the society" or "the association" as may be temporally appropriate. On its founding, see "Organization of the American Sociological Society," *AJS* 11:555–69. I have calculated membership figures from the published statistics in the annual *Publication* of the ASA. There are two reasons for discussing the ASA in some detail here. First, it is important to break the false historicism by which we imagine the professional society of ninety years ago simply as an early version of something familiar. It was not. Second, and more pointedly, the ASA played a central role as the *AJS*'s financial constituency, a topic that will concern us greatly below.

6. In 1910 the membership list includes no fewer than 104 academic addresses ("professor" title or a university mailing address), which is consistent with the statement in text. There were thirteen identified clergy and forty-nine women, 15 percent of the organization (*Publication* 5 [1910]: 261–67).

Despite the coalescence implicit in the existence of a national society, the academic side of sociology was by no means fully organized in 1910. Bernard found pure sociology departments in only 20 of the 173 universities responding to him. Sociology courses were taught in "economics and sociology" departments (thirty-two of them), economics departments (twelve), "history and political science" departments (eleven), "social and political science" departments (twelve), and even in departments like "theology and economics" or "homiletics and applied Christianity." Even by 1928 there were still as many as forty-eight departments combining economics and sociology by comparison with the ninety-nine departments of sociology alone. University faculty thus initiated the institutionalization of the discipline, but they were by no means in a stable position in their home institutions, even by the 1920s.[7]

In short, there was no discipline of which the *AJS* was the journal. Quite the reverse. The *AJS*, with a few other institutions and networks, *created* the discipline.

Editorial Procedures in the Early *AJS*

As the *AJS* developed within this amorphous field of professional activity, it was, like most learned journals of the preceding century, essentially a one-man affair. Medical periodicals—founded by the dozens throughout the nineteenth century—provide the clearest examples of such journals (Ebert 1952; Cassedy 1983). An energetic doctor would collect articles from friends and colleagues, publish correspondence from acquaintances made during his various sojourns abroad, commission some translations, reprint articles from other periodicals, and fill out the rest with his own and others' research, with editorial columns commenting on affairs of professional interest, and with announcements of whatever was going on. Small was admirably situated to run precisely this kind of personal journal. His lengthy stay in Europe (1879–81) left him with dozens of overseas acquaintances, some of whom he published in the *AJS*. His institu-

7. In elite schools, things were different. Columbia with its three full-time and six part-time faculty and Chicago with its six full-time faculty were university departments in the modern sense. As of 1910, however, only five other schools had more than one full-time faculty member in sociology (Bernard 1909). I thank Ronald Durnford of the Division of Social Sciences at the University of Chicago for the department figures, which were compiled from the first two editions of the American Council on Education guidebook, *American Universities and Colleges,* published in 1928 and 1932. I am sorry to bore the reader with figures, but I want to emphasize that the continuous name "sociology" should not beguile us into thinking that "sociology" in 1910 denoted either an institution like the discipline of today but smaller or a "linear ancestor" whose only descendant is the modern discipline. Both of these statements embody assumptions about the social process that are radically ahistorical.

tional position at Chicago gave him access not only to his colleagues at his own and other universities, but also to the city's large and diverse social welfare community. His indefatigable industry (slowed only by the terrible hay fever that made his summers miserable) brought him a central role in the ASA, which he helped found in 1905 and which provided a ready, regular constituency for the *AJS* for many years. The "personal" character of the journal that resulted from these material advantages is evident in the simple fact that Small himself wrote about 10 percent of the published article pages in the *AJS* during his editorship: about 65 pages a year, and often as many as 150.[8]

To help him fill the *AJS*'s pages, however, Small consistently relied on a few others. We can see who these people were by listing those who published more than three articles in each of the journal's first three decades. These authors include Small's Chicago colleagues Charles Henderson and W. I. Thomas, his friend Wisconsin professor E. A. Ross, his (and Thomas's) student Charles Ellwood, and his admired senior colleague Lester Ward. Small also relied heavily on a group of writers on social reform: E. C. Hayes (University of Illinois), Victor Yarros (Hull House), and C. R. Woodruff (a Philadelphia lawyer active in municipal reform). For his European material he generally used translations of work by Georg Simmel or Gustav Ratzenhofer.[9]

Small and this immediate circle contributed an average of about 250 pages a year. In some cases this group contribution came through publication of books in serial form; Ross's *Social Control* and Henderson's *Industrial Insurance* first appeared as *AJS* articles. There are two possible reasons for such serial publication of monographs: to secure a double audience and to fill the journal. The relatively small variance in the total contribution of the core group indicates that the latter is the more probable explanation. When there was a Simmel translation on hand, Small felt less need to pressure Henderson or Ross for material. He probably built the magazine

8. The temporal pattern of Small's personal publishing also bespeaks the *AJS*'s highly personal character. Small published the largest bodies of his own material very early and very late in his thirty-year tenure as editor. Early on, as he said himself, he was desperate for material (Small 1916). Toward the end, he seems to have had personal material that he wanted to publish before leaving the field. Since the number of sociologists was much increased by the latter part of Small's tenure, his taking excess space for himself in the last years can be seen only as personal indulgence. On Small's career, see Dibble 1975 and Christakes 1978.

9. Emerging disciplinary politics in sociology seem the likely reason for the relative absence from the *AJS* of those Small disliked, in particular William Graham Sumner and Franklin Giddings, despite the considerable reputation of both as sociologists, and despite the importance of Yale and Columbia as sites for producing Ph.D.'s in sociology.

around the big serial publications by first blocking out space for them in order to find out how much incidental material he needed.

This foundation material from Small's immediate circle, however, provided only about one-third of the journal's pages. Those who filled the rest were a mixed group. I have built a biographical database including all contributors in the *AJS*'s first seventy years. I have some degree of information on about 1,000 out of 1,200 individuals. (Maximum information is year of birth, of death, of B.A., and of Ph.D., location of B.A. and Ph.D., and complete job history.) Table 1 includes the age information. For ease of reporting, I have collected the authors by decade and dated them all from the midpoint of the decade. (Since many authors contributed several articles, it makes little sense to think about an author's "exact age" when an article came out. The unit of analysis here is the author, not the article.) Thus in the first decade (1895–1905, midpoint 1900) there were 131 different authors. There is age information on 114 of them, and these 114 had a median age of forty.[10]

There is a slight trend here toward publishing later in the professional career. The typical article was published four years post-Ph.D. in the first decade (40–36), eight in the second (43–35), and nine in the third (42–33). But at the same time, these data show that even while Small kept the same group of central contributors, in general he moved with the times. The stability of the average age of writers is remarkable, given the steady aging of his core writers.

10. This biographical directory of *AJS* authors was built on diverse sources at the cost of hundreds of hours of work by Emily Barman and Julian Go, whom I thank again for their efforts. The major sources are the following. Most are standard. I give bibliographical information only for the less common.

The Academic Who's Who, 1973–76.

American Men and Women of Science.

Biographical Dictionary of Social Welfare in America, 1986. Ed. W. I. Trattner. New York: Greenwood.

Directory, American Sociological Association, 1950 and later years.

Directory of American Scholars, 1942 and later years.

"Doctoral Dissertations in Social Work." *Social Service Review,* various years.

International Directory of Anthropologists, 1940 and later years.

Leaders in Education, 1931 and later years. Lancaster, Pa.: Science Press.

List of Doctoral Dissertations in History, various years. American Historical Association.

National Directory of Sociology of Education and Educational Sociology, 1974, 1978.

Sociology Dissertations in American Universities, 1969. Ed. G. Lunday. Commerce: East Texas State University.

Who's Who in American Education.

In addition, we also used general sources like the *Dictionary of American Biography,* the *National Cyclopedia of American Biography, Dissertation Abstracts,* the *New York Times Obituary Index,* and *Who's Who in America.*

Table 1. Average Ages of Contributors to the *AJS*,
1895–1925

| | Decade | | |
	1	2	3
Midpoint	1900	1910	1920
Authors (total *N*)	131	164	136
Age	40	43	42
(*N*)	(114)	(144)	(122)
B.A. age	26	26	25
(*N*)	(70)	(99)	(97)
Ph.D. age	36	35	33
(N)	(55)	(101)	(107)

Note: N refers to the number of individuals on whom the information
listed is available.

Table 2. Higher Degrees of Contributors to the *AJS*, 1895–1965

| | Decade | | |
	1	2	3
Midpoint	1900	1910	1920
Authors (*N*)	131	164	136
%Ph.D. location known (of all authors)	42	62	77
Overseas	22	4	5
Chicago	29	24	30
Columbia	7	18	30
Harvard		10	8
Johns Hopkins	13	5	3
Wisconsin	4	4	4
Yale	4	5	3
Princeton	4	2	
Pennsylvania		4	5

Note: Figures for individual locations are percentages *of those whose Ph.D. location is
known.* Thus Overseas Ph.D.'s were 22 percent of 42 percent of 131.

Of much more interest are the changes in terms of higher degrees. Table
2 contains the important information. Again, I present the number of authors and the percentage of those for whom the location of Ph.D. is known.

A number of facts are clear. First, while overseas Ph.D.'s got Small going,
he quickly turned to the native product. Second, while Johns Hopkins was
a central graduate institution in the United States for a brief period, it was
rapidly eclipsed by other schools; Small's early reliance on Hopkins Ph.D.'s

undoubtedly reflected the fact that he was a Hopkins graduate himself. Third, the emerging dominance of Chicago and Columbia—with fully 60 percent of the known Ph.D. authors coming from those two places by the third decade—shows which institutions replaced Hopkins.

These authors were not, however, necessarily sociology Ph.D.'s, as table 3 shows. Sociology Ph.D.'s did not become the majority of Ph.D. authors whose field is known until after Small's time as editor. The *AJS* was in fact a very interdisciplinary journal, even as it became more academic toward the end of Small's tenure.

The balance among disciplines did change slightly. The generalists in philosophy disappeared. Economics and history were more or less stable sources of authors, perhaps because both became organized disciplines before sociology did. If date of organization is a criterion, however, the relative absence of political scientists seems surprising, for the American Political Science Association also antedates the ASA. More likely these preferences reflect Small's own background in German historical economics. The importance of psychology may very well reflect the influence of his student and colleague W. I. Thomas, although there is no evidence (other than his own publication in the journal) that Thomas was involved in *AJS* editorial procedures.

In summary, through his tenure Small dropped the generalists and picked up the more specialized social scientists as they emerged. Like the

Table 3. Ph.D. Fields of Contributors to the *AJS*, 1895–1925

	Decade		
	1	2	3
Midpoint	1900	1910	1920
Authors (N)	131	164	136
%with Ph.D.	42	62	79
%Ph.D. field known (of all authors)	27	42	54
Sociology	40	34	45
Philosophy	26	12	5
Economics	11	10	11
History	6	7	9
Psychology/Social Psychology		7	8
Education		3	4
Anthropology		3	4
Political science			3

Note: Figures for individual fields are percentages *of those whose Ph.D. field is known.* Percentage with Ph.D. is a minimum figure; undoubtedly there are many Ph.D's unknown to us.

age data of table 1, these figures show a man who moved with the times, despite retaining a central group of cronies to tide him over uneven periods.[11]

Taken together, these tables present another important piece of evidence. They reinforce the earlier argument that while sociology was not an institutionalized, structured academic field when Small and the *AJS* began, it became much more so over the next thirty years. The purview of the *AJS* became sharply academic in Small's time. Authors with Ph.D.'s move from less than half of the total in the first decade to over three-quarters in the third. Another witness to academicization is the declining proportion of female authors. In Small's first two decades of editorship, women were 16 percent and 13 percent (respectively) of the authors with more than one article in a decade. In his last decade the figure fell to 5 percent, a number it more or less reproduced for the next five decades (5 percent, 8 percent, 8 percent, 4 percent, 7 percent are the figures for decades three to seven of the *AJS*'s history). Since university faculties were overwhelmingly made up of men, an inevitable result of the creation of an academic sociology was a gradual exclusion of women, just as the simultaneous institutionalization of social work involved a similar exclusion of men.

The figures also show that the *AJS* was not mainly a house organ in the Small years. To be sure, two of the faculty (Henderson and Thomas) were among Small's core group of contributors. But most of the core were not Chicago faculty, and known Chicago sociology Ph.D.'s made up 5 percent, 5 percent, and 9 percent, respectively, of all authors in Small's three decades and 43 percent, 36 percent, and 36 percent, respectively, of all authors with sociology Ph.D.'s whose location is known. These figures are close to Chicago's proportion of all sociology Ph.D.'s, at least in the first two decades.[12]

These various characteristics of *AJS* contributors are, of course, the downstream result of the grinding little activities that make up being an editor. To see those more clearly, we must look at Small's correspondence.

11. From both Chicago and Columbia, typically half the Ph.D. contributors to the *AJS* were sociology Ph.D.'s, marginally above the general average of 40 percent. It is likely that the percentage of sociology Ph.D.'s is underestimated in this table; mass biographical data sources on "sociologists" are more likely to mention a person's field if it is not sociology than if it is.

12. *AJS* 21:679–83 has a list of doctoral dissertations in progress. Disregarding those at Teachers College—which might more properly be listed as Ph.D.'s in education but with sociological content—Chicago doctoral dissertations in progress are 20 percent of the total. Of course that figure underestimates Ph.D.'s already in the field, since Chicago (and Columbia) had had a bigger share before this time. Small's last decade may show some concentration on the local product; in 1916 Chicago was producing only about 20 percent of new Ph.D.'s in sociology. The turn to locals, if there was one, probably involved more desperation than patronage. Much of the time Small lacked material to publish.

The year 1904—the only year from which Small's correspondence survives—gives a clear picture of his day-to-day activity (or inactivity) as editor. That year was a somewhat unusual one. With Hugo Munsterberg of Harvard, Small was in charge of organizing the social science sessions of the great Saint Louis exposition. These sessions provided him with a surfeit of potential *AJS* material, and he was therefore less desperate than usual. "The Congress together with our usual sources of supply has created a glut just at present which our space cannot easily relieve," he wrote to K. L. Butterfield (30 September 1904). What was Small's idea of a glut? He continues, "I may not be able to use your paper until the March number." In fact this meant almost no delay at all. Small's final copy date for the November issue had already passed (it was 26 September [UCP 3, Standing Orders]) and since the *AJS* appeared bimonthly, only one full issue (January) would pass before Butterfield's paper would appear. What Small saw as a glut—having exactly one issue of a bimonthly on hand—a modern editor (and certainly that editor's publisher) would regard as grounds for panic. Indeed, shortly afterward Small wrote to another author, "If you care to send us the article we shall be very glad to give it space at the earliest opportunity" (Small to R. C. Brooks, 21 October 1904).

Other aspects of Small's experience were far from those of contemporary editors. First of all, Small solicited much *AJS* material. Probably over two-thirds of the journal was solicited in some fairly direct manner. But Small also received a good deal of unsolicited material, which arrived in a bewildering variety of ways and met an equally bewildering variety of fates. One author sent in a manuscript with the note, "Please send me twenty copies of the journal in which it appears, if not, I enclose stamps for its return" (D. M. Blount to Small, 5 July 1904). Another (president of the Rhode Island land grant college) wrote, "The Atlantic is not able to use my paper read before the congress. Do you want it for the journal of sociology?" (K. L. Butterfield to Small, 28 September 1904). Authors were on occasion quite peremptory about submission. J. S. Stevens of 339 Hicks Street, Philadelphia, wrote:

> If you are not open to the discussion of the race question along lines indicated by the enclosed article "Why crime increases among negroes" please *return this article at once.* But if you desire to enlighten the public on one of the most vital and vexing phases of the race question, I am sure that you will find the enclosed article to be all you could desire along this particular line. At all events, please give me your decision at the earliest possible convenience and greatly oblige. . . . (J. S. Stevens to Small, 15 June 1904)

In this case Small apparently did not oblige. Stevens wrote again on 13 August 1904:

> I take it for granted that since I have received no word from you in reference to the article "Why Crime Increases among Negroes," submitted to you June 15, you are going to publish it. [!] I therefore submit you an article "The Negro and Social Equality," thinking that perhaps you would like to follow one article with the other, the two, with the exception of lynching, etc., making the two most vital phases of the negro question. Trusting that you will let me hear from you in reference to both articles at your earliest convenience, I am, . . .

Neither article appeared. Other authors became angry and withdrew papers already planned for publication because the glut of congress papers delayed them. L. B. Ellis of Aripeka, Florida, wrote Small on 25 July 1904: "Please let me know if you have planned my article in [the November issue], as, in case you have not, it will change my own schedule of other articles." Small wrote back that he planned to delay the paper, and although Ellis replied saying, "Trusting that you will do your best for me in January, I leave the article with you," in fact this particular paper of Ellis's did not appear.

With his familiar stable of authors, Small was clearly more obliging. Florence Kelley wrote to the *AJS* on 11 September 1904, "Can you use the enclosed in an early issue of the American Journal of Sociology? . . . I wish very much to get some, at least, of the twelve points embodied in legislation this coming winter, and discussion is the first step." Significantly, the letter was addressed not to Small but to his colleague Henderson, who had even closer ties to the reform world of which Ms. Kelley was a leader. (She was corresponding secretary of the National Consumer's League in New York and had already published four articles in the *AJS*.) The paper appeared in the November issue, whose final copy date was exactly two weeks away, precisely the issue for which the earlier-submitting Ms. Ellis had been turned down.

Small sometimes paid for material. He wrote to R. C. Brooks of Ithaca, New York (21 October 1904), "Our limit for contributions is the magnificent sum of one dollar per printed page including space or inserts for illustrations. We reckon this as simply sufficient to pay on the average the mechanical cost of preparing copy." In fact the journal had (and used) a substantial budget to pay for contributions (see below). With serial articles, Small adopted a pay as you go policy. As his student Howard Woodhead sent in pieces of a multichapter study of German municipal reforms, Small forwarded the payment for each piece, which was promptly spent on expenses incidental to the research (Woodhead to Small, 6 December 1903).

Small's pursuit of material also meant sometimes accepting double publication. Franklin Giddings wanted his 1904 conference paper to appear in *Science* as well as in the *AJS,* and appear it did (Small to H. J. Rodgers, 29 September 1904).

Another correspondence illustrates the intimate scale of Small's ties to the reform community. On 10 September 1904, Small wrote to J. M. Stahl, secretary of the Farmers' National Congress, a reform organization run by Stahl from Quincy, Illinois. He sent Stahl (whom he clearly did not know) a Saint Louis program and invited him to speak briefly "on any topic under the section on the Rural Community." There were various mix-ups; Stahl was ultimately kept from Saint Louis by a brother-in-law's illness and a train wreck (Stahl to Small, 18 October 1904). He sent Small his paper (on the rural school), asking him to arrange to put it in the conference proceedings. Small replied (19 October 1904) that the short papers of the conference would not be published in the proceedings, but that he would like Stahl's permission to use the piece in the *AJS.*

The editor was thus neither a czar nor an Olympian judge enthroned upon double-blind review. He was a hustling wheeler-dealer. He solicited material and sometimes even paid for it. He dodged authors he didn't want and cajoled those he did. The history of one of the published Simmel translations epitomizes the differences between the editorial spirit of the early *AJS* and present scholarly journalism. Charles Ellwood—Ph.D. of the department and professor at the University of Missouri—wrote Small on 20 August 1904 saying:

> I am sending you under separate cover, however, a translation of Simmel's "Der Soziologie des Religions" by one of my students, Rev. W. W. Elwang. . . . I obtained Simmel's special permission to translate it and publish it in the AJS last winter. The translator, The Rev. Mr. Elwang, is the pastor of the Presbyterian Church here (so, my pastor) and has been for four years a student of mine and gives good promise of doing good sociological work in the future. I am anxious to introduce him to sociologists through the Journal, so I got him to make this translation. . . . The Journal need not pay anything for his contribution. Mr. Elwang will be glad enough to see it appear without compensation.

It is hard to know what is more unfamiliar in this transaction: the direct patronage, the paid contributions, the confidence in publishability, the outsider's committing *AJS* pages without asking the editor, or the complexities of the relationship between the pastor-student and the layman-professor. Such was the informal, precarious quality of the early *AJS*.

What did Small actually publish in terms of content and substance? In fact, a retrospective analysis makes little sense of this material, for its organizing principle was fundamentally different from that of professional sociology after the 1920s. This difference was apparent immediately. In the early 1930s, Howard P. Becker analyzed the first thirty years of articles in the *AJS*. He used categories from the twenty-five-year index of the *AJS:* personality, the family, peoples and cultural groups, conflict and accommodation, communities and territorial groups, social institutions, social science and the social process, social pathology, methods of investigation, general sociology. But his analysis was meaningless, for these were not categories that Small understood, and we must categorize the articles as Small saw them if we want to analyze how his journal actually worked. In reality, most of Becker's terms were subheads in the Park and Burgess text of 1921; they were the terms of the professionalizing sociology of the 1920s, not the language of Small and his peers. The Small *AJS* was a mishmash of would-be professional sociology, impassioned progressivist rhetoric, learned European argument, reports on local social problems, legislative programs, and who knows what else. The younger generation was so far from Small's world that even in 1932 it could not see that world for what it had actually been in its own time.

Thus it makes little sense to pursue the issue of topics and trends in material in the early *AJS*. It belonged to a different world, one that seems opaque, confused, and unscientific to us who do not share the conception of sociology common to its readers. We see it through a glass darkly.[13]

The Journal and the Press

But the *AJS* was not merely the personal creature of Albion Woodbury Small. It was also one of ten or so journals published on a proprietary

13. See Becker 1930, 1932. There is also a content analysis of the early *AJS* by Ethel Shanas, published in the fiftieth anniversary volume in 1944. Shanas was more attuned to the realities of the past than was Becker. She documents a distinct change about 1905 toward more formal and academic topics and away from Christian sociology and reform. This makes sense given the foundation of the ASA in that year—an academicizing move. At the same time, there remain fundamental problems in coding and analyzing these articles. The most difficult problem is the large correlation of topics across articles induced by extensive serial publication. I should note, however, that the content distribution of the *AJS* would be very interesting with respect to historical questions other than the one at hand, particularly those involving reform more broadly. Academic sociology is only *one* of the children of the early *AJS*. It just happens to have been the one that inherited the ancestral estate.

basis by the university press. There too its position was quite different from what a progressivist narrative might imagine.

Following Harper's original vision, the University of Chicago Press conceived of the *AJS* as one of its religious journals. As late as 1908 a Press promotional campaign offered each of the ten thousand ministers on the Press mailing list a "buy two get one free" offer on subscriptions to the *AJS*, the *American Journal of Theology*, and *Biblical World*. Indeed, this offer was combined with reduced prices on certain theology books.

That the Press followed Harper and Small in viewing the *AJS* as a religious journal is hardly surprising, given the larger society's concept of "sociology." But just as sociology meant something different eighty years ago, so also did "religion." American church attendance was near its all-time low in 1900, and the clergy's expansion into social welfare in part bespoke a profession looking for things to do. The "religion" connection of sociology happened in the context of a complex social movement whose original intellectual leaders happened to come—not unexpectedly, given their numerical dominance of educated America and their leadership role in the downwardly mobile old middle class—from a clergy largely spurned by its earlier constituency of churchgoers. To say that in this period sociology was religious or that the *AJS* was a religious journal is to say something vaguer, less startling than it would be today. Perhaps calling it a "reform journal" would effectively translate the religious quality of the early *AJS* to contemporary ears. It was the context of the progressive movement that defined the *AJS* as a sort of *Journal of Applied Religion*.

The institutional arrangements of the *AJS* in the early years fall into two clear periods separated by the contract with the ASA in 1905 that made the *AJS* the official journal of the new society. The contract gave ASA members one-half off the price of the journal and included language allowing unilateral abrogation, language that would play a central role in the *AJS*'s later history.[14]

The period before the ASA contract was a time of great instability. The earliest viable circulation figures, for 1898–1905, are shown in table 4.

14. The original contract is gone from Press records but is noted in UCPAR 1907, 8:76. All the later versions can be found in UCP 33:7. Virtually all the figures on the circulation and costs of the *AJS* below are found in the UCP archive series or in PPAB. The annual reports for 1899–1918 have the early information and are found in UCP 3, 4, 5, and 6. After 1918 information is spotty, although many years' records are available in the series "department reports," UCP 9:5, 6 and 10:1, 2. The 1928–29 documents are attached to Bean to E. T. Filbey, 7 February 1930, PPAB 12:10. Later budgets can be found in the same folders. I have also found some annual budget and cost documents in the Burgess and Wirth papers, in particular in EWB 1:4 and LW 17:1.

Table 4. *AJS* Circulation, 1898–1905

Year	Start	New	Discontinued	End
1898–1899	943	175	291	827
1899–1900	827	203	285	745
1900–1901	745	171	189	727
1901–2				688
1902–3				675
1903–4				560
1904–5	560	219	198	581

Note: All figures are numbers of subscribers.

The journal was turning over about one-third of its subscription base annually, the highest figure for any Press journal. Moreover, circulation fell steadily from 1898 to 1905, after which it picked up because of the ASA arrangement. The *AJS* thus did not find a consistent audience in its first decade. Library subscriptions outnumbered individual subscriptions until 1908–9, the year in which a massive joint promotional effort by the ASA and the Press finally brought most ASA members into the fold. (Because ASA members did not get the journal automatically, but merely received a 50 percent price reduction, it was possible for the *AJS* to be the "official journal" yet not have all ASA members as subscribers.)

The Press viewed the *AJS* constituency as far wider than the ASA, however. The promotional mailing lists included membership lists of the National Conference on Charities and Correction and of the National Prison Association, a total of 1,504 (UPAR 1906–7:81), as well as the membership of the American Economic Association, the Press "teachers of history" list, and the subscribers to the Press's Constructive Bible Studies series. But by 1909–10 this wide constituency strategy had been judged a failure, and the Press aimed the journal directly at the professional organization, a strategy that had proved wildly successful with the journals *Classical World* and *Classical Philology* (UPAR 1909–10:102). (Thus the "making of the discipline" was in part "done" by a marketing decision of the Press.) The Press was worried, however, about the consequences of *failing* in this "official journal" strategy, a problem it was then facing with the American Economics Association, which had just founded the *American Economic Review* to compete with the Press's *Journal of Political Economy*. In 1908 and again in 1912, the Press and the ASA actively collaborated on membership campaigns; in the latter year, personal subscriptions were raised by 30 percent (UPAR 1912–13:61).

The Press lost money heavily on the *AJS*. For example, in 1898–99, the subscription price was $2, and the Press in fact collected $1,536 from the

827 subscribers. (The difference between $1,536 and $2 × 827 = $1,654 meant $118 in lost subscription income, partly from failure to collect and partly from the twenty or thirty exchange copies of the journal sent out free to universities sending other journals to the university library.[15] Beyond the subscriptions, the only income was $242 for advertising; total receipts were thus $1,778. Costs of production and distribution totaled $4,125. The resulting deficit of $2,347 was a major loss, about $44,000 in 1996 dollars.[16] This was for the *AJS* alone. The total "subsidy" provided by university funds to all university periodicals was eventually set, by a formal agreement in 1908, at $20,000 current dollars, about $375,000 in 1996 dollars. Such was Harper's commitment to outreach.

Tables 5 and 6 show circulation and financial results for the *AJS* through the First World War. As these figures show, the doubling of the subscription base by the ASA-Press membership subscription drive in 1908–9 did not help the *Journal* break even. Rather, it cut the real deficit to half of what it had been. Thereafter, increasing production costs steadily ate up the "profit."

The relationship between the Press and the editor was then, as today, filled with complications. Despite the university's commitment to the Press, the continual losses of the journals meant that the heads of the Journals Section, of the Publications Division within which it was located, and of the Press itself found the journals a continual embarrassment. Editors were dangerous people given to overspending. Press authorities constantly tried to rein them in.

How did editors overspend? First of all, by paying for papers. All journal budgets at this point provided for paid contributions. "Contributions" costs commanded about 20 percent of the annual Press journals budget, a proportion equivalent to that for promotion and exceeded only by that for manufacturing (40 percent). The *AJS* was no exception in this regard, for although Small usually underspent his contributions budget in the years

15. Library purchasing, because it had to do with books, was located organizationally in the Press. The list of libraries receiving the *AJS* on an exchange basis occasionally reached as many as one hundred names. The involvement of the Press in the library also meant that Press journal editors were required to send excess books (books sent to the journal but not reviewed) to the library for deposit. In fact, journals routinely sold these books on the side, a practice for which there is documentary evidence from the turn of the century and that continued well into the current era. The Press gave up the official policy of deposit about the time it "lost" the library, in the 1920s.

16. This calculation uses consumer price indexes. Gross national product per capita at this time was about $233 (in 1899 dollars [*Historical Statistics* 1976, 1:224]), so the *AJS* loss annually was about equal to ten times the GNP per capita. Ten times today's GNP per capita is on the order of $300,000.

Table 5. *AJS* Circulation, 1905–1918

Year	Library	Others	Exchange	Paid	Free	Advertising	Total Run
1905–6	381	365	79	825	76	110	1,246
1908–9	527	582	83	1,192	24	65	1,550
1911–12	551	658	100	1,309	18	24	1,575
1914–15	352	991	140	1,783	32	10	2,075
1917–18	737	1,099	157	1,993	22	24	2,225

for which we have data (1905–18), that budget grew throughout the period.

Editors also demanded more journal pages than their subscriptions lists could support. This was the heart of the manufacturing costs, which, if they were seldom substantially over budget, were nonetheless conforming to a Press allocation that already assumed that the university would match the journals' advertising and subscription receipts out of its own funds. It was manufacturing cost increase—an increase in the size of the journal—that kept the *AJS*'s subscription expansion from improving its financial situation. (A third major expense—for illustrations—was less relevant to the *AJS* than to other Press journals. Illustrations appeared only in the very earliest numbers of the *AJS*.)

The problems of the editor-Press relationship were encoded in elaborate memoranda. The earliest formal memorandum of agreement between the Press and the editors dates from about 1904 and said that editors controlled "the amount of matter that goes into the journals, the illustrations, the pay for contributions, and the editorial office work." Manufacture, publication, and finance were under the control of the Press. Editors were obligated "to assist in extending the circulation of their journals in reasonable and appropriate ways." The Press reserved the right to set the "maximum aggregate number of pages of printed matter per year," although in practice Press officials had little leverage over editors who exceeded the limit.[17]

Albion Small thus passed on to his successors a problematic relationship. The Press never despaired, as the years wore on, of bringing the *AJS* to the point of profitability. (The Press sometimes did make a little money on the ASA annual *Publication,* which it also published under the 1905 contract; it applied those profits to the *AJS* deficit.) And in total subscriptions, the *AJS* had become the Press's biggest journal by the late 1920s. But the deficits in fact grew steadily from 1918 to 1930. The situation was im-

17. The document is attached to a letter, Chamberlin to President H. P. Judson, 9 May 1908, PP89 42:7.

Table 6. AJS Receipts and Costs, 1905–1918

Year	Total Cost	Total Income	Subscription Income	Advertising	Subsidy	"Profit"	Net
1898–99	4,125	1,778	1,536	242			−2,347
1902–3	3,866	1,602	1,321		4,300	2,036	−2,264
1905–6	3,642	1,401	1,234	167	3,940	1,649	−2,291
1908–9	3,235	2,068	1,877	191	1,800	633	−1,167
1911–12	3,169	2,075	1,974	101	1,350	256	−1,094
1914–15	3,733	2,383	2,273	81	1,350	0	−1,350
1917–18	3,973	2,690	2,607	83	1,350	67	−1,283

Note: All figures are current dollar amounts. The decline in subsidy in 1908–9 was a conscious policy. As of this point the entire Press journals deficit was limited to $20,000. The decline in subscription income in 1905–6 reflects the Press's taking 25 percent of the subscription income for central overhead.

mensely complicated by the fact that University of Chicago sociology faculty not only made up the editorial staff of the *Journal,* but also typically included the secretary, treasurer, and managing editor of the society. (Ernest Burgess, Scott Bedford, Herbert Blumer, and Louis Wirth held these positions at various times through the 1920s.) The ASA managing editor was officially responsible for the annual *Publication* but also often took responsibility for the *AJS* (D. P. Bean to W. Harrell, 9 July 1932, UCP 35:1). The Press executives were thus arguing with people who bore three different relations to them—university colleagues, *AJS* editorial board, and ASA officials.

Conclusion

In summary, a number of conflicting forces shaped the *AJS* in its first thirty years. The *Journal* had its beginnings in the university's outreach programs and in an explicitly religious sense of vocation. Substantively, it was one of many attempts to comprehend the amorphous social concerns resulting from the capitalist transformations of the late nineteenth century by shaping them into a coherent area of academic inquiry. The *AJS* spoke to a diverse and constantly changing constituency within this area, one whose core was a small, devoted group aiming to found within the universities a new social knowledge that would nonetheless support active practice. Throughout the *Journal*'s first decades, this small group persevered in its project of an academic foundation for sociology, succeeding first in founding the ASA and later in installing sociology as a basic liberal arts discipline.

Small's journal played a central role in rallying this core group. He was personally connected with most of its members and organizationally central to all its activities. An energetic and entrepreneurial man, he undertook the creation of the group's public consciousness through the often chaotic task of publishing a journal. With colleagues to report "News and Notes," with dependable friends contributing articles and serials, with solicitations and his own writing filling out the space, Small managed to produce number after number, volume after volume. As time went on, he moved with the discipline, maintaining a flow of younger writers to complement his aging friends, following—and perhaps furthering—the trend toward academicization. He began thereby to absorb the next, much more professionalized generation of what was beginning to be an academic discipline. As his correspondence shows, this was not an easy matter. It called for vision, for tact, for energy and strength.

And Small contrived, throughout this sustained effort, to maintain the financial foundation for his enterprise through deft negotiation with his publisher, the University of Chicago Press. Indeed, he eked out his precarious financial base with large and continuing subsidies from the Press. This too cannot have been easy; Small's *AJS* was an expensive proposition, and as the Press moved away from evangelical outreach toward more sober financialism, he must often have been in a difficult position.

Small's colleagues respected the feat represented by the journal's survival. As we shall see in the next chapter, there was a complete turnover of major contributors in the *AJS* after 1925, as if his younger colleagues swept the board clean. Yet there is no hint of a conflict before the turnover, and indeed the old man (Small was seventy in 1924) was retained at the top of the masthead as "In General Charge" in the last year of his life. He filled his last issues with his own historical reminiscences about sociology, with the last articles of his friends, with all the hodgepodge the *AJS* had published throughout his tenure.

Small bequeathed his colleagues a functioning institution, but only in the loosest sense. There were no editorial procedures, no routines, no hint of a profit. On the contrary, making the *AJS* was as personal and desperate a task as ever. More than anything specific, there was simply a tradition—thirty years of those thick little volumes that new disciplinary historians would rapidly redefine as a trajectory pointing directly toward the newly professional and scientific sociology of the 1920s.

In this sense the *AJS* was not yet a consistent social entity. For the content of the *Journal* bore little relation to the "scientific" sociology that was about to become the foundation of the Chicago school. The Small *AJS* had been the intellectual instrument of a quite different sociology—Small's much vaguer mix of social reform, history, and current research. Yet in its character as an intellectual pillar of this vaguer field, it exercised a profound influence over the emerging scientific discipline by giving it a secure home through a period of extraordinarily intense turnover. In reality the journal of a small inner core of academic sociologists, the *AJS* used its broader constituency to achieve a certain tradition and stability. We shall see in the next chapter exactly how true it was that the *AJS,* far from being the journal "of a discipline," was indeed a journal that "made a discipline."

4 The *AJS* of the Chicago Schools

The early *American Journal of Sociology* was the incarnation of a man. The middle *AJS* was the incarnation of a department. Just as the early *AJS* cannot be understood without understanding Small the academic and reformer, the middle *AJS* cannot be understood without understanding the department whose continuity and balance in the period from 1920 to 1955 supported the *Journal*'s development. Although to some extent split between what came to be called quantitative and qualitative sociology, the department was knit together by a strong and complex network of personal and intellectual loyalties. These made a framework that sustained the *AJS*.

Department and Discipline

The department that Albion Small left in 1926 was quite different from the one had founded in 1892. George Vincent left in 1908, C. R. Henderson in 1914. W. I. Thomas was fired in a celebrated morals case in 1918. The department was now led by Robert Park and Ernest Burgess. Ellsworth Faris arrived in 1920 to replace Thomas in social psychology and became chair when Small retired, remaining in that position until he retired in 1940. Columbia Ph.D. and quantitative sociologist William Ogburn arrived in 1927. Park's students Herbert Blumer and Louis Wirth entered regular faculty positions about 1930, as did Ogburn's student Samuel Stouffer shortly thereafter. The period under Park's leadership (roughly 1920–35) was the heyday of the Chicago school, as we have already seen.[1]

In the mid-1930s the charismatic Park left for Fisk University, anthropologist Lloyd Warner joined the faculty, and Wirth's and Blumer's old friend and classmate Everett Hughes was called back from McGill. The departmental staff now assumed a shape it would retain until the crisis of the early 1950s. The only changes were Faris's retirement in 1940 and Stouffer's departure for Harvard at the end of the war. The department in these later years was quite evenly balanced between qualitative and quantitative work, Ogburn's assertiveness and position as chair tending to offset the nu-

---

1. On the discipline more generally, see Turner and Turner 1990.

merical advantage of the qualitative faculty. The postwar period saw the demise of this balanced department, as we saw in chapter 2.

In this middle period of its own history, the department saw its position in the discipline change radically. Although the dominance of Chicago in Ph.D. production has been exaggerated, the political centrality of Chicago to sociology in the 1920s could not be doubted. With the *AJS* as the ASA journal, Chicago faculty as long-standing ASA secretaries (1912–36) and managing editors (1915–36), and the University of Chicago Press as the ASA's sole publisher, Chicago control was great. And Chicago was one of sociology's two or three principal intellectual centers, as many have noted.

All of this was challenged in the 1930s as sociology came to institutional maturity. National Ph.D. production was now about forty a year (Marsh 1936). Of 236 colleges and universities surveyed by the American Council on Education in 1928, nearly half (99) had departments of sociology. Most of the regional sociology associations date from the 1930s, as do the Population Association of America (1932), the Rural Sociology Society (1937), and the American Catholic Sociological Association (later the Association for the Sociology of Religion, 1938). More important, at least for the *AJS,* while such general journals as *Sociology and Social Research* and *Social Forces*—one-person journals like the *AJS*—dated from 1916 and 1922, respectively—the 1930s brought a host of specialized journals aimed at differentiated clienteles: the *Journal of Educational Sociology* in 1927, the *Journal of Social Psychology* in 1930, *Population* in 1933, *Rural Sociology* in 1936, *Public Opinion Quarterly* and *Sociometry* in 1937, and the *Journal of Marriage and the Family* in 1939. Thus, by the 1930s sociology had stabilized as a social phenomenon, turning itself into a fully structured and internally differentiated academic discipline.

Stability requires not only institutional structure but also institutional boundaries. And thus it was in the 1930s too that the last of the do-gooders drifted out of the ASA. The survey movement that had bridged academia and social work was dead. Social work itself was successfully and separately professionalized in its own schools. Separation, and with it institutionalization as a fully academic field, was complete.[2]

Intellectually also, the discipline moved ahead strongly through the 1930s and 1940s. As Stephen Turner has argued, a central force was the

2. It is probably this separation, as much as the depression, that accounts for the fall in ASA membership in the 1930s; some social activists were still on the rolls in 1932 (see the supplemental list in the ASA *Publication* of that year; *Publication* 27:4–11), and their monetary contributions were highly appreciated (Odum to Burgess, 15 May 1930, EWB 2:3). Observers at the time set the membership decline down to general penury (see the interviews cited in Lengermann 1979), but personal cost cutting may have differentially forced out the residual

sudden success of quantitative social research in attracting money from both commercial organizations and government. By the postwar period sociology was big business, and until well into the 1950s market research remained something of a sociological preserve. At the same time, the grand theorists somewhat unexpectedly seized disciplinary center stage both intellectually and politically.

In the middle period of 1925–60, then, the disciplinary context around the *AJS* changed radically. As the discipline became a secure, independent, and intellectually differentiated fiefdom in academia, the *AJS*—like the Department of Sociology—lost its privileged status. It then had to find a place for itself among a host of new specialty journals as well as vis-à-vis its new central competitor, the *American Sociological Review* (hereafter *ASR*).

The Founding of the *American Sociological Review*

Like the Small period, the middle period began with a founding—in this case not of the *AJS* but of its rival the *ASR*. The founding of the *ASR* is of interest not because it had so many bad consequences for the *AJS*, but rather because it had so few. As I shall show, the founding of the *ASR* actually caused an increase in *AJS* subscriptions, a rise in *AJS* profitability, and a clearer formulation of long-run *AJS* editorial policy. But the *ASR* affair also led to the first appointment of external advisory editors and thus testifies to a sense, enduring to this day, that although the *AJS* is no longer the official journal of the ASA, it is governed not merely by departmental will but also by the emerging national norms of disciplinary life. The episode delineates the curious nexus of profit, intellectual life, and organizational structure that is at the heart of scholarly publishing.

The founding of the *ASR* was part of a broader anti-Chicago politics within the ASA, a transformation that began about 1930 and continued until the vote establishing the *ASR* as the ASA's official journal in 1935.[3] Lengermann (1979) notes five forces conducing to the revolt against

___

social activists. The same separation came to the department somewhat earlier: the "activists"—all women—cut their affiliations with it when they founded the university's School of Social Service in 1920.

3. The story is told well by Lengermann (1979). I have not read the sources she cites in the Bernard Papers, but the article is impressively researched and squares well with what I have seen in the Chicago sources. (Lengermann did not, however, read primary sources on Chicago's reaction to the episode.) As she shows, the "rebellion" was led by a small core of dissatisfied sociologists who had no obvious connection other than personal alliance: Luther Bernard, Jerome Davis, W. P. Meroney, Newell Sims, and H. Phelps. These were unlikely rebels. The group included some Chicago Ph.D.'s (Bernard and Meroney). They were not all "Young Turks" (Bernard and Sims were over fifty). They were not particularly linked to either of the then emerging paradigms of structural functionalism or positivism.

Chicago. The first were purely personal hatreds, the most important being the feud of Luther L. Bernard with *AJS* editor Ellsworth Faris. A second force was disciplinary growth and differentiation, which, as I have already noted, had long since eclipsed Chicago's pivotal role; in the decade 1925–34, Chicago produced only 17 percent of sociology Ph.D.'s (Marsh 1936, table 13).

For Lengermann's third factor—a lessening of internal cohesion at Chicago—evidence is weaker. The Chicago faculty lined up uniformly on the Chicago side of the dispute over the *AJS;* moreover, the internal disagreements at this time have been considerably overstated, as Bulmer (1984) has argued.[4] Rather than a loss of cohesion, the Chicago group had suffered a loss of nerve. Its crucial intellectual paradigms—human ecology, institutional studies of social organization, and Thomas-Mead style social psychology—were either in retreat or abeyance during the 1930s, while other disciplinary paradigms were on the increase.[5]

As Lengermann points out, the new quantification was actually on the Chicago side. But its consequences were negative, making it a fourth reason for the rebellion. The rebels feared that the alliance of the new scientific elitism with the old organizational power of Chicago would lead to complete elite control of the discipline. A fifth factor was the Great Depression, which exacerbated fears among the professional rank and file of elite control of avenues of professional advancement. It was this factor, Lengermann believes, that gave the rebels the votes they needed to break the Chicago coalition. From the rebel viewpoint, the deep issue was equity versus elitism.

How did this revolt appear in Chicago? The Chicago faculty was in an

4. Most descriptions of Chicago in the 1930s have relied heavily on student memories, which have overemphasized the quantitative/qualitative split. After all, Blumer was Hauser's M.A. adviser and close friend, and both were very intimate with Wirth and with Burgess, whose methods were eclectic to say the least. There is some evidence for intradepartmental hostility—mostly in Ogburn's pontifications and in his attacks on the students of Blumer and Hughes at proposal time. But there is also evidence that the split was taken with a large grain of salt; for example, Hauser (personal communication) reports the existence in the 1930s of quantitative and qualitative softball teams. When serious divisions emerged, after the war, they were between Warner and Hughes on the one hand and Blumer, Hauser, and Wirth on the other. There is no hard evidence for why Bernard hated Faris. The feeling was partly intellectual (Faris was a Meadean and Bernard a strict behaviorist), but more likely Bernard had simply wanted the Chicago job that Faris got in 1920.

5. Human ecology was under the attacks that would culminate in the "ecological fallacy" debate. Studies of social organization had been seized by anthropology departments and business schools. Social psychology was awaiting (as it always would) Blumer's full-scale exposition of symbolic interactionism. The new quantification was by contrast very much at the beginning of its life, and its limits were by no means yet apparent.

awkward position. While on the one hand they were fighting the ASA rebels for control of the *Journal* and the society, on the other they were defending the *Journal* and the ASA against their own Press's increasing demands for solvency. But even the Press was ambivalent toward the ASA. Originally the Press saw the ASA simply as a marketing device. However, once the ASA reached its mature size (one thousand members) and its turnover stabilized (in the early 1920s), it grew too slowly to pay off the annual deficit run by the *AJS*. Worse yet, the ASA was perennially late in paying its bill for the publishing of its annual *Publication*—the proceedings of the annual meeting. For example, Press Managing Director Donald Bean wrote to University Business Officer Harrell on 9 January 1933 (UCP 35:1), "I am still working hard on the American Sociological Society and will go after Tyson on my trip to New York City this week. Only $1294 of this account is due, but that much I will insist on promptly." In 1935, while the ASA debated the issue of establishing a new journal, Bean humiliated the organization by imposing substantial interest charges on its debts to the Press. The ASA was forced to sell bonds to its members to avoid legal action (ASA *Publication* 29, 1:14 and 29, 2 [1935]).[6]

Despite these difficulties, the Press had a strong positive interest in the ASA both for its subscription base and for the symbolic capital that came from publishing the flagship journal for a prominent discipline. The *AJS* was by 1930 the Press's largest single journal, with 2,851 subscribers; the next largest Press journal had only half that. And by 1932 a combination of reduced costs in house and a rise in non-ASA prices had brought the journal very close to the black. University subsidy per subscriber was down to about fifty cents. This situation led Bean to be extremely conciliatory in the early stages of the conflict, in fall 1930 and winter 1931; he would simply demonstrate the financial foolhardiness of the ASA's striking out on its own. Thus his subordinate, Press business officer R. D. Hemens, wrote to the Press's New York publicity agent urging a careful attempt to find "the right people to cultivate" at the upcoming ASA meeting (14 December

6. As it happens, we know very little of faculty members' emotions during this battle; all were in Chicago and all communication was oral. Between the department and the Press, however, communication was written. So we can reconstruct the situation from the Press's, and through it the department's, point of view. The Press was securely on the department's side throughout the controversy but always mindful first and foremost of the university's pecuniary interests. The Press's campaign was directed by Donald Bean, its tough, wily managing director, who studied the ASA/*AJS* situation in depth in early 1931 and decided ahead of time "when to hold 'em and when to fold 'em." But Press-department relations could be incestuously complicated. Throughout the years of the *ASR* controversy, Herbert Blumer as managing editor and later secretary-treasurer of the ASA spent endless hours fighting off Bean's insistent demands that the ASA pay its overdue bills.

1931, UCP 33:1): "The relationship between the Society and the University or at least between a small group in the Society and the University are [*sic*] somewhat strained. Whatever we can do to relieve this strain will be of assistance in renewing our contract for publishing. . . ."

On the other hand, as Bean made clear in his long confidential review of the situation, which was released to the ASA on vote of the Chicago Sociology Department (2 November 1932, K. E. Niles to Bean, UCP 33:7), ASA members got a great bargain for their half-price rate. As he dryly noted, "The contract has not been a source of financial profit to the University." Bean's recommendation to the ASA rebels was that they ignore the fact that Press ownership meant that a University of Chicago faculty member had to be editor of the *AJS* (this was the central rebel objection) and concentrate instead on the contractually guaranteed right of the ASA to elect advisory editors annually. These editors, Bean said, could "take a more active participation in the editorial policies of the journal." This conciliatory gesture failed because the real target of the rebellion was the department, not the *AJS* in particular. By 1933 Bean was more cynical. He wrote to his secretary on 7 February 1933 (UCP 35:1):

> Mr. Simms [*sic*] of Oberlin is the new chairman of the Reactionary [!] Committee in the American Sociological Society to start their own official journal. . . . Mr. Burgess suggests that the next time I go east I stop off at Oberlin and have Mr. Wilkins introduce me to Brother Simms. Will you put a note to that effect in my New York folder?

As Lengermann notes, December 1933 to December 1934 was a period of Chicago "counterattack" under Burgess, who had by then become ASA president and was working his usual interpersonal and political magic.[7] But Burgess had his work cut out for him. For, having taken advice from the university lawyers, Bean wrote to Burgess (in the latter's capacity as ASA president) on 24 January 1934 unilaterally removing the ASA from any role in the *AJS*.

> In view of the disposition of certain members of the Society to misinterpret the present contractual relations between the University of Chicago Press, as publishers of the *American Journal of Sociology* and the Society, the University hereby serves notice of its desire

---

7. Shils's condescending portrait of Burgess (Shils 1991) as a gentle, shy man overshadowed by Park could not be further from the truth. Burgess was a subtle handler of people: quiet, but very effective. Lengermann (1979) rightly sees him as a master interpersonal tactician.

to cancel these contractual relations as of January 1, 1935. . . . The *American Journal of Sociology* will continue its editorial policy of serving the vital publishing ends of Sociology to the fullest extent of its financial resources. We believe that most of the members of the Society have appreciated this tradition in the past and will agree that this should be its continuing ideal.

The Press, he said, was not dissatisfied with the current situation but undertook to do this "to free them [the Executive Committee of the ASA—largely made up of Chicago faculty] of all possible sources of embarrassment" (UCP 33:1).

It is not clear whether this sudden strike was Burgess's idea or Bean's, although it is clear what Bean was responding to. The "reactionary" committee headed by Newell Sims had reported in December 1933—at Faris's suggestion (in his capacity as *AJS* editor)—that members ought to have an option of taking *AJS, Social Forces,* or *Sociology and Social Research* as their "society" (half-price) journal. Officially this disestablished the *AJS,* although in a practical sense it did not, since 85 percent of ASA members still elected the *AJS* the following year, only a little less than the percentage subscribing to the *AJS* in a "normal" year (Bean to Harrell, 24 November 1934, UCP 33:1). But in Press eyes, if the ASA was not a captive market, there was no point in any formal relationship, for the main effect of the contract was to constrain the Press's ASA price for the journal. Moreover, the declining membership of the ASA (as the depression wore on), coupled with the fact that non-ASA subscriptions now nearly equaled ASA subscriptions in numbers, meant that Press revenue from the *AJS* was far less dependent on ASA members than before. In fact by 1934 less than one-third of *AJS* revenue came from the ASA (*AJS* budget in EWB 1:4). Hence, when the ASA voted for free choice, Bean canceled the contract within three weeks.

Thus the university, not the ASA, actually ended the special relationship of journal and discipline. There is no indication in Lengermann's account that anyone in the ASA other than Burgess knew during 1934 that the Press had already exercised its option to end the contract or that by doing so the Press had already refused to publish the ASA *Publication* after 1 January 1935. President Burgess apparently said nothing to anyone about Bean's letter. When, nearly a year later, Blumer (as ASA secretary) wrote to Press business officer Hemens informing him that the society wished to cancel the contract for publishing the *Publication,* Hemens politely pointed out (22 January 1935, UCP 35:1) that the *Publication* was published under the general contract, which had long since been canceled by the Press. Not only had Blumer known nothing about this, neither had the ASA Publications

Committee (the "rebel" committee of Newell Sims, Read Bain, Luther L. Bernard, and W. P. Meroney), which at the annual meeting in December 1934 recommended that the Press be notified of the termination of the contract for the *Publication* and put Blumer to the humiliation of writing his letter to Hemens in the first place. Burgess, who had known about the abrogation for a year at that point but had apparently said nothing, must have been amused.

The final ASA report declaring the separation from Chicago was filled with polite noises about the "helpful service" of the *AJS* and the "cooperation" of the Press. It did not mention either the Press's underwriting the ASA's budgets or the Press's decades of carrying the society's debts without interest. For the record, the total direct Press subsidy to the ASA between 1905 and 1932 was worth $715,000 in 1996 dollars, an average of $25,500 a year. (For a full listing, see the Bean memo in UCP 33:1.) This amount does not include forgiven interest or the time devoted to faculty administrative and editorial service, except for the secretary-treasurer, who was paid off the ASA budget. (The ASA report on this matter is at *Publication* 29, 1:19, 1935.)

Taken in total, in the 1920s the Chicago subsidies averaged about 35 to 40 percent of the society's true budget (the titular budget plus the Chicago contributions). Financially, therefore, the ASA was basically a client organization of the Press and the department through its first thirty years. It thus seems better to regard the *real* foundation of sociology as a profession in America as taking place in the 1930s, with the wave of new journal foundings and the freeing of the ASA from its Chicago overlordship, rather than dating it from 1905. It is also crucial, as I noted earlier, to recognize that part of "making a discipline" was in fact accomplished by the desire of third parties to create a captive market.

The Press accompanied its abrogation of the ASA agreement with a stronger campaign to retrieve its debts from the ASA (the legal threats mentioned above), but it also promised the ASA some money to search for new members if it would formulate a definite plan to pay off its $2,517.87 debt (Hemens to Burgess, 28 November 1934, UCP 35:1). Bean was still willing to deal if the financial results were good.

For itself, the Press spent 1934 making its plans for the financial and editorial future of the *AJS*. Bean informed Press editorial director Gordon Laing (16 August 1934, UCP 35:1) that Faris, who wished to step down, was recommending Ogburn as his successor. Bean was reluctant to lose Faris, who nonetheless continued to urge Ogburn's candidacy through the fall. But Laing left the issue up to the editorial board of the *Journal* (Laing to file, 15 October 1934, UCP 33:1), and at some point between then and 6 February 1936 (Burgess to department, WFO 29:2) Burgess emerged as the central figure. He then became the next editor, expected by Press and department to save the day.

Meanwhile, ASA fulminations continued. During the first flush of their victory, the rebels planned both to continue the annual *Publication* and to start a new journal. However, the low bids that had lured them away from the Press suddenly doubled after the split, when the society finally asked publishers for solid, realistic bids (ASA *Publication* 29, 1:8, 1935, forwarded to Bean and commented on by him; see UCP 33:1). As reality set in, the ASA *Publication,* already quarterly—was simply redefined as the bimonthly *ASR* (ASA *Publication* 29, 4:3–10). This ancestry was emphasized by the rule that the *ASR* would have first refusal of any presentation at the annual meeting, a rule rebel editor F. E. Hankins gleefully imposed on Chicagoan Philip Hauser in the *ASR*'s first year.[8] The *ASR* was thus *not* a new journal, but simply the old *Publication* issued in installments under a new name and without a Chicago managing editor.[9]

In fact, the Chicago faculty had founded the *ASR* in all but name. It had been Burgess who in 1930, before the rebellion began, started negotiations with the Press to publish the *Publication* quarterly, transforming it from a proceedings volume into a journal. This move, he felt, would allow con-

8. Hankins to Hauser, 13 January 1937, PMH 14:8. Hankins's letter was coolly insolent: "The paper presented by you at the Chicago meetings of the ASS has not yet reached the editorial office. Will you kindly send same at your early convenience? If you desire other disposition of this paper please inform us. You probably know that acceptance of a place on the program entitles the *Review* to first claim on the paper presented." Hankins's editorial in the first number of the *ASR* referred to other sociological journals "to which we may appear to be a competitor" but pointedly did not mention the *AJS* by name.

9. The *ASR* rebellion did little to exclude Chicago and its allies from ASA journalism. By year two of the *ASR* Stouffer was on the editorial board. Year three brought Charles S. Johnson, year five Pauline Young, and year six Leonard Cottrell. The *ASR*'s fourth editor was Chicago's staunch ally F. Stuart Chapin. On the financial side, the creation of the *ASR* was a major handicap to the ASA. The 1935 Publication Committee's notion of 2,000 subscriptions within two years was overly optimistic given that the society's membership was down to 1,141 by that year. The same report also noted that the ASA would allocate $4 of each full member's $6 dues to the *ASR;* in the last year of the old arrangement with the Press (1932) the subscribing ASA members had paid the Press only $2.50. The new *ASR* thus actually cost society members 60 percent more than had the *AJS.* Moreover, without the massive nonmember support of the *AJS,* what was from the member's point of view more money bought less journal. In 1932, when the *AJS* cost ASA members $3,750, its actual expenses were $12,582. The rebel Publications Committee planned to replace this journal with an outlay of $3,800 to $4,600. The consequences in size and physical quality of the two journals were obvious at the time and endured for decades. The *ASR* went to glossy covers in 1987, for example, twenty years after the *AJS.* However, the long-standing size difference, at least, is now gone; the *AJS*'s page number advantage is offset by the larger and more densely printed *ASR* pages.

centration of particular areas into "special issues" that would then acquire separate monetary value (Burgess to R. D. Hemens, 28 February 1930, UCP 35:1). The *Publication* moved onto that quarterly basis under Blumer and Wirth, the managing editors in the early 1930s. The journal was simply renamed and made bimonthly to begin the *ASR* in 1936. The occasional acceptance of papers not presented at the annual meetings was the only new policy.

The rebellion's effect on *AJS* finances and distribution was to make the journal profitable and to increase its circulation, for it forced the Press to aim its promotional efforts entirely at full-rate subscribers and to give up its attempts to expand an ASA membership that paid only half-rate. Free to set the price of the *AJS* to ASA members, the Press raised that price 40 percent in one year and lost perhaps 10 to 15 percent of ASA subscribers; the raised price made the change revenue-neutral.

Table 7 shows the circulation information. The *AJS* recovered almost all the ASA as subscribers within a few years of the *ASR* debacle but lost

Table 7. *AJS* Circulation, 1928–1951

Year	Paid Full	Paid Special	Exchange	Free	Pages	Total Subscriptions	% ASA
1928–29					1,212	2,572	
1930						2,851	
1934–35	998	1,124	98	33	888	2,122	88
1936–37	1,092	785	92	53	1,014	1,877	67
1937–38	1,191	812	92	55	1,116	2,003	78
1938–39	1,233	900	90	65	1,092	2,133	87
1939–40	1,168	1,040	86	90	1,020	2,208	99
1940–41	1,264	916	84	93	990	2,180	
1941–42	1,435	844	81	92	1,076	2,279	
1942–43	1,421	910	81	82	726	2,366	84
1943–44	1,602	757	81	80	592	2,369	
1944–45	1,430	896	81	83	600	2,366	75
1945–46	1,537	925	80	84	632	2,502	
1946–47	1,725	1,445	74	95	606	3,197	80
1947–48	-----3,261-----		76	95	568	3,261	
1948–49	-----3,877-----		68	101	936	3,877	
1949–50	------------4,101------------			108	764	4,101	
1950–51	------------4,407------------			112	688	4,407	

Note: In 1942 the *AJS* changed format, resulting in a sharp page decline. The excess pages in 1948–49 include an index. The % ASA figure is an estimate of the percentage of ASA members subscribing to the journal, estimated by dividing the number of special-rate subscribers by the number of ASA members. Since the *AJS* was on a July fiscal year and the ASA was on a 1 January membership year, these have had to be interpolated, but they are probably accurate to about 5 percent.

ground in the early years of the war, ground that was then regained in the postwar period. Note that the depression itself had already cost the *AJS* nearly 25 percent of its subscription base between 1930 and 1934.

The financial results of the debacle were even more satisfactory. Table 8 gives the details. As I noted earlier, the *AJS* cost the Press an average net loss of about $1,500 a year in its first thirty years. From 1925 to 1932, the deficit averaged $3,600 a year. But the deficits declined from 1930 onward, reaching $1,044 in the last year of affiliation with ASA (the "free choice" year, 1934–35). After the founding of the *ASR,* the *AJS* had only two deficit years (1938–39 and 1948–49) in the next fifteen. The average annual profit was $1,100. Part of this income change can be attributed to advertising income and sales of special issues. But the deep foundation for this solvency was a steadily increasing subscription base and, in particular, growth in the full-rate subscription base. This was a matter of aggressive merchandising to non-ASA faculty and to libraries.

The *ASR* episode shows well the powerful forces pushing for an institutionalization of academic disciplines independent of particular universities. Domination of the society by one university's faculty could not persist. The Chicago faculty could not simultaneously argue for the society against the Press and for the Press against the society. Once it had become clear that the ASA's interests were not identical with the department's, the Chicago faculty position was untenable. A first sign of this recognition was the appointment of non-Chicago faculty as advisory editors to the *AJS,* first done in 1933. (The list included one or two rebels, a trick that did not forestall the rebellion.)

Like the Press, by 1934 the department began serious planning for the future. As I noted above, there is no evidence of how or why Burgess replaced Ogburn as the potential *AJS* leader. But Burgess redrafted the letter Faris proposed sending to every alumnus of the department, and from that point forward he seemed in control. The letter (WFO 29:2) clarifies the Press position, listing the immense Chicago donations to the ASA, not only in Press money, but in departmental time (of faculty) and money (for fellowships for students working on the *Journal*). It also discusses the history of the various votes, the "year of free choice," and the fact that 85 percent of the ASA elected the *AJS* during that year. Burgess then goes on to define the new situation explicitly in terms of standards:

> This change in status, however, may, we believe be turned by our collective effort into an inviting opportunity for developing a more vigorous publication of superior merit. Hitherto there has always been an obligation to give representation to the diverse interests

Table 8. AJS Receipts and Costs, 1928–1951

Year	Cost	Income	Subscriptions	Advertising	Back	Price per Subscription	Net
1928–29	13,588	9,446	9,152			4, 2	−4,112
1934–35	8,493	9,537	8,057	574	590	5, 2.50	−1,044
1936–37	10,317	10,759	8,325	543	1,425	5, 3.50	442
1937–38	10,158	10,309	8,944	670	513		151
1938–39	11,268	10,911	9,504	686	403		−357
1939–40	11,219	11,687	10,100	689	738		468
1940–41	10,957	12,045	10,116	775	648		1,088
1941–42	12,728	13,273	10,383	724	1,862		545
1942–43	13,108	14,020	10,681	319	1,673		912
1943–44	10,854	12,605	10,804	308	1,281		1,751
1944–45	12,536	14,170	12,354	528	1,064		1,634
1945–46	14,638	17,274	14,645	1,075	1,009		2,636
1946–47	15,521	19,499	16,006	1,530	1,752		3,978
1947–48	18,062	20,572	16,284	1,608	2,371	6, ?	2,510
1948–49	26,744	26,460	20,279	2,162	3,786		−334
1949–50	24,862	25,516	20,544	2,057	2,504		654
1950–51	22,947	23,974	20,346	2,003	1,270		1,027

Note: All figures are current dollar amounts. The prices are noted only when they change. The first price is the general price, the second the price to ASA members.

and claims of the membership of the Society. It is now possible to improve greatly the character of the articles and the book reviews and to publish a Journal which will merit an even more enthusiastic support than has been accorded in the past.

Unlike the rebels, who posed the issue as equity versus elitism, Burgess posed it as quality versus representation.

The department also drafted a mission statement for the *AJS* (LW 17:1). The journal would focus on "cultural or group behavior," because that was the area of the department and "has a further advantage of being the common area of sociology and cultural anthropology." Areas of interest would be race relations, communication, the community, crime, population, social movements, social trends, personality, and the family. The *AJS* expected to solicit some articles and to devote at least one issue a year to a special subject. Major articles were to present the findings of research and were also to be significant, readable, and, preferably between ten and twenty printed pages. The *AJS* also hoped to print minor articles—summaries or abstracts, brief statements on new methods, outlines of promising research, and reports from meetings. The "News and Notes" section would be continued. Book reviews would become fewer, longer, and more critical. The editors expected more from the advisory editors than they had in the past, and to achieve this they set up a formal system of rotation.[10]

As a sign of the new regime, the first luncheon meeting of advisory editors was held in December 1936 (EWB 1:4) and touched many of the same themes. But the advisory editors also suggested taking other new risks that prior association with the ASA had forbidden. They urged a more controversial letters section, more pointed reviews, omission of articles justifying sociology, and trying out longer articles "rather than publishing several short articles of more dubious merit" (the last comment was Pitirim Sorokin's). The meeting the following year brought many of the same suggestions, plus the new one that some articles be published that did not "proceed smoothly from a statement of the problem through the procedure to conclusions and interpretations without any statement of the method-

10. For years, editors of the *ASR* tried to get the *AJS* to give up the "News and Notes" section, and for years *AJS* editors and managing editors refused (see, e.g., editorial board meetings notes for 14 May 1951, LW 17:1). Helen Hughes and R. E. L. Faris, at the helms of the two journals in the mid-1950s, discussed the change, but it was ultimately Peter Blau who removed "News and Notes" from the *AJS*.

ological and technical problems involved" but rather were "diaries of headaches" (a suggestion made by Robert Lynd).

It is striking that overall this list of special policies has been more or less the line of differentiation between the *AJS* and the *ASR* to the present. Longer articles, fewer but longer reviews, explicit controversy, and strong special issues became the hallmarks of the *AJS*. In this sense, the fight over the *ASR* produced a differentiation that has endured for half a century.

But the department was very bitter. On 8 January 1936, days after the final ASA vote establishing the *ASR*, the department discussed the matter and decided to reduce the *AJS* price to $4 a year for all subscribers, abolishing the ASA discount (8 January 1936, MDS). Managing director Bean, however, forbade a vendetta. The *AJS* stayed at $5 for the general subscriber, but the ASA price went up only $1 (40 percent) to $3.50.

Editorial Succession

During this long controversy, the routines of editing had nonetheless to march along. The *AJS* saw several official editorial successions in the middle period. When Albion Small retired in 1926 he left the journal to an "editorship of the whole" by the department. In 1933, halfway through the *ASR* controversy, the collective editorship was replaced by Faris as editor-in-chief. (In fact Faris was de facto editor by 1929 at the latest: see Ogburn-Faris correspondence in WFO 29:4.) In 1936, at the beginning of direct competition with the *ASR*, Ernest Burgess took over the *AJS* for four years, as I have noted, to be followed in 1940 by Herbert Blumer, who was the editor until he departed in 1952, at which time he was replaced by Everett Hughes, who remained editor until *his* departure in 1961. The names on the masthead meant little, however. Louis Wirth was de facto editor for extended periods between 1926 and his death in 1952, and Helen MacGill Hughes was de facto editor for various periods during her stay with the *Journal* (1944–61).

Whatever the titles, every one of these people was a Chicago Ph.D., and all but Faris were Chicago sociology Ph.D.'s. All of them were personal friends, on intimate terms with each other, and four—Blumer, Wirth, Helen Hughes, and Everett Hughes—were graduate-school classmates and close friends. The *AJS* was no longer a personal journal; it was, in these middle years, a primary group journal.

We know little about what caused the editorial transitions. Faris, as I have noted, wanted Ogburn to take over from him, but Burgess in fact did so, despite great reluctance (Burgess to Ogburn, 28 October 1939, EWB

1:5). At this time the editorial director of the Press was the ultimate authority on who should be editor and was lobbied in this matter by individuals rather than addressed formally by the department as a whole. There was no department vote proposing Burgess nor, to my knowledge, any proposing his successors Blumer or Hughes. (Formal department proceedings arrived during another controversy, this time involving young faculty in the late 1950s. See chapter 5.)

After four years, Burgess felt confident that the *AJS* was in stable condition and resigned, recommending that the new editor be Wirth, who "has borne the heaviest editorial responsibility which he has discharged with great effectiveness." Chair Ogburn tried to persuade Burgess to continue, because Wirth had other administrative chores. But Burgess was adamant. With Ogburn in the chair, Faris retiring, Burgess resigning, Wirth unavailable, and Hughes just arrived (1938), there was basically no other candidate than Blumer. Blumer and Wirth had figured out that he would be the editor long before either Burgess and Ogburn did (Blumer to Wirth, 30 May 1939, LW 1:8).[11]

Ten years later, Blumer himself tried to resign a year before leaving Chicago. He was to be on leave in Hawaii in 1950–51 and had also had a number of serious conflicts with the Press (Editorial Board Minutes, 11 April 1950, LW 17:1). But Wirth and Helen Hughes handled the *AJS* for the year, and Blumer did not actually resign until he left the university (1952). Again, there was little choice. This time the editorial board itself made the decision, meeting 22 May 1952 at the Windermere Hotel (Editorial Board Minutes, 22 May 1952, EWB 1:7). Wirth was dead, Blumer leaving, Burgess and Ogburn retiring. Of the tenured faculty, only Hauser, Warner, and Hughes remained; the first was out of town consulting on the Burmese census, the second was an anthropologist. Hughes, who had fortunately been an active member of the editorial board for some years at this point, was the only real possibility.

These editorial successions show the largely adventitious character of the *AJS* editorship. Albion Small appears to have been the only editor in *AJS* history who retained the editorship when other faculty wanted it. The position is onerous, and faculty have avoided it at all times since 1925. In the middle period, however, it was seen as an important duty, and central departmental faculty did the job—either officially like Burgess and Blumer or unofficially like Wirth. With the accession of Hughes, who was peripheral

11. Also, Blumer was single at the time and perhaps was therefore considered readier to take on such an obligation. Ethel Shanas (personal communication) reports him sometimes at work at 6:00 A.M. and notes that his editorial style presumed immense personal effort.

to the department in many ways when he took over, there began a drift of the *AJS* toward the periphery, a move that would accelerate in the *Journal*'s later period.[12]

Another important "editorial transition" took place at this time: the transformation of the office and editorial routines by Helen MacGill Hughes as assistant and later managing editor. In the years 1925 to 1944, graduate student assistants were responsible for the day-to-day management of manuscripts and books. Typically the responsible student held a departmental fellowship, as did Nathan Bodin, Robert Winch, and Ethel Shanas, although sometimes the department applied to the dean for scholarship money to fund such a position. The student assistant maintained card files on manuscripts, sent overdue notices on book reviews, and generally maintained manuscript flow. There was at this point no regular editorial meeting. Business and policy matters were discussed (rather cursorily) at faculty meetings, and the editor personally made all manuscript decisions.[13]

In 1944, two years after Shanas had departed for the West Coast, Helen Hughes became editorial assistant and gradually transformed the office structure. As she later pointed out (and as I noted in chapter 2), the editors were simply not present much of the time. Blumer became arbitrator of the postwar steel strike in Pittsburgh and spent substantial parts of several years there. Stouffer, Burgess, Ogburn, Everett Hughes, and Warner were all involved in war-related research. After the war, Everett Hughes spent extended periods at the University of Frankfurt, and Wirth was active around the world for the Social Science Research Council and the International Sociological Association, which he helped found. Hauser was often away at the U.S. Census Bureau or at other consulting jobs.

12. In an interview with me, Philip Hauser stated emphatically that department members looked on editing the *AJS* as a "patriotic chore" and in particular that no one who had serious grant resources could afford the time away from research. "I certainly don't remember any classic battles of people competing to get the editorship," he said sarcastically.

13. We do not know who did the clerical work for Small. Small was dean of the faculty during much of his career and probably had his personal secretary in that office do the *AJS* clerical work. For the later period, on fellowships, see Shanas (personal communication) and department minutes for 11 April 1929 and 9 October 1936 in MDS. The faculty minutes show numerous discussions of *AJS* business and policy matters—on the "Social Changes" issues, the preparation of indexes, the institution of a bibliography of current literature (see also Lindstrom, personal communication). Both Ethel Shanas (speaking of 1940–42) and Philip Hauser (speaking of 1947–51) were explicit that Blumer made all his own decisions, with a few exceptions in the quantitative area, where he tended to seek advice (as from Shanas, who was well trained in quantitative work). Also, the available evidence argues that Helen Hughes (1972, 767) was mistaken in recalling that the editorial assistants on the *AJS* were more likely women than men.

But it may also have been, as Helen Hughes (1972) noted, that she found new things to do. The number of manuscripts was not overwhelming. The *AJS* got about 150 manuscripts a year in the mid-1930s and accepted one out of three (Advisory Board Meeting Minutes, 29 December 1936, EWB 1:4). Ten years later Helen Hughes was not dealing with a substantially larger number of manuscripts, but she did more with them. Both her own and others' recollections note her activities in copyediting; she extensively rewrote many articles, sometimes to authors' chagrin. She also instituted formal editorial board meetings (every month or two as business demanded) and more efficient manuscript tracking procedures.

Hughes was in many ways ideally situated to take this next step in the institutionalization of the *AJS*, the creation of a professional office staff. She was a Ph.D. classmate of Wirth, Blumer, and Everett Hughes. After she and Everett Hughes married, they went to Canada (she was Canadian), where he was on the McGill faculty. There she (more than her husband) maintained close ties with Chicago, mostly through long intimate letters to Blumer and particularly Wirth, from whom she cajoled book reviews to keep herself busy as a scholar.[14] On their return to Chicago, Hughes wanted part-time work; her youngest child was in nursery school. She took the *AJS* position and turned it into a position for a combination copyeditor, managing editor, and on occasion scholarly editor. Although there is little documentary evidence, the recollection is widespread that once Everett Hughes became official editor (1952), Helen Hughes was to all intents and purposes the actual editor of the *Journal.*

Thus the editorial structures of the journal changed considerably in the middle period. Once run by an individual, the *AJS* was now run by a primary group who deputed one member to run it at any given time. The religious calling of Albion Small was replaced by a sense of duty to the

14. It is not clear why the extraordinary youthful intimacy evident in Helen Hughes's letters to Blumer and Wirth while the Hugheses were in Canada gradually cooled to something close to stiffness in the late 1940s. Thus a letter to Blumer (25 May 1933, LW 5:3) closes with "Give Dr. Faris a kiss for me, on the back of the neck, Love, Helen." Or to Wirth (19 October 1934, LW 5:3), "Here are a lot of books I am dying to have and my thoughts naturally flew to you [Wirth was book review editor] in the hopes of getting them for nothing. If any of the following come in, could I have them for review?" She wrote to Wirth on 11 January 1938 (LW 5:3) about Everett's breaking his glasses in a striptease parlor in Atlantic City. Yet in the late 1940s her memos to Wirth are occasionally addressed to "Professor Wirth," not the "Dear old Louis" of the 1930s. In part this reflected departmental politics; Hughes allied with Warner and others in the Committee on Human Development and was strongly affected by anthropologists, whereas Blumer and Wirth were central to sociology itself and somewhat suspicious of anthropology. It is also true that Blumer didn't think much of Hughes's work and said so publicly, at least by the early 1950s. There were political differences as well. But the estrangement seems to have come earlier.

discipline, best exemplified by Burgess's stepping into the breach in 1936, but also by Blumer's tireless hours reading all *AJS* submissions himself. But the disruptions of the war, coupled with the increasing obligations of faculty away from Chicago, required another transformation: the creation of a permanent office staff, with someone to maintain and sustain editorial processes. From these came some of the routines that constitute the modern journal.

Reviewing

New office routines were complemented by new review procedures. It is easy to imagine middle period reviewing as a not yet fully fledged version of "true peer review." In this view early reviewing seems, as does the *AJS*'s editorial process more broadly, simply a mass of quiet nepotism. But middle period reviewing should rather be seen in terms of what lay behind it and of the specific editorial problems it aimed to answer. The due process conception of scholarly publishing lay far in the future.

Reviewing probably arose during the late 1920s. Small may have asked for occasional outside opinions, but his enduring loyalties to long-standing friend-authors suggest that solicitation continued to be his main way of acquiring manuscripts and that, having solicited them, he published them more or less without revision. It seems clear that reviewing arose under Faris and dealt with specific areas of expertise, the most crucial being the new statistics. All the refereeing documents that survive from the 1920s and early 1930s are from Ogburn, are addressed to Faris, and concern statistics:

> Miss Jennison's paper on Religious Views of Contemporary Sociologists: There is nothing particularly bad about the statistical work of this paper. It is orderly and clear. The only doubtful point is that of selection, which is a point in connection with most questionnaires that the author of course recognizes, but I wouldn't consider it an especially serious defect. Otherwise, the statistical part is clear, orderly, and seems to be very well done.
>
> I would raise a question about this paper, however, as to the importance of the subject matter. Perhaps one's opinion is as good as another's on this, but it doesn't interest me greatly and I don't know whether it would interest the readers of the Journal very much. (Ogburn to Faris, 27 April 1929, WFO 29:4)

Several characteristics of this letter are common throughout early refereeing documents. First, it relates to a quite specific expertise of the referee; Ogburn was the department's best statistician. Second, it directly raises the issue of reader interest. Ogburn urges against publication of what was com-

petent but uninteresting. Third, it assumes a close personal relationship between referee and editor. This assumption is clear in the lack of technical detail, the almost contentless quality of the criticisms, and the nonbureau-
cratic format (this is written as a letter, not a form). The receiver (Faris)
trusts the sender's (Ogburn's) judgment absolutely; as Faris says in a later
request for a review, "I seem to have serious doubts on the soundness of the
argument and hope you will be willing to enlighten me" (Faris to Ogburn,
28 May 1930, WFO 29:4). But it is equally clear that other experts may be
necessary; in another review letter Ogburn writes, "Perhaps [this manu-
script] ought to be read by some member of the law faculty if it is accepted"
(Ogburn to Faris, 30 November 29, WFO 29:4).

   In part this tone is very much a personal style of Ogburn's: short, suc-
cinct, sardonic. But we see the same kinds of assumptions in a review of a
book-length manuscript (for an *AJS* monograph) done by Wirth in 1936
for Blumer (not Burgess, who was "officially" editor). Like Ogburn, Wirth
speaks to the size of the paper's audience. He too suggests other relevant
experts. He even apologizes for making comments on the manuscript
that extend his remarks beyond a single page ("I should like to add a few
comments on the manuscript"). He also deliberately limits his scope:
"There are numerous questions of factual criticism and of point of view in
the generalizations and of sources and of style that I presume you do not
wish me to touch on here, but that I think a thoughtful reader should call to
the attention of the authors before the manuscript is finally published. This
would take more time than I can give to the manuscript" (Wirth to Blumer,
17 July 1936, LW 1:8). Note the presumption that detailed commentary is
the *editor's* prerogative and that it is not the reader's responsibility to point
out all failings, but simply to give a judgment. In making this judgment,
Wirth invoked the same central criteria as did Ogburn: quality of writing,
timeliness, and clarity and success of the argument. The audience for the review, as with Ogburn, is the editor alone, who can be expected to help the
authors improve the manuscript *only* if the manuscript will ultimately be
published. Indeed, other correspondence (Winch to Wirth, 29 January
1940, LW 17:1) shows that referees were occasionally asked to specify the
exact changes required, but only *after* acceptance.

   The social structure of reviewing was thus as follows. An editor asked a
personal friend, whose expertise and idiosyncrasies he knew well, for an
opinion of the timeliness, audience, and quality of a piece of work. This
judgment was delivered, without much evidentiary justification but guaranteed by personal trust, and then, if the judgment was positive and the editor concurred, the exact problems and detailed changes required would be

worked out. If a faculty member did not consider himself competent, he referred the editor to an outsider, generally someone he knew personally, but not necessarily an outside advisory editor. There was thus a two-step flow of expertise.

The key to this system was the editor's absolute trust in the referees, since judgments were accepted with minimal evidence. Indeed, into the late 1940s referee judgments within the faculty were often delivered orally (Hauser, personal communication). Also, there was no particular rule at this point about conflict of interest; Faris asked Ogburn for an opinion of a submission by (Ogburn's student) Samuel Stouffer in the mid-1930s (22 June 1935, WFO 29:4). The whole situation was thus defined within an arena governed by collegiality and trust rather than by formal norms and procedures.

The faculty itself did most of the reviewing. On 29 January 1940, student assistant Bob Winch timidly wrote to Wirth prompting him for judgments on the *ten* articles he has been assigned to read, one dating from nearly a year before (LW 17:1). This situation persisted. A decade later, 15 June 1949, Helen Hughes was badgering Ernest Burgess for the seven he owed (EWB 1:7), and a year later she was hounding Louis Wirth (14 July 1950, LW 17:1) for five. Then, as later, reviewers were picked by area of specialty. Ogburn got most statistical papers. Burgess's seven in 1949 included four on the family, Wirth's five included four on race and ethnic relations and one on the sociology of knowledge.

But refereeing was a small business. If, as the evidence suggests, individual faculty were reviewing about fifteen papers a year, then the extended faculty could easily have reviewed between one hundred and two hundred manuscripts a year, since it included not only the six or seven tenured professors but also that many or more assistant professors, instructors, and research associates. (Also, there is no indication of papers' being reviewed by *two* people other than the editor until the 1950s.) Moreover, Blumer rejected a substantial proportion of manuscripts by himself, without referees. The *AJS* received only 150 manuscripts a year in the late 1930s. Therefore a maximum of thirty to fifty manuscripts went to the outside advisory editors annually in the 1930s and 1940s. (There were fourteen such outsiders in 1940. In many cases, manuscripts going outside went to faculty-indicated experts not on the masthead.) It is unlikely that these figures changed much before 1946.

This entire system of refereeing presupposed a network of personal connections. A short judgment works only if the editor knows the reviewer and trusts him absolutely. And the practice of short, terse reviews continued well after the war; Wirth responded to Helen Hughes's July 1950 letter on 28 August (LW 17:1) with three-sentence judgments on each of four manuscripts (see also Burgess to Blumer, 26 August 1948, EWB 1.6).

But other parts of the general structure of reviewing had begun to shift by the 1950s. By 1951 Helen Hughes wrote letters apologizing to authors for late reviews, a courtesy of which there is no earlier sign. Moreover, she sent marked copies of these letters to delinquent faculty (EWB 1:7). Second reviewers seem to have appeared for a substantial number of manuscripts by this point (e.g., examples in EWB 1:7). To be sure, the interactional structure—reviewers spoke to editors who spoke to authors—remained, as did the fact that virtually all *AJS* reviewing was done by about twenty-five people and a few others known personally to the Chicago faculty in that group. But the presence of a managing editor introduced a new formality and a new emotional-normative structure into the relationship, a structure that created new disciplinary rules of civility for editor and referee.

The force behind this change was not necessarily the personality and imagination of Helen Hughes, although they undoubtedly played a part. Rather, with Blumer absent for extended periods, there was no faculty editor present to make the multiple personal judgments on which the earlier system depended. (Wirth usually filled in for Blumer but was vastly overextended and often out of town himself.) To be sure, Helen Hughes was permanent party on the *AJS* and a sociology Ph.D., but she lacked the authority—faculty status—to make these personal decisions. She must then have introduced routine editorial practices to create the necessary official bases for editors' judgments. When Blumer returned to town, he seems to have put the older, more ad hoc system back in place (Hauser, personal communication). But by 1952, when Blumer left for Berkeley, a new and more formal structure had been tried out and was available. Indeed, although we do not know for sure, the number of manuscripts must have seriously increased by this point, for the ASA doubled in size between 1945 and 1950 and again between 1950 and 1956.[15]

15. Helen Hughes's relationship with the men of the faculty was of course complicated and difficult, as she later noted in print (1972). In her correspondence at the time, she often seems torn between exasperation and respect. Sometimes she was lighthearted, mocking her own prodding of the "big men" ("I am back from Vancouver full of zest and energy to resume my old nagging" [HMH to Wirth, 12 May 1947, LW 17:1]). At other times she seems cold, perhaps reflecting the complex relationships between the Hugheses, the Wirths, and the Blumers noted above. What is central to my story here, however, is that it was Helen Hughes who by her existence and actions as a permanent party managing editor established the normative routines and the overt enforcement of guilt (on faculty delinquents) that had been impossible for her graduate student predecessors.

To some extent these changes applied to the book review section as well. From 1930 onward the book reviews had been in the hands of Louis Wirth. Wirth ran the section very informally, sending books to people who asked to review them, particularly if he knew them, like Helen and Everett Hughes during their Montreal years. At the same time, the section caused occasional trouble. Blumer got into much difficulty as a result of a hostile review of a book by Howard Odum, who complained bitterly in private to Ogburn and Burgess (Odum to Burgess, 21 May 1930, WFO 29:10), and indeed the *AJS* may have first alienated Newell Sims, who played a large role in the *ASR* controversy, by blacklisting him as a reviewer after an extremely hostile review of a Chicago stalwart in the mid-1920s.

Helen Hughes tried to regularize book reviews as well. She organized the faculty into regular sessions to assign books to reviewers (Helen Hughes to various faculty, 18 November 1949, LW 17:1). She seems also to have generated some kind of database and tracking system. Nonetheless, book reviews have never achieved the same regularization as manuscripts. Not all of Helen Hughes's prodding could keep reviewers on time, deal with the authors whose books got ignored (they wrote to the faculty, who then contacted her), or find the books that got lost in the mill. Book reviews remained in chaos at the *AJS* well into the contemporary period.

Solicitation and Contributors

Throughout the first period the *AJS* contained much solicited material, as I noted above. But there are infinite shades of "solicitation." Small might hear about a piece from a colleague to whom it had in fact been sent either blind or based on personal connection. By the end of Small's term, this kind of referral was routinely coming through younger faculty (see the Park-McKenzie correspondence discussed by Gaziano 1996), producing networks of manuscript recruitment that may have persuaded the faculty they could do without an editor-in-chief immediately after Small's departure. (This fits the notion that an editor's main task is to recruit manuscripts, which had been the Small model.)

In the early years of the middle period, and indeed continuing through it, many papers came to the *AJS* via "faculty referral." Usually these were papers sent to a faculty member interested in the paper's substance with the hope—sometimes expressed, sometimes implicit—that the paper would be sent on to the *Journal* if deemed worthy. This avenue, which seems to us like an oblique approach to submission, might have been followed because the author did not know who the editor was or because he thought it might be helpful to have a "friend in court." But most often authors regarded this means of submission as a kind of prescreening, since they assumed (rightly) that the interested faculty member would be asked for his opinion. (The faculty member involved often sent his opinion along with the referral; Ogburn to Faris, 30 November 29, WFO 29:4.) One should also recall, however, that making multiple copies of papers was by no means easy until the 1960s, and that many authors may have felt they had only one copy to send to colleague, department, and journal. But it is also clear that the masthead in the first decade after Small—which listed no editor-in-chief—enforced this kind of submission, although such referrals did not stop after 1934 when a single, named editor reappeared on the masthead.[16]

Sometimes such faculty referral was clearly a matter of patronage. Thus Edward Sapir, a former department member, wrote to Wirth (in one of his editorial moments; 12 June 1935, LW 17:1):

> I wonder if you mind my coming to you with another manuscript for the American Journal of Sociology, and I hope this time you will be more interested. The enclosed paper on "Sanctification in Negro Religion" is by a Negro graduate student at Yale University who is specializing, I believe, in education and who is at present at Tuskegee Institute, Alabama. . . . I hope you and others in the department will be attracted to it.

From 1949 we have a similar referral from Wirth, although now, with the office changes, the route is no longer directly through the editor, which profoundly changes the nature of the contact.

> I think this article which represents a summary of Miss Cohen's thesis would be quite suitable for the Journal. I commend it to the editors for their consideration. If you want an outside reader, I suggest Mr. Coleman Woodbury of the Urban Redevelopment Project at 1313 E. 60th St (Wirth to Helen Hughes, 16 June 1949, LW 17:1).

But while the letter *sounds* quite distant and formal, in fact "the editors" means Wirth's old friends Blumer, Hauser, and Hughes, and the outside reader is in sight across the Midway. This tells us not that Wirth was a nepotist—an anachronistic judgment—but rather what "outside" meant in the 1940s: someone not in the immediate circle of those who ran the *AJS*. At the same time, some faculty did conceptualize conflict of interest in something

---

16. Examples of this "faculty referral" are legion and involve most of the faculty. An interesting case is Ogburn to Faris, 23 April 1929, WFO 29:4, conveying a paper by Dr. Herz of Vienna (see also Herz's letter to Ogburn, 7 January 1929, WFO 29:4). For another case, see Burgess to Blumer, 26 August 1948, EWB 1:6.

like modern terms by the late 1940s. Burgess, in a similar referral through Helen Hughes, writes, "Some other reader should read it since I am rather prejudiced in its favor, however" (11 May 1948, EWB 9:3).

Papers referred by faculty did not necessarily receive preferential handling. Thus Blumer as editor wrote to Wirth on 10 February 1943, returning a paper Wirth had referred: "This is an impossible paper. It is full of naivete, dogmatic assertion, and ethnocentric perception. He knows not morale or motivation. Will you please return it to Masserman [possibly Jules Masserman, a psychiatrist]—give him any excuse you wish." This short memo also shows that faculty-referred papers did not necessarily merit a formal reply from the *AJS* editor. One of the difficulties with estimating the *Journal*'s manuscript flow in the middle period is that many or perhaps even most manuscripts about which the editor made a decision actually arrived at the *Journal* in this way rather than through the *AJS* mailbox. It is quite likely that the student assistants, and later Helen Hughes, did not even know about many such manuscripts, which could be received, referred, read, and rejected without any official appearance in the *AJS* office or files. Ironically, the *AJS* official notice about manuscripts, published in the front of each issue, specifically told authors to send their manuscripts to the editor, "not to an individual." The effect of this prohibition was apparently nil; twenty years later, in Peter Blau's time as editor, the "not" was italicized! Maybe that did some good. But up until 1960, many or most papers arrived through the faculty.[17]

Referral became particularly important for the *AJS* after the founding of the *ASR*, with its proprietary claim over all papers at the annual meeting. It is probable that the *AJS* lacked sufficient high-quality manuscripts in the late 1930s, driving it to undertake its long series of special issues.[18]

Changes in patterns of manuscript origins had definite effects on the overall pool of contributors. I define as "major contributors" any authors who published in the *AJS* four or more times in any decade. By this definition, there were fourteen, sixteen, and nine major contributors, respec-

17. Only rarely, outside special issues, did the editors deliberately solicit an article by a particular author and give him carte blanche. One such instance was the attempt, managed by Wirth and his friend Louis Gottschalk in 1938, to get an article from Leon Trotsky. The latter agreed, in principle, to write a reply to Gottschalk's article on him (in the *AJS* issue for November 1938), but he did not do so before his murder two years later (Gottschalk to Wirth, 25 July 1938, LW 1:8).

18. At the same time, however, the special issues were part of Burgess's planned strategy to make the *AJS* the intellectually dominant journal in sociology. The controversy, breadth of interest, and intellectual depth Burgess had urged became the hallmarks of the special issues, which I discuss below.

tively, in Small's three decades. Of those who were major contributors during the Small tenure ($N = 32$, since some people repeated), few remained so in 1925–35; only Ernest Groves, F. Stuart Chapin, and ironically, the rebel leader Luther L. Bernard.[19] Even the Chicago faculty who were major contributors were new to the role; Park, Ogburn, Wirth, Burgess, and Faris published a total of twenty-nine articles in 1925–35. None was a major contributor before that point.

The journal's fourth decade was thus a period of great contributor democratization; thirty-six people had four or more articles in the *AJS* in this ten-year period. Beyond the eight just listed, they also included prominent national figures like Pitirim Sorokin, local graduate students like Ruth Cavan, anthropologists like Melville Herskovits, nonsociology Chicago faculty like Charles Hubbard Judd, and leaders of the ASA rebellion like Read Bain and Howard P. Becker. Only eight of the thirty-six were Chicago graduates or faculty. These major contributors wrote a total of 177 articles, about 40 percent of the total number in the journal in this decade. Thus democratization in the central group came somewhat at the cost of the profession's periphery.[20]

This democratization at the top declined sharply after 1936. There were only twelve major contributors in the next decade, who contributed about 20 percent of the total number of articles. The decade 1935–45 was dominated by locals. Of the twelve major contributors, five were Chicago sociology faculty, one was Chicago psychology faculty (Edward L. Thorndike), and four were graduates or research staff of the department (H. Warren Dunham, Ethel Shanas, Abe Jaffe, Edward Reuter). In the subsequent decade (1945–55) the contribution by such major contributors grew even less. Nine people contributed about 10 percent of the total number of articles. Of the nine, three were faculty (Ogburn, Bogue, and Burgess) and four were recent graduates (Ralph Turner, Arnold Rose, Ronald Freedman, and Reinhard Bendix), In the *AJS*'s seventh decade, this measure inched up again. Sixteen people provided about 15 percent of the articles. Faculty in this group included James Davis, Otis Dudley Duncan, Peter Rossi, Anselm Strauss, and Leo Goodman, and graduates and other locals included Howard S. Becker, Stanley Lieberson, Murray Wax, and Sanford Dornbusch.

19. For all his bellyaching, Bernard in fact published more pages in the *AJS* over the past century than anyone else except Albion Small, Small's friend E. A. Ross, and Small's colleague C. R. Henderson. It was not lack of airtime that drove him to rebellion.

20. A substantial amount of this "democratization at the center," however, reflects repeated authorships in the annual "Social Change" volume.

Thus, the decade during which the *ASR* rebellion grew was in fact the decade in which non-Chicagoans played the *largest* role among the *AJS*'s core contributing writers. After that time, although concentration in general fell, the Chicago group commanded a far larger portion of the central group's input.

The gradual fall in overall concentration of contributors bespeaks a trend of democratization consistent with the increasing size of the discipline as a whole. The age data on contributors in table 9 also tell a simple and consistent story of normalization and professionalization. The age figures start low; the dropping of the old Small core made the *AJS* look young again. Then they rose as a new elite stayed in control, but they fell after the war, when sociology began rapidly expanding. The fall in the three decades to 1965 is striking. The B.A. and Ph.D. figures show the emerging stability of the sociological career. B.A. age of contributors fell steadily as uninterrupted schooling became the norm. Ph.D. age has fallen five years over the history of the *Journal,* again reflecting a stronger pattern of uninterrupted schooling and professionalization.

A similar regularizing and institutionalizing process is evident in the disciplinary focus of the *AJS,* shown in table 10. During the middle period the *AJS,* having begun to academicize by 1925, became a specifically sociological journal. From its fourth to its seventh decade the *Journal* moved steadily toward concentration on sociology, the percentage rising slightly to 56 percent during the fourth and fifth decades, then jumping to 75 percent in the sixth and seventh. Other disciplines were kept visible by the special issues in the fourth and fifth decades, but the inward turn of these issues after 1950—to topics like family and industrial sociology—began to reduce the nonsociology contribution. By 1965 the *AJS* was finally a pure sociology journal.

Table 9. Average Ages of Contributors to the *AJS,* 1925–1965

	Decade			
	4	5	6	7
Midpoint	1930	1940	1950	1960
Authors	282	328	383	451
(total *N*)				
Age	41	45	41	39
(*N*)	(248)	(290)	(328)	(388)
B.A. age	25	24	24	23
(*N*)	(206)	(220)	(272)	(348)
Ph.D. age	34	33	33	31
(*N*)	(229)	(276)	(337)	(408)

Note: N refers to the number of individuals on whom the information listed is available.

Table 10.   Ph.D. Fields of Contributors to the *AJS*, 1925–1965

	Decade			
	4	5	6	7
Midpoint	1930	1940	1950	1960
Authors (*N*)	282	328	383	451
% with Ph.D.	82	84	88	91
% Ph.D. field known	67	67	82	86
(of all authors)				
Sociology	56	57	73	76
Philosophy	2	3		1
Economics	8	5	6	3
History	3	2	1	1
Psychology/Social Psychology	6	6	8	9
Education	3	3	2	1
Anthropology	4	7	4	3
Political science	6	3	1	4

Note: Figures for individual fields are percentages of those whose Ph.D. field is known. Percentage with Ph.D. is a minimum figure; undoubtedly there are many Ph.D's unknown to us. The Ph.D. can come after publication, and thus successful graduate students are included.

This move was temporarily accompanied by a renewed focus on Chicago itself. The percentage of all sociology Ph.D. authors who were *Chicago* sociology Ph.D.'s stayed at Albion Small's level of 36 percent in the decade 1925–35. But after that, with the loss of the possibility of publishing polished versions of annual meeting papers (which now went by rule to the *ASR*), and with the profession shrinking, editors turned inward, and the rate rose to 42 percent in 1935–45. After the war, the rate returned to 37 percent between 1945 and 1955. After 1955 there was clearly a new regime, as we shall see below: the rate fell to 22 percent in 1955–65.[21]

However, the overall pattern for sources of Ph.D.'s, shown in table 11, is somewhat more complex.[22] By comparison with earlier epochs, the relative concentration of Chicago Ph.D.'s (of all fields) in the *AJS* became greater during the middle period until 1955. Chicago Ph.D.'s stayed at 30 percent of

21. My figures are higher than Evans's (1986–87) because I have separated authors by institution and field. He finds lower Chicago figures because of the many non-Chicago nonsociologists in the special issues. As I have noted, the special issues to a certain extent skew all general statistics on the *AJS*. It is in part for that reason that I do not really consider content here. For a general study of the content of the *ASR* and *AJS* based on a fairly careful aggregate level analysis, see Kinloch 1988.

22. For comparison, in the decade 1929–38, Chicago produced 12 percent of sociology Ph.D.'s and Columbia 10 percent. In 1948–55, Chicago produced 15 percent, Harvard 12 percent, and Columbia 6 percent. In 1953–62, Chicago and Harvard each produced 9 percent, Columbia 7 percent. These figures are from various editions of the American Council on Education's *American Universities and Colleges* (Brumbaugh 1948; Irwin 1956; Cartter 1964).

Table 11. Higher Degrees of Contributors to the *AJS*, 1925–1965

	Decade			
	4	5	6	7
Midpoint	1930	1940	1950	1960
Authors (*N*)	282	328	383	451
% Ph.D, location known (of all authors)	81	84	88	91
Overseas	5	12	8	7
Chicago	30	30	32	20
Columbia	20	13	12	10
Harvard	5	6	7	9
Johns Hopkins	2	1	1	1
Wisconsin	3	4	5	4
Yale	4	3	3	3
Princeton	1		1	2
Pennsylvania	3	4	4	2
Minnesota	5	4	3	3
Michigan	1	2	3	5
North Carolina	1		1	3
Washington	1	1	2	3
Berkeley	2	4	2	3
Cornell	2	2	1	3
Stanford	2	1	1	
NYU	1			2

Note: Figures for individual locations are percentages *of those whose Ph.D. location is known.*

authors even in the face of decline in the Chicago's share of new Ph.D.'s. (Of course, the *full* pool of potential authors changed against Chicago much more slowly because of Chicago's *prior* Ph.D. output.) Columbia's place was increasingly supplied by a second generation set of state universities—Wisconsin being joined by Minnesota, Michigan, Washington, and Berkeley. The elite private schools continued to provide a small, fairly steady contribution, mostly coming from Yale and Pennsylvania. Overseas scholars become important after 1935, as one would expect given the prewar migration, and outnumber all but two or three other sources until 1965.

In general this pattern reflects well the *Journal*'s editorial practices and manuscript supply. The Chicago portion did not really fall until 1955–65, after the discipline had quadrupled in size from its wartime level. By then Chicago has producing fewer than 10 percent of new Ph.D.'s, and the *AJS* itself had acquired an editor who, for the first time since Albion Small, was not himself a Chicago Ph.D.

As I have noted, the *AJS* was basically a personally run, face-to-face affair until the mid-1950s. There was little change in the structure of article referral networks, and there was still a substantial amount of direct solicitation. Thus, while the *Journal* became considerably more open in the years 1925–55, it opened mainly to an elite directly and personally connected with the editors. As the figures show, *AJS* authors tilt a bit toward the state universities, again fitting Lengermann's (1979) notion that the *ASR*, by contrast, became something of a Harvard-Columbia preserve; the data show Harvard and Columbia slipping precisely when the *ASR* was founded, losing ground to the state university departments.

Special Issues, Monographs, and Promotion

The intellectual diversification of the *AJS* under Burgess and Blumer was not the *Journal*'s only approach to its newly competitive context. As in earlier years, there were strong promotional efforts. The first of these were the special issues, which served a combined need to fill space, reach new constituencies, and expand the range of sociology.

From 1929 to 1952, there were a total of twenty-one special or symposium issues, typically one a year. There were two in 1942, when the editors were undoubtedly desperate for manuscripts, with half the ASA off to war.

The first seven special issues, starting with May 1929 and ending with May 1935, were on "Recent Social Changes." Introduced by Ogburn, these were collections of review articles in the modern sense, although Ogburn himself clearly saw them as research articles. They were in-depth reports of the impact of social trends in a wide variety of areas: family, labor, production, foreign policy, earnings, employment, community organization, race relations, education, government, status of children, status of women, and numerous other topics.

The "Social Changes" issues were obviously timely and useful. They were also relatively remunerative, for the Press bound them as freestanding books and sold them to marketers, planners, and others interested in social trends. In 1936, however, faced with the sudden problem of creating a clear differentiation from the *ASR*, Burgess chose a radical approach. The next special issue—"Social Psychiatry," May 1937—reached well outside professionalized sociology to the vibrant area of psychiatry and psychoanalysis, then approaching the midpoint of a forty-year dominance of American cultural criticism not unlike the present tide of postmodernism. Burgess tapped the cream of American psychiatry: Alfred Adler, Franz Alexander, Trigant Burrow, Paul Schilder, and Harry Stack Sullivan. To this group were added Elton Mayo and Edward Sapir. Herbert Blumer completed the issue with an extended response to the papers in it.

The "Social Psychiatry" issue was timely, exciting, and challenging. It apparently took Burgess and the department a year to realize they were onto a good thing. But from volume 44 there started a series of remarkable issues, one per year, on current, sometimes controversial topics, featuring the best of social science in America and abroad. In 1939, authors on "Individual and Group" included Florian Znaniecki, Bronislaw Malinowski, Maurice Halbwachs, Kurt Lewin, Floyd Allport, Harry Stack Sullivan, and Louis Wirth. Only three issues later, an issue on the death of Freud featured papers from prominent psychiatrists and psychoanalysts (Karen Horney, Fritz Wittels, S. E. Jelliffe, A. A. Brill, Gregory Zilboorg), sexologist Havelock Ellis, delinquency specialist William Healy, political scientist Harold Lasswell, anthropologist A. I. Kroeber, and literary critic Kenneth Burke. An issue on war in 1941 assembled Lasswell, Alexander, Malinowski, human biologist Raymond Pearl, jurist Hans Kelsen, historian F. J. Teggart, and sociologist Hans Speier. This time it was emeritus professor Robert Park who provided the Chicago response. Authors on "Prospects for the Postwar Period" in 1945 started with former Czech president Eduard Beneš and included Hans Kelsen, Charles E. Merriam, Frank Knight, Carl Friedrich, Pitirim Sorokin, W. E. B. Dubois, Franz Alexander, and Lawrence Frank.[23]

Some special issues avoided the "great man" strategy. An issue on "War in American Life" featured Chicago and its graduates: Hauser wrote on war and vital statistics, Burgess on war and the family, Hughes on war and American institutions. Around these faculty were old students: E. Franklin Frazier on the war and minority groups, Walter Reckless on war and crime, and H. Warren Dunham on war and personality disorganization. An issue on "Morale" in 1941 contained an astonishing diversity of authors—social workers, deans of law schools, professors of philosophy, clergymen, newspaper reporters, generals, psychiatrists, and officials at the Federal Communications Commission. The return of the servicemen in 1946 led to an issue on "Human Behavior in Military Society," featuring short articles

23. Behind the parade of great social scientists through the pages of these special issues lay systematic personal connections. Sullivan, the *AJS* broker to psychiatry and psychoanalysis, knew W. I. Thomas through a collaboration in the late 1920s, and Thomas had never dropped his personal connections to Chicago. More generally, both were connected with the Social Science Research Council (in New York—not the one in the Social Science Division at Chicago), where Louis Wirth was also a central figure. In other cases the connection is even more immediate. Franz Alexander ended up at the Chicago Psychoanalytic Institute; Lasswell was a former Chicago faculty member, as was Sapir; even Burke had been at the university for a time. Note that authors were clearly encouraged to make major statements; Lasswell's paper in volume 44, number 6, "The Garrison State," became one of the foundational texts of the totalitarianism literature.

and aiming not to report developed research but to feature many voices "from the front." Five papers were personal memoirs, two of them anonymous. A rehabilitation counselor at Fort Knox wrote on group psychotherapy and soldiers. An occupational counselor at the discharge center at Fort Leavenworth wrote on discharged servicemen. A few of these articles were by sociologists, but even these were largely based on reflections about military experiences.

After the war the special issues continued, although becoming more narrowly disciplinary. But there were issues on the family, on fertility and marriage, on industrial sociology, on the sociology of work, on public opinion and propaganda.

The beneficial effect of these issues on *AJS* finances is clear; a new column for back issue and single issue sales was added to the budgets of the *AJS* by the early 1930s. Such sales produced from 7 to 10 percent of the journal's receipts. The financial report on the May 1948 special issue on "The Family" showed 886 single copies sold and a total of 293 new subscriptions brought in, for total receipts of $2,265 ("G.W." to EWB, 12 July 1948, EWB 1:6).

Moreover, to the extent that this series was designed for product differentiation from the *ASR,* it was an enormous success. The *ASR* ran only two special issues in this entire period—both in the 1950s. The *ASR* did make "substantive issues" by assembling research papers on common themes in a single issue, something the *AJS* did as well. But there was nothing in the *ASR* like the *AJS* special issues. Profits and product differentiation, however, were undoubtedly not the only reasons for special issues. As any editor knows, the most common reason for special issues is dearth of routine material. The 1930s had seen ten major or minor sociology journals founded, even while the ASA dwindled steadily from 1932 to 1946. It is probable that the *AJS* special issue series stems as much from manuscript desperation as from intellectual ambition.

Another attempt to deal with new competition was a renewed effort to locate the *AJS* within a comprehensive program of sociology publishing. This program had a prehistory. During the Park years, the Press had issued the University of Chicago Sociological Series, in which many of the classic works of the Chicago school appeared. This series slowed in the mid-1930s after Park's departure. Late in the decade, Burgess persuaded the Press to set up a "sociology book of the month" promotion, the Sociology Book Plan. On this plan, one to four volumes would be selected from existing Press series and sold to *AJS* subscribers at 50 percent of list price. The books were automatically sent, and the receiver returned them if they were not wanted.

The works selected were largely the empirical products of the Chicago school; for example, the 1938–39 selections were Clifford Shaw's *Brothers in Crime,* Faris and Dunham's *Mental Disorders in Urban Areas,* and Frazier's *The Negro Family in the United States.* The book plan did not fare well, lasting about seven years before failing sometime in the mid-1940s. Sales never reached the five hundred mark required to break even ("B. E. R." to Burgess, 26 March 1940, EWB 1:5).

But the failure of the book club plan simply led to another expedient, the publication of "*AJS* monographs" as journal supplements. A number of these were printed in the late 1940s, with mixed results. By 1950 the ever hopeful Burgess was pressing for a revival of the book club (Burgess to Couch, 10 January 1950, LW 17:1). Far from being interested, the Press tried to cancel all monographs, book clubs, and similar strategies (Helen Hughes to Wirth, 3 April 1950, LW 17:1). The *AJS* was on a very firm financial footing, and such expedients were not felt to be necessary.

Like most Press programs, the comprehensive sociology publishing program had various special constituencies. One was the Society for Social Research, the association of graduate students, alumni, faculty, and friends of the department that Park had founded in 1921. During the 1930s and 1940s, the SSR served as a discount buying service for department graduates, who routinely sent their book and journal orders not to the Press, but to the current SSR secretary (SSR Minutes, 6 May 1926, SSR 1:2; on sales, see these files more generally).

Another constituency was graduate students, both at Chicago and elsewhere. During the *ASR* crisis, the *AJS* editors had gotten the Press to keep student subscriptions at 50 percent of full price. Not only were all new sociology students at Chicago circularized (memo, n.d., EWB 1:5), faculty also pushed for student subscriptions elsewhere, urging friends and acquaintances to have their students subscribe.[24]

Faculty and editors played a personal role in subscriptions. Louis Wirth's letter to those who let their subscriptions lapse was a pastiche of persuasion and flattery, "looking forward to your continued presence in our common enterprise" (28 May 1940, EWB 1:5). Blumer wrote the equivalent letter to new subscribers, who got a discounted rate and a free copy of the latest special issue (21 May 1940, EWB 1:5). The *AJS* also offered a continuation rate equivalent to the ASA discount rate.

24. Ernest B. Harper, head of the sociology department at Michigan State, wrote Wirth (1 August 1941, LW 17:1): "You and Burgess have *both* written me about student subscriptions. Is this 'high pressure publicity' rather than duplication? . . . In any case, I have as usual canvassed our advanced students and will have at least one subscription I am sure."

Faculty were able to sell the *AJS* to such diverse groups in part because it remained so multifarious. In this middle period it contained "News and Notes," abstracts (*AJS* had taken up abstracting after the failure of F. Stuart Chapin's *Social Science Abstracts* in the early 1930s), letters (a section of controversy), and book reviews as well as articles and special issues. All these special services attracted their own constituencies.

Thus, very much in contrast to the modern situation, the editorial staff and more broadly the faculty of the department were actively involved in sales and promotion efforts for the *AJS*. This too fits the model of what we might call a "primary group enterprise."

Conclusion

In the middle period, the *AJS* was carried on by a tightly bound department. Department and editorial staff saw minimal changes. Although the arrival of Ogburn created a slight quantitative/qualitative split, the department viewed the *Journal* with pride and a feeling of true collective ownership. Faculty sacrificed substantial time and effort to review manuscripts, to organize the occasional special issue, even to sell the *AJS*. The smaller editorial group—a group of old friends—ran everything from subscriptions to book reviews to publicity campaigns. The journal was run informally because of long-standing personal relationships that generated, if not absolute trust in each other's judgment, then at least very clear knowledge of where that judgment could not be trusted.

When confronted with disciplinary expansion and differentiation, this tight group rallied to the local cause by recasting the *AJS*'s referral networks, entering seriously into marketing, and inventing the general-interest special issue. By all indications, the result was both a financial and an intellectual success. At the same time, the complications of disciplinary life gradually removed editors from day-to-day involvement and made an office staff inevitable. But the permanent staff person—Helen Hughes—was in fact another member of the group of old friends, so despite her gestures of rationalization, the journal continued to be very much a primary group enterprise.

All this would change when the department imploded in the early 1950s. Helen Hughes had laid foundations on which rationalization could build when the department became as eclectic as the national discipline. But for the moment—and it was a long one—the middle period *AJS* was a surprisingly unified and occasionally quixotic intellectual endeavor. It was very much a department venture rather than a disciplinary one, the more so after the bitterness of 1936. It was personal, clubby, and quite successful.

The Chicago school had made Albion Small's grab bag into a collective voice for its view of the world.

Through a larger lens, we can see these events at the *AJS* as part of the structuring of a broader disciplinary field. This chapter adds firm evidence to the sense emerging from the previous one that the *AJS* was in many ways the maker of a discipline. The University of Chicago Press turns out to have been the ASA's single major financial supporter over its first thirty years, and indeed I have made a case that the discipline's first reality was as a marketing structure for the Press. The division of the *AJS* and the *ASR* was turned by Burgess into an explicit differentiation between a broadly representative journal and an intellectually elite one. Burgess (and Blumer) emphasized this position with their long string of special issues. Note that there was nothing inevitable about this differentiation. It was the Chicagoans' policies that produced it. Traditions do not always simply drift into existence. They can also be actively created, as was true of the *AJS*.

5   The *AJS* in Transition to Professionalism

The *American Journal of Sociology* of the late Hughes years remained a premodern journal. Many of the qualities we take as definitive were absent from it: double-blind reviewing, formalized submission procedures, editorial accountability. But the journal was nonetheless a very consequential and established social actor. If it was not the mouthpiece of the second Chicago school—*Social Problems* took that role—it was clearly differentiated from the *American Sociological Review*. But the transitions discussed in chapter 2 could not but have drastic effects on the *AJS*. Through them, and through later changes in the department, the *AJS* left its primary group heritage behind and emerged as a fully bureaucratic, nationalized institution.

Department and Discipline since 1955

The dissolution of the primary group journal came in the first instance because of the dissolution of the primary group itself. The 1950s brought a long twilight to the Chicago school. By 1953 Blumer had gone to Berkeley, Wirth was dead, Burgess and Ogburn had retired, and the department was in receivership. As we have seen, the dean and the chancellor pursued—to no avail—star hires like Samuel Stouffer, William Sewell, Robert Merton, and Paul Lazarsfeld. At the junior level there was steady but eclectic hiring, while a lateral move brought David Riesman in from the College faculty.

But the new mix did not gel. The battle-torn department of the late 1950s had many new faces, most of them from Columbia: Peter Blau, Peter Rossi, Elihu Katz, and (briefly) James Coleman. It was a heavily quantitative department, for in addition to the Columbia quantitative hires (e.g., Coleman, Rossi, Katz) there also arrived in the 1950s James Davis, Leo Goodman, and Donald Bogue. Edward Shils reentered the department in 1957, to be sure, but only part time.

The new emphasis proved problematic. From the mid-1950s there was constant faculty turnover. In the 1960s there were crises: a tangled conflict over NORC that led to Rossi's departure, Blau's move home to Columbia, a stormy chairmanship contest that left the department under caretaker management, and finally the Marlene Dixon tenure case (and consequent student strike) in 1969. It was only in the early 1970s that Morris Janowitz assembled a team of faculty that would lead the department through another long period of stability. Coleman, William Wilson, Edward Laumann, and Gerald Suttles were added to Bogue, Goodman, and Hauser to make, with Janowitz and Shils, a group that would last largely unchanged to 1990.

The broader discipline also went through major changes in this period. The huge growth rates of the 1950s slowed in the 1960s, but the rapid expansion of higher education kept demand for new faculty high. By 1972 the ASA had reached its peak membership of nearly 15,000, ten times the 1,500 member ASA that had supported the middle period *AJS*. A huge cohort of new faculty began inundating the journals with papers.

At the same time, sociology's long-standing place at the left edge of the social sciences drew to it a strongly activist cohort of students. These students pushed the discipline toward political and historical sociology, toward Marxism and other nonmainstream theoretical traditions. Functionalism vanished. Sociology also provided an early home for students of gender, partly because the new empiricist paradigm made it painless to add gender as an extra variable in one's models. But when the job market plummeted at the end of the 1970s, sociology very quickly feminized, although without the intellectual transformation that feminization occasioned in other fields (Roos and Jones 1993; Stacey and Thorne 1985).

The late 1970s also brought financial hard times as government funding for research fell rapidly. The market for Ph.D.'s turned sour and never recovered. At the same time, the ASA fragmented into isolated special interest groups. Many subfields built their major intellectual venues elsewhere (e.g., the sociologies of crime, religion, science, even of organizations, as well as fields like network analysis and parts of historical sociology). Populist politics removed the discipline's intellectual elite from any significant role in the ASA.

Indeed, by the 1990s the discipline's position in the university division of labor had begun to seem shaky. In a few highly visible cases, there had been attempts to remove sociology departments from universities. Attempts to combine or recombine sociology with anthropology departments were common, particularly in four-year schools. At the same time, heirs of the creative and offbeat graduate students who had flocked to the discipline in the 1960s and 1970s were turning to anthropology, history, and cultural studies. Worse yet, quantitative sociologists were in many areas being beaten at their own game by the swelling tide of econometricians.

Two particular aspects of these national trends affected the *AJS* directly. First, those interested in building factions within the discipline nearly always tried to found their own journals. Some of these new journals were not serious competitors but rather helped the *AJS* by providing new outlets for middle-quality papers in areas where the *AJS* and *ASR* still received the top-quality manuscripts. But there were some new competitors—*Rationality and Society, Theory and Society,* and *Social Studies of Science* are examples—that removed the best papers in their areas from the *AJS* and other general-purpose journals. Second, the newly huge demography of the profession was directly responsible for a flood of new manuscripts and indirectly responsible for the transformation of the journals into the central arbiters of tenure decisions.

The national trends notwithstanding, in the long period from 1965 to 1995 the *AJS*'s history tracks the "crisis followed by stability" experience of the department rather than the boom-and-bust history of the discipline. The disciplinary boom years brought crisis for the *AJS,* which went through a long transition from the late 1950s until the editorship of Charles Bidwell in the 1970s settled it into its present stable pattern. I therefore consider the modern *AJS* in two periods, the first covering the long transition and the second the more or less stable journal under the current regime.

The Onset of Transition: Rossi and Hughes

The transition began with an intense conflict between Everett Hughes and Peter Rossi during the latter's year as interim *AJS* editor. I examine this conflict in detail because it raised many of the issues that have preoccupied *AJS* editors throughout the current period.

In 1957–58, after editing the journal for five years and chairing the department for three, Everett Hughes spent a year in Germany. Strauss, Blau, and Rossi had all acted as associate editors, but Hughes recommended Rossi as his stand-in. Before leaving, Hughes sent the department a general memo outlining the relation of the *AJS* to the department (ECH, 20 September 1957) and telegraphing his intention to step down in two years' time. He also proposed a thorough discussion of the *AJS* on his return in fall of 1958, for he was very worried that the increases in both the diversity and the size of sociology would make it "very easy to fall into a policy of accepting only articles which have a certain form or which use certain techniques rather than others."

Rossi, for his part, took command unequivocally. By January 1958 he had designed a reader questionnaire to help improve the *AJS*. Commenting on it, Hughes politely but firmly pointed out that Rossi was assuming a purely professional audience for the *AJS,* and that with the rapid—and in Hughes's view pernicious—professionalization of sociology, the *AJS* had a duty to speak more broadly and to recruit articles more broadly. He wanted to know more than "how they rate us with other rather narrowly professional journals" (ECH to PHR, 7 January 1958).[1] In forwarding this note for her husband, Helen Hughes made her own comment:

> I was under the impression that the list [of typical articles, supplied by Rossi with the questionnaire] is a bit overweighted on the side of fact-finding contributions and a little underweighted on the theoretical articles and articles which would interest our marginal readers.

Not waiting for either these reactions or responses to the questionnaire, on 23 January 1958 Rossi sent the department a memorandum proposing a total overhaul of the *AJS.* He began with a general review. The editorial policy was completely passive, a mere waiting for submissions. There were an ever increasing number of submissions, he noted, but "the proportion of acceptable articles to total flow is so low that we are always in a position of worrying whether we will have enough articles to fill the issue currently being worked on." (The journal was receiving about two hundred submissions a year and accepting about 20 percent of them.) Rossi liked special issues, with their proactive editorial policy and strong reception, but he felt the book review section was hopelessly overloaded by its attempt to review everything. Subscriptions stood at 4,439 (about the same as in 1951; see table 7), but Rossi was mystified about the identities of many of the *AJS*'s readers, since by his calculations they were not members of the ASA, which he assumed contained "most sociologists of any worth."

Rossi proposed many new policies. He would continue special issues and would focus them not on "big shots" but on "medium shots in the process of expanding." He proposed active solicitation: "We should know who is doing the exciting work and should ask such persons to send stuff to the Journal." He proposed commissioned review articles on what would later be the *Annual Review* model. He proposed administrative reforms: faster decisions, flexible length, less "professionalism" in editing. He proposed longer book reviews, by "topnotch experts," of fewer works and also review arti-

---

1. Hughes had in fact refused to run for ASA president that year on the grounds that he found the drive for professionalism by ASA staff and officers deeply repugnant. Later letters make it clear that his objections began with the separation of sociology from anthropology and history. Letter citations without dates refer to materials in the *AJS* archives. As noted in "Sources and Acknowledgments," these have no location because the locations will be changed when (if) the files are opened.

cles covering a number of books and short book notes. He proposed dumping both the "News and Notes" section and the dissertations list.

But Rossi's big plans were for the editorial structure. He proposed restricting the editor to a three- or four-year term and instructing him to "carry out in detail the broad editorial policies laid down by the department." There should also be two associate editors appointed by the department, who with the editor would constitute an editorial committee that would have authority over what books got reviewed, who was asked to write commissioned pieces, and so on. (The editor, however, would have final authority in case of dispute.) Rossi proposed to rotate advisory editors faster and to make them read two articles a month. He also proposed using graduate students as "journal fellows." Finally, he urged the adoption of double-blind reviewing in imitation of the *ASR*.

This document was an overt attack on nearly everything Hughes and the older *AJS* had represented. Hughes took it mostly in good part, with the exception of Rossi's comment about "less 'professionalism' in editing." Rossi had said the *AJS* should "at least give the author the impression that his work is being given an editorial treatment by someone competent to judge the sociological content of his article." It was painfully obvious what Rossi meant. Hughes waited till he was in Chicago on a visit and then angrily demanded whether Rossi had meant to imply that Helen Hughes actually made publication decisions. Rossi said yes, and Hughes denied it furiously in a memo to the department (ECH to department, 6 March 1958). But even worse, since Helen Hughes's degree was from the same time and place as her husband's, attacking her sociological expertise was equally an insult to Hughes's own.

In his long memorandum, Hughes pointed out that a number of Rossi's facts were wrong. The article supply was not so low that standards were violated. Informal solicitation had long been practiced. The *AJS* had for at least a decade reviewed only a small fraction of the books it received. There was no length restriction. Graduate student fellows had long existed but had lately been forbidden by income tax provisions.

On several policy matters, moreover, Hughes took strong issue. He defended Helen Hughes's editorial activities: "Some people write enthusiastically when their papers have been turned into English; others say they will not change a word." He opposed Rossi's desire to dump the news and dissertation sections, desiring to keep "a certain human flavor about the journal." And he opposed all proposals to limit the editor's discretion. One could not ask for a clearer contrast between the new professionalized model for a journal and the older less formal one.

The correspondence between Hughes and Rossi continued through the year. Hughes wrote as cordially as ever ("Dear Pete") despite his anger. (Rossi and Hughes were planning a book together!) In time Rossi himself became less contentious, although he maintained:

> Even before I came here to Chicago, the reputation of the *Journal* as an unpleasant organization to deal with was quite familiar to me. I know, personally, of many authors, including myself, who had vowed not to submit any further material to the *Journal*. (PHR to ECH, 12 May 1958)

Hughes of course dissented. But in reply he pointed to a problem that was to assume major proportions over the next twenty years:

> There is one rule which I think causes a good deal of misunderstanding, yet must generally be held to—the rule not to tell the author why you don't accept his article and not to enter into any argument on the point. People won't love you for not telling them, but they will go wild with anger if you do tell them.

Hughes saw the editor as a sole authority. He often called himself "an SOB" and said that it was best that editorial responsibility rest on one person so that person, not the whole department, got all the blame. The editor should be a wise but quite inscrutable autocrat: fair but neither questioned nor constrained.

In early summer, chair Philip Hauser wrote Hughes one of his characteristically blunt letters (PMH to ECH, 14 June 1958), making it plain that the department had taken advantage of Hughes's absence to have precisely that discussion of the *AJS*'s future that Rossi had promised to avoid until Hughes's return.[2] In quick bureaucratese Hauser informed Hughes that "we are recommending that you be appointed as editor for the academic year 1958–9 under the old regulation with respect to the Journal." (Hughes himself had given the job to Rossi for the year with the clear expectation of his own return to a full, enduring editorship at the end of the year; now the department would "allow" him to return for one more year.) Hauser went on to tell Hughes that the department had "tentatively agreed" to give the editor a three-year term and to elect independently an associate editor with a *longer* term "to stagger the term of the associate editor so that there would be continuity between successive editors." Then the

---

2. Hughes and Hauser had been opponents through most of the debates in the early 1950s, and indeed Hauser had opposed Hughes's chairmanship, having been passed over (that time) for the same position himself.

editor could choose a *second* associate editor, and the three together would be the editorial board of the journal.[3]

Shortly after midsummer, Rossi wrote to Hughes somewhat disingenuously, saying that he hadn't changed the consulting editors because "you would prefer to do it yourself. I don't think very much harm is done by keeping over a set an additional year" (PHR to ECH, 22 July 1958). Hughes wrote back, cordial as ever, that

> you made a good deal of the point that you were to be the editor, not acting editor. . . . It now looks as if you [are] taking the tack of being an acting editor and leaving the chores to be done when I come back—as I am told—to be editor for a temporary term of one year.

Hughes was, as usual, upset about the offense against politeness:

> The least that we can do is to write the advisory editors, those whose terms were up at end in May, a courteous letter thanking them for their services and asking them whether, owing to special circumstances, [they] are willing to continue to serve until May, 1959.

He closed with sad confusion:

> I am sure there is some reason for your extraordinary bursts of energy and interest in the Journal combined with attacks on me, followed by lack of interest and desire to hand it all back to me, but I do not yet understand the whole affair. Perhaps you can explain it when I get home. In the meantime, peace be unto you.

Hughes knew very well what had happened but apparently was wise enough to know that he could do nothing about it. The *AJS* of the middle period was gone. A new small group wanted the *Journal* and would do with it as they wished.

The Double-Bind of Double-Blind

Probably no issue better symbolized the different paradigms of the two generations than double-blind reviewing (then called anonymous reviewing). As I noted above, universal review of formally submitted papers

---

3. Conveniently, Hauser dictated his letter two days before leaving to spend the summer in Japan. The younger group was in a big hurry. Hughes would be forced to retire in 1962 in any case by the university's age restrictions. Apparently three years was too long to wait for the change of regime. Rossi had the good grace to be embarrassed by Hauser's letter (PHR to ECH, 18 June 1958).

seems to have been the creation of Helen Hughes, who had aimed thereby to avoid the accusation that Rossi was to make in 1958.

But early reviewing had never been double-blind. Double-blind reviewing was first tried in sociology by Leonard Broom. When Broom took over the *ASR* in 1955, he "became aware that some of the reviewing was of persons rather than of submissions." He conducted a test of the affiliations and backgrounds of authors in the major sociology journals and found that "some journals looked like house organs."[4] Reading old manuscript files, he found that "some of the editorial reviews were exemplary, others betrayed small-minded and spiteful displays or apple-polishing." (All quotes from Broom to Abbott, 4 January 1993.) In response, Broom initiated double-blind reviewing shortly after he took over the *ASR,* about 1956. Within two years (in January 1958), Rossi proposed it for the *AJS.*

Given our current presupposition of the validity and, indeed, the moral righteousness of double-blind reviewing, it may seem strange that a strong case was argued against it by leading sociologists. But Hughes so argued to both Rossi and, later, Peter Blau.

> There are many reasons why [anonymous judgment] does not appeal to me. It is a matter for discussion. I would rather have an article judged by a reader who knows he knows the author than by one who only thinks he knows who wrote the piece. There is also no reason to believe that a man would rise above his prejudices any more in judging an article whose author he is not sure of than in the other case. The problem of judgments on merit (universal*istic*) [Hughes's emphasis; Rossi had used the word universal] is a difficult one. On the other hand, most people write judgments that are—within their own lights—judgments of merit. A reader may think that all technically competent bits of research, no matter how slight, should be published without respect to space and other problems of the Journals. Others will want a ground-breaking piece of work in print, even though there are unsolved problems of method in it. Some will blast us if we publish an article which, in their view, used a device which he [sic] doesn't like. Some write with a school-teaching philosophy, saying tell this man that we will publish the article if he changes this, that, etc. (ECH to department, 6 March 1958)

Thus the case against double-blind reviewing was that reviewing based on guesses was worse, that there were other, worse prejudices than those

---

4. Recall that 30 percent of *AJS* contributors in the period 1935–55 had Chicago Ph.D.'s, well above the background disciplinary percentage. Broom might also have been thinking of *Social Forces* and *Sociology and Social Research.*

about authors, that beliefs in universalism were dubious and diverse, and that referees inevitably encoded their own editorial policies into their reviews. But Hughes could only put off, not prevent, the change. Peter Blau enacted double-blind reviewing when he took over the *AJS* in January 1961. The policy was complete in its present structure, with separate forms for editor and author. The issue had been previously discussed at the *AJS* lunch at the New York ASA meetings, at which Hughes had not been present.[5] "Most editors were strongly in favor of anonymous readings," Blau wrote to Hughes (PMB to ECH, 16 February 1961), "although a few were strongly opposed to it." Hughes tried one last objection, writing in response to Blau's form letter to all editors in January 1961.

> You give as one of your reasons for anonymity, bias against an author. But bias against an author is only one of several kinds of bias of which any one of us may be guilty. We are biased against topics, against style of writing, against ideas. It is not likely that reading an article anonymously will eliminate these other biases which may be, at least taken together, a good deal more important than bias against a particular person. A second thing which is in my mind is that people will almost certainly guess who wrote articles in the field in which they are familiar. A wrong guess could do a good deal of harm. Unless people can keep themselves from guessing, anonymous reading may be worse than reading with the name known. Finally, I come to what I consider an even more important item. Anonymous reading is done on the assumption that each article is an independent item, not related to what a man may have done before and what he may do in the future. This is an entirely false assumption. A given piece of a man's work has to be judged not merely by itself but as one item in his complete or growing production. It fits into something that he has done before. In some cases the article may be an isolated piece of work which the man will not follow up, but in the cases of the better articles, I think we will find that it is best understood as part of a man's ongoing work, and a

5. Curiously, the *AJS* long had the policy, started by Blau (see PMB to David Street, 22 June 1962), of identifying authors to the referees when the latter were told the final disposition of the paper. This policy was not questioned until at least twenty years later. It is hard to guess Blau's intention. He seemed to assume that his elite reviewers needed to be protected from their own biases in the phase of judgment but would find it useful afterward to know who wrote good material and who bad. Some people specifically liked this policy, such as David Riesman (Riesman to PMB, 18 June 1962). On the matter of the *AJS* lunch, the editor did not always attend the meetings (see ECH to PHR, 25 June 1958, and PHR to ECH, 22 July 1958). In 1958 Rossi said he couldn't afford it. Hughes later remarked, "I make it a point to go only once in a while" (ECH to PHR, 29 July 1958).

man's ongoing work is by the nature of the case a very personal product and by no means anonymous.

Thus, in addition to extending and clarifying his earlier arguments, Hughes now added one against the conception of disembodied work. It was meaningless to understand work either as an anonymous contribution to some greater scientific whole or, worse still, as an isolated bit of decontextualized knowledge. Hughes's position rested on the classical Chicago conception of social facts as situated, a position diametrically opposed to the new decontextualized sociology of variables represented by Blau and Rossi (cf. chapter 7).

Blau's response was statesmanlike: "I do realize that there are disadvantages to the policy I have introduced. On the other hand, so far I feel the advantages outweigh the disadvantages. I may find out that I was quite wrong, and if I do find out I hope I have enough sense to change back." But neither Blau nor anyone else ever thought of going back. The day of a personal sociology was over.

The controversy over double-blind review reveals a watershed in sociology. Hughes was correct to see the depersonalization inherent in the new ethic, but he did not see the curious combination of motives behind that depersonalization. For Broom, double-blind review was a populist policy, a blow against the establishment. For Blau and Rossi, by contrast, it was a matter of scientism, which was itself an ideology of the establishment. (Double-blind reviewing at the *AJS* may also have reflected coercive isomorphism, since the *ASR* had already changed.) What neither side saw were the consequences of double-blind reviewing in a sociology that was becoming substantively diverse. Oddly enough, it was the Tory Hughes who throughout the controversy recognized that diversity would be lost through double-blind review, not gained.[6]

The Editorship in Transition

Rossi's behavior in 1957–58 had made one thing very clear. The postwar-trained, professionalizing sociologists of the late 1950s saw the *AJS* editorship as an important position, not to be left in the hands of an aging eccentric. But at the same time, nobody really wanted to do the job. Herbert Blumer had been among America's leading sociologists when he was editor. Hughes too had been a major figure by 1952. But Peter Blau in 1962

6. To my knowledge there is only one experimental study of the effect of double-blind reviewing on diversity. The American Economic Association did a randomized test and found that double-blind reviewing slightly favored central institutions over peripheral ones (Blank 1991).

was just nine years post-Ph.D., not yet the major figure he would later become. He was followed by C. Arnold Anderson, a sociologist in the Education Department whom no one considered a major figure in any field. Anderson was followed in 1972 by Charles Bidwell, another professor in the Education Department only recently (1969) admitted to associate status in Sociology (MDS, 6 May 1969).

Not surprisingly, these editorial transitions were sometimes ad hoc. When Hughes wanted to step down, he suggested Blau. As Hauser remembered it, Blau was eager to take the *AJS*. However, Blau says (personal communication) that he was willing, to be sure, but more or less got the editorship as a booby prize with tenure (a sentiment Roger Gould would later echo). When Blau left Anderson was chosen, but there is no evidence on why or how. Although Anderson had been Blau's stand-in for one leave year, the department at the time of his selection contained Janowitz, Rossi, and Hauser, all reasonable possibilities for editor.

Charles Bidwell was the first *AJS* editor actually recruited by a routinely convened faculty committee. There was a reason for the renewal of faculty interest. The Anderson regime had produced a crisis. The issue, once again, was the role of the managing editor. There was a predictable history. Blau and Helen Hughes had fought from the start of his editorship over the line between managing and academic editorships, and although he allowed her to stay until she and her husband left for Boston, he thereafter replaced her with an "assistant editor" whose position was more limited. But this person (and her position) lasted only a year. For the rest of the Blau years, the *AJS* made do with an "editorial assistant."

When Arnold Anderson took over, he went through five such editorial assistants in two years. Manuscript flow was rising quickly. The office fell into chaos. So in mid-1968 he revived the position of managing editor. His choice was a middle-aged woman with much publishing experience, fresh from the antiwar and civil rights movements, who was deeply interested in social science. Florence Levinsohn seemed ideal for the job. She was energetic, smart, and determined to make the *AJS* intellectually exciting. It was a fateful combination. Although kindly and well-meaning, Anderson was an ineffectual editor. Levinsohn expanded into the vacuum.

The years from 1968 to 1974 (the year Charles Bidwell fired Levinsohn) were, of course, an exciting time. For the department, they reached an early climax in 1969 with the denial of tenure to Marlene Dixon and the consequent student seizure of the university's administration building. These events led to a complete transformation of graduate education in the department, worked out by faculty-student committees under the leadership of Morris Janowitz and (on the student side) his dissertation student William Kornblum. In addition, the department lost some faculty members (Rossi, Duncan MacRae, Blau, Suttles), and gained others (Coleman, Wilson, Laumann, Stanley Lieberson, Barry Schwartz), in effect seeing a major turnover.

In the midst of this, the *AJS* had its own revolution. Students flocked to Levinsohn's coffeepot in the basement of Foster Hall ("the Left Bank at the U of C," recalled one student). Levinsohn made friends with the Press advertising office and peppered the scholarly journals with ads for the *AJS*. She produced an immensely successful special issue on women. She gave lavish parties at the ASA. She redesigned the journal's physical layout, against serious opposition from Anderson, the editorial board, and numerous subscribers. The results of all this were exciting, at least to the Press, which cashed in on 2,200 new subscriptions (about a 25 percent jump) in the two-year period 1969 to 1971 alone. Press and editor were pleased indeed.

At the same time, the flamboyant Levinsohn very nearly became the scholarly editor of the *AJS*. She read many of the papers before review and rejected some of them without further ado. She sat in on—indeed more or less presided at—editorial board meetings. She suggested reviewers, partly because she alone knew who worked fast and who slow, partly because her energetic ASA activities left her with far-flung personal connections. She solicited papers. She organized special issues and recruited editors for them. Indeed, her views were so important that Anderson scotched one faculty member proposed as associate editor, saying to chair Janowitz that "the proposed person would be uncongenial and unacceptable to other peers— and not particularly welcomed by the office manager (not wholly irrelevant)." By the time Anderson announced his desire to step down, Levinsohn felt powerful enough to dicker with Janowitz about his successor.

A good illustration of Levinsohn's power was an episode in which she blew up at the book review editor for leaving a window open, driving the young faculty member off spluttering to Anderson. Anderson quietly calmed him down and smoothed the whole episode away. Better that Levinsohn not be disturbed. The breadth of Levinsohn's conception of her role is clear from her letters to authors. These read like Maxwell Perkins's correspondence: confident, thoughtful, occasionally brash. She clearly saw herself as mistress of a major intellectual magazine.

> What I personally miss is some sense of yourself in the setting. Surely this idea did not arise out of purely intellectual preoccupations. All of us have feelings and attitudes towards schools. . . . I

hope you will be able to intrude some of that into the final version of the paper. (To an author)

I am continually plotting new publications events that have changed the *AJS* from a dull plodding journal read by 7000 to a lively controversial one read by 10,500 with more advertising than ever before. (To the Press journals manager)

Yes, we'll consider your manuscript and the strong recommendation of our good friend [X] makes it all the more attractive to us. (To an author asking if a piece might be considered)

If [the newspapers which the military controls] are your only source of information, then you cannot learn more about the military than the military wants you to know, which is not sociology as we practice it here. (To an author rejecting a manuscript)

We regret very much that we have decided we cannot publish your piece on Goffman. It simply is not sufficiently analytic for us to publish this as a review essay. (To an author rejecting a manuscript)

This is just a note to say thank you for the gorgeous essay on [X]. I hoped that the book would stimulate in you that kind of brilliance. That you would get so fully to the heart, that you would strike exactly that flame, was marvelous to behold. (To a book review author)

Anderson was very clear about his debts to Levinsohn.

All the smug satisfaction generally at how well *AJS* is holding up to the competition and just now over the special July issue—for both of [these] Mrs. Levinsohn deserves much credit. (CAA to Press journals director Jean Sacks, 24 May 1972)

Levinsohn had some help in her attempts to transform the *AJS*. Associate editors, whom Anderson quite deliberately selected from the young faculty, were often kindred adventurous spirits, and some of them helped her turn what Janowitz called "the good, gray *AJS*" into a lively and exciting, as well as prestigious, journal. Some of them, too, were bored with the endless short articles of survey analysis that constituted the majority of submissions. Although they may not have shared all of Levinsohn's goals, they were willing to support her strongly, as was Anderson.

All this might have mattered less had Levinsohn not played with fire in terms of topics. But she found and promoted controversial papers—papers from Marxists and papers on racism and sexism—and also esoteric papers on topics like the sociology of odors or tourism. She steered papers she liked to people who would treat them well and papers she didn't to those who would treat them badly. Eventually a few of these episodes—particularly the controversial articles—got the attention of the department. There were meetings and scenes. When Anderson stepped down, Charles Bidwell was brought in to remove Levinsohn from power. By telling her not to read the manuscripts and removing her from editorial board meetings he returned the job to a clerkship. By mid-1974 Levinsohn left the *AJS* for another Press journal. Later she became a freelance writer.[7]

Thus the two transition editors had completely opposite editorial styles. Blau was firmly and absolutely in control. He read every paper himself, wrote all correspondence himself, and made all acceptance decisions alone (PMB to CAA, 16 November 1970). He was on first-name terms with all of his consulting editors. When he went on leave in 1962–63, he insisted that his name remain on top of the masthead as editor, with Anderson listed below him as acting editor.

By contrast, Anderson was content to be a delegator who ran the *AJS* in a very easygoing style. He sought advice on papers from many people. He did not write all the formal article correspondence himself but shared it with his managing editor and his associate editors. He did not know his consulting editors personally before they joined the journal. He occasionally let Florence Levinsohn reject manuscripts on her own. He was the first to send papers to students for review, and during the complex student-faculty negotiations of the Marlene Dixon crisis, he wrote to chair Janowitz that

> when you lay things before the student members of the student-faculty committee you may mention that we are prepared to make suggestions of ways in which students may share in the operating of the Journal . . . we would entertain arrangements for more regular membership on the Editorial Board.

In fact, he even considered allowing students to sign formal article correspondence (CAA to Jean Sacks, 29 September 1969). Of course the stu-

7. Levinsohn's departure was clearly a relief to the department as a whole. Their visions of the *AJS* were widely divergent. In the end (the protagonists' memories are unclear on this) it seems that Bidwell fired Levinsohn, but she went to the Press to resign before the firing became official. When I sent Florence Levinsohn a copy of this chapter, she objected that it portrayed her as much too dominant. She saw the *AJS* in the late 1960s as a team effort led by Anderson and supported by junior faculty associate editors whom she admired very much. I may have underplayed the warmth of fellow feeling she recalls. But judging from her own earlier reminiscences, from the correspondence, and from others' remarks, I feel justified in seeing her as the central figure in the *Journal* in this period.

dents saw all this openness as a great honor and concession, and certainly Anderson's desire to help and support graduate students was sincere. But taken in context, it seems in many ways more a sign of Anderson's casual approach to the editorship.[8]

Manuscript Demography and Processing

The emergence of a dynamic managing editor was not the only crisis of the Anderson regime. There was a manuscript crisis as well. The demographics of manuscripts had changed sharply in the transition years. The *AJS* averaged a little over two hundred new manuscripts a year through the early 1960s.[9] This number moved very sharply up to three hundred in the middle of the decade, thereafter drifting slightly upward until it abruptly climbed to six hundred between 1971 and 1974. Disciplinary expansion cannot explain so rapid a growth in submissions.[10] It seems likely that the enormous expansion in the early 1970s reflected Levinsohn's outreach activities and in particular her conspicuous openness to nonmainstream papers, a fact underlined by the special issue "Changing Women in a Changing Society" in January 1973.

But the flood of manuscripts found the *AJS* completely unprepared. Manuscript processing time rose from thirteen weeks to twenty-four between 1970 and 1972.[11] The *AJS* files were filled with complaints about refereeing time.

> To receive a form rejection slip after five months is not what I expected from the best of the profession I am about to enter.

8. Anderson also ran some part of the *AJS* occasional budget through his personal checking account. Astounding as it seems, the canceled checks are still in the files—checks to the British Sociological Association, Florence Levinsohn, Peter Blau, various typists, the Press, and many others. This seems not to have been simply petty cash, but regular operating expenses. According to Florence Levinsohn, however, these checks involve the book sales "slush fund."

9. Recall that at this time the ASA annual meeting acceptance letter still emphasized submission to the *ASR*: "The editors of either the *Review* or *Sociometry* will be pleased to consider your paper for publication. It may be submitted in its present form, though in most cases a somewhat expanded version would be desirable for appropriate evaluation. Manuscripts may be submitted prior to the Annual Meeting" (form letter dated 28 April 1961, in *AJS* files).

10. The ASA grew rapidly in the mid-1960s, about 10 percent per year from 1964 to 1968. But growth slowed quickly and stopped completely by 1972.

11. Barry Schwartz and Steve Dubin (an assistant professor and a graduate student) collaborated on a study of manuscript flow that remains in the files. This section relies heavily on that study, to whose authors I am greatly indebted.

I should note that from here on in the text I shall be quoting letters from authors and reviewers both extensively and anonymously. The reasons for anonymity are obvious; many of the writers are still active in the discipline, and there is little to be gained by identifying them. Occa-

> I am dismayed by the rejection of my paper—and not only because
> it took over seven months to review it.

Not for nothing was the *AJS* "turtle" letter—the letter urging referees to hurry up—invented in this period.

The easiest way to cope with the flood of submissions was to reject papers without review. (I use the local neologism "prejecting" for this action.) Reviewing was itself a recent practice at this point, and prejection was and is standard throughout the commercial magazine world from which Levinsohn drew much of her inspiration. Thus it is not surprising that the *AJS* prejected nearly 30 percent of papers in the period 1970–72. Typically these were papers from outside sociology as generally defined or papers hopelessly unprofessional in writing and thinking. Some were simply felt to be uninteresting or "not yet ready." The *AJS* was thus prejecting many of the very papers that Levinsohn's efforts were attracting.

But even with high prejection, numbers of manuscripts to process were rapidly increasing. Given the relatively constant journal space, this fluctuation in manuscript numbers of course imposed a downward trend on acceptance rates. These reached their low point of 7 percent in the middle 1970s when submissions were highest. The Press did increase the page allotment by about 50 percent during the Levinsohn years, but this expansion was almost completely absorbed by growing article length. In 1962 the average *AJS* article was 10.5 pages (*ASR*'s was 10.9). By 1971 the average length was 18.2 pages. Although this number must be deflated for the format change in 1970, the deflated figure of 14.25 old pages was still a 40 percent increase in article size. The new pages simply lengthened the old articles.[12]

Managing the higher manuscript flow required bureaucratization. This period saw the overhaul of many of the *AJS* boilerplate forms as well as a new manuscript tracking system. Even these changes were unsuccessful, however, and by the end of Levinsohn's tenure office slipups had become routine. Acceptance letters got sent to people who were supposed to get rejections, marginalia got mistaken for text and were published, papers got lost, and correspondence was mailed to the wrong people.

---

sionally I have referred to someone as "an eminent sociologist," a "struggling young author," or some other semi-identifying phrase. The reader will simply have to accept my judgment on these matters. I cannot divulge identities. (Indeed, I have used the universal masculine pronoun to cover gender identities.) At the same time, I cannot support some of my claims about the *AJS*'s experience without using direct quotes. I hope I have safely walked the line between reticence and publicity.

12. Figures are partly from *AJS* annual reports and partly from an *ASR* report, *ASR* 26 (1961): 983.

Referee and Discipline

The increased flow of papers, given a policy of reviewing most of them, meant a vastly increased burden on referees. In the Blau years, with 150 to 200 manuscripts reviewed per year, the *AJS* needed about 350 first-time reviews and a handful of reviews of revisions. Blau got by with the editorial board (the faculty), sixteen consulting editors, and fewer than a hundred ad hoc reviewers. When Anderson took over, he stuck with the old levels of referees for a year. But in his second year the *AJS* jumped to about 190 ad hoc reviewers, the following year to 270, and eventually to 400 in 1972.

The shift to ad hoc referees—possibly a conscious policy of Anderson's—was a major change. For all his scientism, Peter Blau had been a Hughesian autocrat, soliciting reviews as advice from friends. There were no editorial board meetings: "I read the reviews; I made the decisions" (personal communication). The Blau *AJS* was still the organ of a small community of shared values organized around a central authority. But Arnold Anderson not only was not widely connected in the elite, he was also driven by inclination and necessity to vastly broaden the base of reviewers. By the time he stepped down, the *AJS* was reviewing 450 manuscripts a year, needing 900 first-time reviews and another hundred or so for revised manuscripts. (Actually, many papers got only one review in this period, so the total number of reviews needed was probably about 750.) The numbers meant that far less than the majority of the reviews were coming from people he or his managing editor knew at all well. The *AJS* had democratized, something Anderson wanted very much. But in the process reviewing had become a faceless exchange.[13]

13. One might have thought that this relatively sudden and enormous demand for refereeing would be met by turning to the younger members of the discipline. Sociology was still growing rapidly (although less rapidly than immediately after the war), and such a high "birthrate" meant that most sociologists were young in professional terms. But in fact the average professional age of referees at the *AJS* in the Anderson years was a steady ten years post-Ph.D. Although that figure was probably less than the age of the more elite group that Blau had been able to rely on, it still represented nothing like an overwhelming reliance on young people. However, the "ten years post-Ph.D." figure is somewhat high because one group likely to be unidentified from the data is graduate students who never finished. At about this time, other journal editors were writing to the *AJS* wondering how to use students in the journal process, which was seen as a "way to keep one's graduate students abreast of what is going on." "It is likely," one editor wrote, "that most of our clan would not like the idea of callow graduate students reviewing, not to say refereeing, manuscripts they had submitted."

These figures on reviewer age conceal a vast effort. There are no computer records of referees until after 1980. I scanned all the published referee lists, corrected the scan, sent students to the field, and identified, in all years 1972 to 1996, the Ph.D. dates of over 80 percent of the referees. These are reliable figures. Any biases are likely to be systematic and constant over time.

The move to widespread ad hoc reviewing produced chaos, not so much because Anderson and Levinsohn couldn't decode the messages referees were giving them, but because the new referees simply didn't know how to behave. Indeed, one of the reasons Levinsohn got so far behind in editorial work (most of the delays took place *after* the reviews were in) was that she had to edit many referee reports to make them less callous and contemptuous. A sampling of responses from authors:

> Never have I received such dubious editorial comment as yours with respect to your rejection of my paper.

> My experience with your journal is enough to discredit it in my eyes as well as those of others.

> Let me finally add that my feelings were badly hurt by the patronizing and caustic tone of this comment. As you know, I read dozens of papers for you each year, . . . and I think you will find I am very careful to make my comments to the author as tactful as possible.

Again and again Anderson found himself defending his journal. "We do not, out of consideration for the author's feelings, include anything [as comments returned to authors] but constructive criticism," he wrote one disgruntled author on 7 July 1970. To an author protesting that he got no comments that would help him do better next time, he wrote: "Very often our readers do not write comments for the authors and, at other times, we exercise our editorial judgment about whether to send their comments on to the author." He told the author to send the rejected paper back to *AJS* and one of the editors would comment on it constructively (4 December 1968).[14]

Throughout these letters we find editor and authors groping toward a conception of what refereeing should be. While this problem might seem to arise mainly from rapid disciplinary growth and factionalization—a problem of socialization under a regime of rapid differentiation—in fact the correspondence shows that there was from the start no clear idea of the moral

14. According to Levinsohn, she drafted these letters and signed Anderson's name. Anderson was clearly overwhelmed by what was going on. He wrote to Everett Hughes on 4 June 1970 asking for a paper for the *AJS*'s seventy-fifth anniversary, saying: "I get the impression a larger variety of people from more varied schools are now submitting material. But I think fewer people have read anything. I think professional manners and normal courtesies in letter-writing have deteriorated. But on the other hand, you may choose to emphasize the way an editor can shape trends in the field, or is that an illusion?" About the letter writing, he was certainly right. Anderson seems to have had little idea, when he pushed democratization of the *AJS*, of the astounding diversity—of interests, talents, training, and personality—among the referees he was reaching out to.

structure of reviewing, particularly with respect to the emotional rights and responsibilities of double-blind reviewing. The discipline's diversity was extraordinary, to be sure. But more important, nobody had a clear idea of what were the norms of civility in such a diverse world. As a result, author after author waited forever and was then personally bludgeoned. Indeed, this personal assault was what Hughes had sought to avoid by leaving rejection unexplained. In sending on the comments, Blau, Rossi, and their generation had disagreed, believing that common principles—the "scientific sociology" with which their generation stormed the ramparts of their elders—would provide a moral foundation for universalistic reviewing, reviewing that would be acceptable to both sides because of its appeal to shared norms. But it was the luck of Anderson and Levinsohn to confront the impact of double-blind reviewing in a world that lacked not only common principles, but often basic courtesy. Letter after letter invoked moral arguments to challenge the reviewing process.

> It seems to me . . . that you do indeed *owe* an author more than a "courtesy quick reply," you *owe* him the reasons (as given by the reviewers) why his work is judged in a particular way. And I see no reason why such comments should not be passed on to him or her. (Emphasis added)

Others attacked the logical structure of reviewing:

> The size of the sample was an apparent and unalterable fact when we first submitted the paper. If this were a serious consideration warranting rejection of the paper, it could have been done after the first reading. (To CAA, 6 June 1969)

Similar letters made precisely the reverse argument, that manuscripts should not be rejected up front based on "screening," for example, for low response rates. Others attacked the moral failures of referees:

> His review is almost exclusively concerned with that tradition rather than with the merits of the paper. It is not a publication review, but an opportunity to attack a line of research with which he disagrees. (To CAA, 17 December 1969)

Note the assumption that arguing against a particular line of research is immoral, that it is not conceivable that a whole line of research could be wrong. Thus, substantive differences could be claimed as differences of taste and could therefore not legitimately serve as a basis for rejection. The disappearance of common principles was an established fact.

Still another view was that the referee functioned as an officer of the *AJS*. One author had received a letter from Levinsohn saying, "If [the referee] is satisfied that you answered him, we will be happy to publish the paper." But the referee found further problems and the paper was turned down. The angry author wrote:

> When a responsible person in your organization says that you will publish a paper if certain revisions are made, I think it is unfair to later reject that paper on the basis of a new set of criticisms generally not related to the revisions themselves.

Levinsohn replied:

> This is not the first nor will it be the last time that a reviewer has found errors in a paper on a second reading. . . . We said we would publish if you could satisfy the reviewer. Clearly you have done something far short of that. [From now on] I will not even suggest [the] possibility of publication until I am certain that the paper is ready.

In this exchange, we find a full-blown due process view of refereeing, as if the ultimate criterion for publication were not the quality or interest or importance of a paper, but rather whether certain procedures had been followed. There was a sense that the *AJS* could not reject any paper that it did not affirmatively demonstrate to be incompetent or rejectable. Publication had become a rebuttable presumption.

As part of this sense, we find authors regarding the "interest" of their paper as irrelevant to the publication decision. Competence alone should decide. Thus Anderson found himself apologizing profusely for a negative review whose entire text read as follows: "There is nothing wrong with this paper, except possibly that it would have been of interest in 1955 and at this time [1969] should be superfluous." The reviews that survive from the 1930s and 1940s usually read exactly like this review. The referee's quality judgment was taken completely on trust; no justification was given to author or editor. The real issue was whether a paper was found interesting by a competent judge. Now authors began to perceive the interest, timeliness, and even creativity of papers as something outside the due process judgment of competence. Interest was not only irrelevant as a criterion, it was illegitimate.

Many authors, of course, recognized the contingent nature of the moral contract of journal and prospective author. "By the way, it is not my habit to bitch. I have had rejected papers which I thought deserved it," wrote one author. "However, I do feel injured in this case." Some even had a sense of humor about the long waits. A well-known scholar wrote:

> My records indicate that you sent me a postcard on December 12 1972. . . . Please let me know whether [the paper] 1) has been read and there is now a furious argument going on within the editorial staff about it, 2) it has been read and you haven't had an opportunity to let me know about it because the office has been flooded due to the heavy spring rains, 3) it has been sent to a reviewer three months ago who has run off with one of his students and is traveling somewhere through the south seas, 4) it was eaten by a dog who happened to walk into the office, 5) it is alive and well but covered with peanut butter.

The new moral contract was not only with authors, but also with referees. Blau and Rossi had begun the policy of cold-mailing manuscripts to reviewers (sending them out without warning the receiver they were coming), a practice Hughes had singled out as conspicuously impolite. The old generation's attitude was made clear by one former ASA president's replying to a cold-mailed manuscript from Bidwell early in 1974: "Damn you, Charles, I never do this kind of work. The next time you ask me to do this, I shall throw the ms unread into the wastebasket." Another aspect of the situation was an emerging sense that the journal was serving the teaching function Hughes had anticipated long before. One rejected author wrote:

> I hope it is some reward to you and your readers that your efforts are appreciated, even when the decision is negative. Sometimes, it seems like the only way to get a professional evaluation is to do it this way, especially in a relatively remote department like ours. (To CAA, 30 March 1969)

But *referees* could object to this function:

> More to the point, I am really holding out on him. I see no reason why I should hand him the specific ideas that can be gleaned from the interactionist literature. . . . I'm not inclined to do the work for him. (To FL, 18 December 1972)

Moreover, the only way to discipline referees was to drop them:

> As for the comments you enclosed [from our reviewer] they are really dreadful. My first reading of them is that this reviewer is really not competent to handle manuscripts and I am going to send Arnold Anderson a note to discourage him from using that reviewer again. [Editorial assistant to an author, 28 December 1972]

And some referees had their price. In response to a cold-mailed manuscript, one famous figure replied:

> Don't make me laugh. You haven't printed my review of [one of his own colleagues]. Why should I work for you unless I happen to feel like it? (To CAA, 11 November 72)

The problems of refereeing thus had several dimensions. Authors wanted publication most of all, but since that was chancy, at the least they wanted speed, due process, and consistency. Often they wanted to learn something, to be "improved" by an encounter with one of the discipline's best journals. Finally, authors wanted not to be wounded, not to feel personally attacked. The objectification implicit in double-blind reviewing vastly increased the likelihood of this negative experience, and in the early years it was clearly a *very* common one.

The referees had much more diverse interests. Some sought to teach, some resented having to give others "information they should have known." Some found refereeing an honor (particularly students), some considered it a chore, some saw it as a moral imperative. A few found it a chance to even scores with opposing people or arguments or research traditions at the expense of a third party. The referees were also people of very diverse skills—increasingly so as the net spread wider and wider—who had to be asked to work for no reward. They too expected a compact with the *AJS*—not to overuse them, not to bury them with poor work to weed out.[15]

The editors stood in the middle. They had obligations to advance the field, to uphold its standards, to treat authors fairly, to even out the load of refereeing (both for justice and for self-interest) and to prevent the emotional damage that double-blind refereeing regularly seemed to produce. But their central interest lay in producing an exciting and important journal. Yet the single-minded pursuit of interesting material characteristic of the magazines Levinsohn admired sat ill with the sober disciplines of research and the thin skins of people unused to the writer's market. Worse

---

15. With the proliferation of journals, overwork became a problem. There were probably about thirty sociology journals at this point. Assuming a rough mean of 150 manuscripts per year at each, we have 4,500 manuscripts, each requiring two reviews, plus probably another 1,000 reviews for revisions. The total is about 10,000 acts of reviewing. The ASA had only 13,000 to 14,000 members, nearly half of whom had been members less than five years. If we are to assume that, to quote the rejected author above, "the best of the profession" was doing the refereeing, the best of the profession was already being seriously overworked. In practice, what these figures meant was that disciplinewide many, indeed probably most, manuscripts were reviewed by people at or only slightly above the competence level of their authors. In this sense—and the numbers are worse today—the whole "teaching function" argument is a myth.

still, in the new expanded world of sociology, not only were editors unlikely to know authors at all, they also knew little about their referees. Every review was an indexical argument; what it meant was conditional on the unknown refereeing style of the reviewer.[16] The resolution of this tangle of conflicting interests and obligations would come only in the Bidwell years and would have important costs. More than any other thing, this jumble of issues—more moral and emotional than intellectual—overshadowed the history of the transition *AJS,* and no doubt that of other sociological journals at the time.

Contributors and the Problem of Interesting Papers

By the mid-transition period *AJS* editors and many others were already worried about what they saw as one particularly ominous effect of the double-blind reviewing system on the nature and types of contributors. The flight of major authors from the refereed journals became a topic of conversation quite early, being mentioned by Hughes in his 1958 letter to the department about *AJS* policy (ECH to department, 6 March 1958): "There is a great tendency for leading sociologists to publish only in symposia these days . . . the papers in symposia are soon buried, because symposia go out of print." At the time, people like Rossi felt that some, at least, of this hesitancy could be attributed not to the reviewing process but to what was perceived as Helen Hughes's interventionist editing. As time passed, however, this explanation became less tenable.

There were some conspicuous examples. One of the defining figures of modern sociology wrote, "It was not until I was eminent that either journal [*ASR* and *AJS*] started giving me hassles in the form of sheaves of ill-considered comments and suggestions by people ill-equipped to comment or suggest" (personal communication, 25 May 1993). It is not clear now whether the flight of the leaders was a reality or some kind of widespread belief. Blau deliberately courted major figures for the *AJS* and published large numbers of their articles. Under his editorship, articles appeared from Angell, Bales, Coleman, Costner, Coser, Duncan, Hollingshead, Hughes,

16. Everyone who worked with journals at the time was well aware of these problems. Blau, not surprisingly, took a scientific view of them. In his first year as editor, he initiated a study of reviewing practices. The *AJS* at this point had a six-level recommendation scale, and Blau found referees in perfect agreement 35 percent of the time. They were no more than one point apart 67 percent of the time. Detailed figures showed that referees were far more likely to agree on rejection than on acceptance and that even the middle levels produced more agreement than there was at the very top (Blau, Special Report appended to AJSAR 1962). Not surprisingly Blau, with his vision of a relatively unified discipline, interpreted these results as a glass half full rather than half empty.

Parsons, Sewell, Sorokin, Taeuber, and Williams—certainly a list of well-established, senior figures. But at the same time the *AJS* files hold numerous letters from well-known sociologists testifying to their authors' anger over rejections (note also Rossi's comments to Hughes above):

> I am afraid this recent incident has not helped our negative stereotype about submitting papers to the *AJS*. I will of course refrain from submitting anything else I write for consideration in your journal.

Along with the flight of major authors went a flight of those outside what some saw as a narrow definition of professionalism. As Hughes wrote to the department (20 September 1957):

> My view of the Journal is that it should not be too professional. By this I mean that we should keep our frontiers open. Since we are not the organ of any professional society we are in an ideal position to be the ground-breaking Journal; the one in which new ideas can be presented, in which new fields of study can be opened up. Work of an essentially sociological character is being done in many organizations other than universities. We should keep our frontiers open not only with respect to method and subject matter, but also with respect to the kinds of people from whom we get manuscripts and [to] whom we address what we publish.

But in the new dispensation, unusual work could fare badly. As Anderson wrote to one author, "We welcome articles that challenge shibboleths, but then we treat them with great caution, lest we be called irresponsible" (10 March 1970). Levinsohn preserved such papers only by maintaining special channels for them. One well-known author wrote after a rejection:

> I do appreciate the fact that you are sympathetic to getting different kinds of papers and I am sorry that I did not alert you personally to this paper instead of sending it directly to the editor. Next time I will know better.

At the same time, the transition editors did have some latitude. One of the foundational papers of modern sociology was accepted without refereeing or comment other than "Dear X: Of course we'll publish your paper" (this was not, incidentally, a paper by a Chicago faculty member).

Thus, while there were real concerns that some important work was disappearing from the *AJS*'s purview, the situation was not desperate. But the relation of interest and importance to competence remained a nagging problem, perpetually setting at odds the three crucial actors in the publishing nexus: author, reviewer, and editor.

Even while these concerns arose, the overall pattern of contributors did not change substantially. The age of contributors did indeed fall, but well before the transition period (see the previous tables). Most of that drop reflected rapid disciplinary expansion rather than changing likelihood of submission, and in any case it had occurred by 1955. The general pattern of contributors to *AJS* had reached its modern form by 1965. As the tables show, the average age of authors in the decade 1955–65 was thirty-nine, their average age at B.A. twenty-three, and their average age at Ph.D. thirty-one, numbers that confirm fully professionalized careers among writers. A minimum of three-quarters of the contributors were sociology Ph.D.'s, making the journal fully professionalized in that sense as well. Finally, the proportion of Chicago Ph.D.'s among authors had fallen back to 20 percent from the 30 percent figure that had obtained for the previous four decades; the *AJS* was now considerably more national and probably more democratic than before.

Taken together, this evidence all suggests integration of the *AJS* into a stable national profession with routine careers and a considerably more democratically organized publication system. There is also some evidence of this integration in intellectual terms, for a newly "professionalized" rhetorical structure seems to have become slightly more common in the *AJS* between 1955 and 1965 (Abbott and Barman 1997).

Minor Matters

The book review section of the *AJS* in the transition period functioned increasingly as a separate operation. Although Levinsohn was deeply involved in the "big name" reviews, as she often was in "big name" papers, the main operation ran separately under book review editors. In substantive terms, the *AJS* and *ASR* book review sections had diverged substantially by the 1960s. A study the *AJS* did in 1967 found that the two journals reviewed only 305 books in common in 1962–65. The *AJS* reviewed 546 books that the *ASR* did not and the *ASR* 495 books that the *AJS* did not (AJSAR 1967). The *AJS* pattern of not reviewing the majority of books received thus was not unique.

But the percentage of books received that were reviewed fell steadily through the 1960s and 1970s. There were several reasons. For one thing, more and more books came to the journal. The *AJS* was receiving about 600 books a year in the early 1960s, about 1,000 in the late 1960s, and 1,500 by 1972. The number of reviews at first kept a proportionate pace, but the Anderson regime started with a dramatic cut in the number of reviews (from 209 in volume 71 to 121 in volume 72 and 87 in volume 73).

Apparently there was a conscious choice to make reviews longer. In 1967 reviews averaged 0.96 page, about the same as in 1962. (Even then the *AJS* reviews were longer than the *ASR*'s, which averaged 0.65 page in 1962.) But in 1972 *AJS* reviews averaged 2.3 pages. As a result the *AJS* went from reviewing about a quarter of the books it received to reviewing a tenth. Levinsohn sold the leftovers to build a slush fund for new office furnishings, air-conditioning, and the occasional party. It seems clear that this change was part of Levinsohn's general strategy to increase controversial, intellectual content at the expense of short, informational reviews. The split of *Contemporary Sociology* out of the *ASR* in 1972 made the *AJS*'s move seem prescient, since one of its aims was to provide space for more substantial review essays.

The era of annual special issues came to a close early in the Hughes editorship. Special issues still occasionally appeared, and one of them, "Changing Women in a Changing Society" proved the scholarly equivalent of a best-seller. The issue originated with Levinsohn, who recruited Joan Huber—then an assistant professor at the University of Illinois—to edit it. Huber struggled through the inevitable editorial problems, which included turning down some well-known figures for the issue, most of which was filled by open submissions. With her eye on what she correctly saw as a rapidly breaking market, Levinsohn bet the ranch. There were 122,000 brochures, 57,000 direct mailings, and hundreds of letters to feminist organizations and publications, plus an arranged review in *Ms.* magazine. In the end, the doomsayers of the department were humbled by the issue's extraordinary success. The first print run sold out before it was produced, and a paperback was brought out two months early to fill the demand. Eventual sales were well over 20,000, not to mention the subscribers who got the issue automatically (CEB to EOL, 21 August 1979, with the AJSARs). This success helped persuade the Press to create *Signs*. But the other special issues did not fare as well. "The Changing Face of the Suburbs" and "Turning Points" (a life history issue) were by comparison minor successes, both reaching about 1,800 copies in their book manifestations.

The transition era came to a close with Charles Bidwell's firm reassertion of the purely professional character of the *AJS* after 1974. Both transition editorships had produced hybrid journals. The Blau *AJS* instituted the new discipline of double-blind reviewing and had a more narrowly professionalized focus than the Hughes *Journal*. But it was still a small-time affair, an elite autocrat and his peers producing a focused journal. The Anderson *AJS* was democratized beyond anyone's wildest conceptions: in editorial practices, in contributors, in reviewers, in topics. Returning to the broader

Hughesian conception, it reflected Florence Levinsohn's drive to create a readable professional magazine of a type not successfully produced in the social sciences until the *Journal of Economic Perspectives* appeared in 1987. But the Anderson *AJS* was buried under an avalanche of submissions that questioned the entire practical and moral structure of reviewing as Blau and Rossi had imagined it. It was Charles Bidwell who returned the *AJS* to a more conventional structure and, in so doing, resolved some of the basic dilemmas in the moral relations between editor, authors, and reviewers.

6   The *AJS* in Modern Form

Since many of the participants are still active sociologists, my discussion of the *American Journal of Sociology*'s recent years must of necessity be less focused than that of earlier periods. The central intellectual interest of the *Journal*'s past twenty-five years lies in the establishment, by Charles Bidwell and Edward Laumann, of the current concepts of the editor's role and of the *AJS*'s publication policy. A discussion of these leads naturally into a conclusion examining the role of journals in the current discipline.

Editors and Their Workload

The Department of Sociology's continuing difficulty in finding editors for the *AJS* is evident in the list of prominent Chicago faculty over the past forty years who did not edit the journal. One can understand why quantitative specialists like Bogue and Goodman did not become *AJS* editors, and perhaps Suttles for the equivalent converse reason. But that the *AJS* was never edited by Hauser, Coleman, Wilson, or Janowitz proclaims an obvious message. Scholars with large administrative responsibilities had little time for editing. This ruled out heavy grantees like Hauser and Coleman, as it did department chairs like Hauser, Wilson, and Janowitz. Of these men only Janowitz undertook a substantial editing task, and that was his attempt to bring the Chicago school back to life through the Heritage of Sociology series. With all their alternative avenues of power, Hauser and the others apparently felt neither an interest in editing the *AJS* nor an obligation to do so.

One sign of the wearing nature of the job was the shortening of the editorial term. Faris, Burgess, Blumer, and Hughes took the *AJS* through thirty-six years. The next thirty-four years saw six editors: Blau, Anderson, Bidwell, Laumann, William Parish, and Marta Tienda. (By comparison, the ASA journals have had three-year editorial terms throughout the past forty years.) The job would have been much worse but for the energetic efficiency efforts through which Charles Bidwell created a structure that, undergirded with computer databases introduced by Laumann and extended by Parish, made the job a reasonable task for a working faculty member.

Bidwell's efforts arose from more specific concerns than simple manuscript efficiency. In the mid-1970s the *ASR* considered introducing page charges, a standard policy throughout the heavily grant-funded sciences through which grant money helped support journals. The ASA eventually settled for submission fees, which began in late 1978. Such journal fees radically changed the submission incentives for authors. Bidwell feared inundation at the feeless *AJS*. In continuous consultation with Everett Wilson at *Social Forces,* Bidwell introduced manuscript processing fees in 1977, before the ASA discussions were final. Both men worried about the effect on impecunious scholars, but at the same time they recognized that there were savings to the broader group of subscribers, who had effectively been subsidizing prospective authors. Above all, Bidwell said, "it seemed better to fall in step—in part because otherwise we were afraid of a heavy increase of trivial and inept manuscripts" (CEB to Everett Wilson, 2 November 1977). Since the *AJS* was quite marginal financially at this point, the money would be helpful, too.

The results were dramatic. From the peak level of about six hundred manuscripts a year, which obtained throughout the mid-1970s, the submission rate quickly fell back to about three hundred in 1980. Half of this fall came in the first year of the submission fee policy. With occasional digressions, the submission rate has stayed at about three hundred manuscripts a year ever since.

Another result of this policy was the virtual disappearance of rejections without refereeing. When he first took over, Charles Bidwell continued the practice of prejection, although not at the earlier draconian level. In 1974 there were 643 manuscripts processed, of which 17 percent were rejected without review. But the papers for which prejection was deemed appropriate simply disappeared under the new policy. (Perhaps only ten to twenty such papers were now received each year.) *AJS* practice thus came into line with what was emerging as a norm in the field; universal review would eventually be all but explicitly mandated in the ASA Code of Ethics (2.C.1, 2).

Another result was the recovery of acceptance rates. These returned to their long-term average level of about 14 percent by 1980. This figure drifted slowly back down through the 1980s, however, and in the late 1980s and 1990s began to dip below 10 percent again. The culprit was article length. Articles had gained about 40 percent in length between 1962 and 1971. By the time of Tienda's editorship (1992), the figure had again risen by 40 percent, with articles averaging about thirty (new) pages, roughly twice as long as the articles thirty years before.

A not insignificant part of the increase in length of *AJS* articles was caused by the expansion of reference lists, which contributed length both within the article and at its end. The average number of items cited in a published *AJS* article nearly doubled between 1973 and 1992, going from a little over thirty to just under sixty. Most of this change came at the bottom of the distribution. The *AJS* has always had a few massive reference lists; lists of 160 items or more appear as early as the mid-1970s. But the tiny lists disappeared. In my sample, the shortest list in a given year typically cited ten to fifteen items in the mid-1970s. By the 1990s it was twenty-five to thirty.[1] The number of full-page tables also increased sharply, a change with even more dramatic implications for article length.

Like other editors before and after, Bidwell tried to tame the page expansion by encouraging authors to turn routine papers into research notes. As always, this policy proved a failure. Authors simply took their articles elsewhere or injected a new theoretical twist to justify their length. Replication has never become a sociological genre.

Even more important for public relations was Bidwell's near obsession with time to review. Concerns about time to review dated from well back into the Hughes editorship. In the Levinsohn era these continued, with department faculty among the worst offenders. When Bidwell took over, median time to decision was about 20 weeks, with many manuscripts waiting over six months. Bidwell got the time down to a mean of 5.3 weeks in 1974–75, but much of this was achieved by up-front rejections. Reviewed manuscripts took an average of 7.1 weeks. By the late 1970s, prejection had been abandoned. Mean review time had again edged up over three months.

Over time, Bidwell was helped by the decline in submissions. When he took over there were a grand total of about six hundred referees used in a given year, which, as he told the consulting editors frankly, led to distinct quality problems. But declining submissions meant less need for ad hoc referees, which Bidwell hoped would free him from reliance on the slow and the bad. Indeed, he was able to trim about 20 percent of his ad hoc referees in the wake of the imposition of submission fees. Moreover, the load was shifted to the consulting editors, who were told—for neither the first nor the last time (recall Rossi's 1957 plan)—to expect two papers a month. All papers would be sent to one consulting editor and one ad hoc reviewer. In the three years before 1974, consulting editors in fact read only 5 percent of papers, editorial board members (department faculty) 13 percent, other

---

1. I considered the first ten substantive, nonreview articles in each volume's March number from 1973 to 1992.

university staff or students 7 percent, and ad hoc readers 75 percent. By 1976, consulting editors read 27 percent, editorial board 8 percent, staff and students 8 percent, and ad hoc readers 57 percent. The figures changed further as the consulting board was expanded.

As it happened, the reallocation of reviewing had little direct effect on review time, for mean reading times were roughly comparable in all four groups and changed little over time. But the reallocation meant much better quality control, which in turn meant fewer referees' comments to ameliorate and fewer split decisions. As a result, Bidwell made dramatic cuts in the time to decision once reviews were received. Together with a faster allocation of articles to reviewers, these cuts allowed him to accept an unchanging period for refereeing itself (about one month median time from mailing the documents to receiving the review) and still achieve a large reduction in overall turnaround for fully reviewed papers.

Bidwell's quality control efforts apparently led him to favor older scholars. The average professional age of referees rose to thirteen years post-Ph.D. in the early Bidwell years. But it plateaued or fell slightly at the end of Bidwell's tenure, reflecting his increasing penchant for student reviewers. (Staff and students read as many as 11 percent of papers in his later years as editor.) After this point the ad hoc referees, like the discipline as a whole, grew slowly older as the input of new young sociologists slowed. The figure drifted upward under Laumann and Parish, hitting eighteen years post-Ph.D. at the end of Parish's editorship. Put another way, the percentage of ad hoc referees within six years of Ph.D.—the assistant professor ranks—fell from about 40 percent under Anderson to about 20 percent under Parish.

As the correspondence between Bidwell and editors of other major journals indicates, the problems of overload and review quality that the *AJS* confronted in this period were quite general to sociology journals. Indeed, these common problems were discussed at regular group meetings for sociology editors held at the ASA meetings. The "high wall" between the *AJS* and the *ASR* created in the 1930s had endured at least twenty years; Helen Hughes had made much of a secret visit to the *AJS* by R. E. L. Faris, former classmate and *ASR* editor in the 1950s. But by the 1960s annual ASA sessions—now involving editors of a wide variety of journals—were a regular event with an extensive agenda. That agenda was organized mainly around the problems of overload and review quality. But in many ways the most important issue was the problem of what exactly were the obligations of editor, author, and reviewer in the new world of scholarly publishing.

Disciplinary changes had run this question together with the old worry about the flight of senior papers and creative work.

The Emotional Economy of Contributors and Manuscripts

Probably more important than his taming of the submissions surplus was Charles Bidwell's settling of the *AJS* editorship into a consistent moral and emotional stance toward these questions of journal obligation. The structure he created was then consolidated and extended by his successor Edward Laumann. Central to Bidwell's changing of the editorship was his recognition that the journal's heavy freight of moral obligations had increased, since it had become apparent to him as to other journal editors that the modal would-be author was now a young person whose career was at risk.

It is difficult to establish exactly how far young people became relatively more likely to submit to the *AJS* in the years after 1970. For one thing, the demographics of the discipline guaranteed increasing dominance of the journals by the young. The high disciplinary birthrates of the 1960s meant a "baby boom" and a young discipline, and this alone meant relatively more young submitters. Even more important, in the 1960s these young scholars had been absorbed with eagerness and little question by the rapidly expanding universities. But expansion slowed as the 1970s wore on, and well before the professional baby boom had fully traversed the Ph.D. pipeline, the level of talent required to remain in academics began to rise. Moreover, a wide range of universities and even four-year colleges took advantage of the market to recast themselves in the research mold, broadening the research ethic with its emphasis on publication at the expense of teaching. Although this eased the employment market slightly, it meant publications became even more widely important. Yet except for those whose patrons could slip their work into edited volumes, members of these new large cohorts had no access to publication other than refereed journals.

For all these reasons, a dominance of the journals by younger authors from the 1970s onward was guaranteed. The forces pushing the young into the journals were aided by what seemed to be the continuing withdrawal of the senior, famous members of the discipline. Usually one bad experience was enough to send them scurrying to the security of edited volumes and solicitations.

The review process is intolerably slow and not notably better than that of other journals of comparable standing. I have no illusions my soft annoyance will weigh any more heavily on you than that of more cantankerous authors . . . but it gives me pleasure to "punish" you. It adds to stories to tell friends and grandchildren—the time we deprived nice Charles Bidwell of a chance to publish something interesting. (Very famous author withdrawing a manuscript that got an R&R [revise and resubmit] judgment, 1977).

I have not submitted a paper to *AJS* for many years—not since an experience where one review accepted the paper with no qualifications, and the other damned it. I countered the poor reviewer's comments—to no avail. (Well-known author, as an addendum to a review document, 1980)

Laumann wrote to one consulting editor in 1980: "Many established authors stop trying the major journals because they feel they are likely to be ill-used by overly critical referees. I think, unfortunately, this is the price we pay for the anonymity of the review process."

Prominent authors were helped in this flight by the curious fact that despite the glut of papers at the major journals, editors of new, struggling journals were often desperate for papers, and particularly for prestigious papers. Direct solicitation of papers from eminent sociologists was common. There was, too, a rapid spread of "special issues," which for most journals were essentially a means by which an editor short of material got someone else to produce an edited volume using journal space. Special issue editors always wanted a few high-profile authors, and indeed such issues often started as (solicited) conference sessions, with the same needs for visibility. Another important factor was the burgeoning market of almost completely solicited annuals. Although the *Annual Review* stuck to true review articles—which had never appeared in the *AJS* or the *ASR* to any great extent—quite a number of other annuals began to appear, all publishing theoretical pieces and current research. With their need for visible names, these annuals gave major figures an easy outlet for articles that would otherwise have gone to refereed journals. Between the second-tier journals and the annuals, well-known scholars could publish most or all of their work on a solicitation basis if they so chose.

Given these incentives, senior writers seemed in the 1970s to be deserting the journals faster than before. Those who remained were much more likely to be joined by junior coauthors, for authorship lists show a distinct rise of coauthorship by the mid-1970s. The trend may in part have reflected a true increase in collaborative work. Yet in many cases the division of labor was exactly what it had been in the 1950s and 1960s. By the late 1970s it had simply become normative to give the research assistants who ran the regressions a share of the marquee billing, no doubt in part because the scholarly market had become so tight.[2]

With the young people flooding in and the established ebbing out, by the late 1970s journal publishing was clearly a young person's game. Journals like the *AJS* therefore became the main judges of young people's work for tenure. Correspondence in the files underscores this fact. On 2 December 1977 Bidwell answered the dean of a major university with the assurance that X's paper was indeed under review at the *AJS*. In 1981 Edward Laumann received a letter from an author whose paper had already appeared in the *AJS:*

> Within my department, faculty members are, of course, familiar with AJS and perceive it to be of highest quality. However, officials outside my department who are involved in tenure and promotion decisions (e.g., college committees, deans, etc.) are not necessarily familiar with AJS or any other journal in which sociologists publish. One bit of information which seems to aid these individuals in evaluating the quality of a journal is its acceptance/rejection rate. . . . If you happen to know what the rate was for [X] (the year my article was published) it would be most helpful.

It would be hard to imagine Peter Blau receiving or replying to such a letter, but Laumann dutifully sent off the rejection rate of 85 percent.

Such documents were the visible tip of a monstrous iceberg calved from the glacial flow of tenure proceedings. It was painfully clear to the editors who received these letters that deans and their committees were unable or unwilling to read candidates' scholarship, mistrustful of their own departments' judgments, and disinclined to do more than count numbers of entries on vitae. Young people's professional lives rested on the journals in an immediate sense. Due process had very high stakes.

For their part, young authors widely believed in the randomness (at best) of reviewing. One exasperated positive referee, himself in early mid-career, was contacted through the *AJS* by a rejected young author and wrote back: "Do not be discouraged by difficulties in publishing. I have published 29 articles in the last nine years and from this experience I can tell you in all seriousness that publication is a result of 'pure chance' aided by the selective processes of reviewers, without any reference to the quality of material" (1977).

2. This change of mores regarding coauthorship is yet another reason it is extremely difficult to estimate whether there "really was" an increased dominance of the journal by the young beyond that expected by the demographic changes. The rise of coauthorship is overwhelming in the modern period.

The situation would have been comical had it not been so sad. Prospective senior authors fled the journals to spare themselves the hassle of referees, thereby hiding their work from most colleagues. Prospective junior authors felt the article process to be absolutely central to their careers but more or less random. Meanwhile, editors felt an enormous responsibility, even an obsession, for fairness.

The extraordinary complexity of these issues was evident to Bidwell immediately on taking over the *AJS* in 1974. His response was to surround the editor's role with a nimbus of ethics. He wrote to one referee who complained of getting too many bad papers: "Even though the Associate Editors and I try to screen out the weakest, we are reluctant to be too harsh without the benefit of referees' comments." Not only was he worried about the quality of the papers, he was also concerned to smooth the feathers of troubled referees and deeply worried about the morals of deviating from explicit process. This cajoling, caring tone runs throughout his correspondence, whether with authors, reviewers, or editors.

> I am sorry to tell you we cannot consider papers as sets. If you want them to be considered individually, we should be very pleased. . . . I'm always pleased to know of persons interested in reviewing manuscripts at AJS. (To someone who volunteered to review)

> We draw widely on colleagues for review, so I am happy to have this useful intelligence. (To another volunteer)

> It's full of interesting things but I'm afraid speeches are speeches and articles are articles. (To someone asking him for a quick judgment)

When attacked, Bidwell took his stand on the clarity and consistency of his ethical position. To an author claiming that "it was professionally irresponsible and unethical for you to take 7 months to review my article," Bidwell wrote:

> This review took five reviewers. Had we failed to keep you informed of our difficulties in review, you would have been right that we were unethical. I believe we did our best and fulfilled our obligations. You were kept informed of the slow progress of your paper through review. Had you chosen, you could have withdrawn your paper at any time after the three months' limit.

The sheer subjunctivity of this passage underscores the extraordinarily self-conscious moral care with which Bidwell surrounded the editorship. His emphasis on cleaning up problems like that of undisciplined reviewers was evident in his discussion of the *AJS* policy of sending copies of all referees' comments to author and other referees: "We do indeed send all referees' comments to authors. The only exception would be an obviously irresponsible or ad hominem review, and I have not seen one of these since I began editing the Journal." In fact they had existed, but Bidwell quickly stamped them out.

But if moral regularization steadied the relations between author, referee, and editor, there remained, increasingly annoying, the problem of the flight of interesting and senior work. Surely some of this feeling of loss—how much we cannot know—was attributable to the perpetual sadness of aging. Editing is an activity of middle age, and nothing we know in middle age can have the unquestioned greatness we assigned to the things we read in our first professional years. But though well aware of this tendency, Bidwell and Laumann were still both convinced that they faced a dearth of good papers.

In hindsight, it seems clear that the flight of this work was in part driven by the necessities of public due process for papers, as Hughes had predicted it would be. Moral regularization was the solution for one set of problems but in part the origin of others. Eminent people wrote a disproportionate amount of important and interesting work but now had little incentive to send it to the *AJS*. But the flight of interesting work was also furthered by the fact that several of the new hot areas of sociology—particularly political sociology, historical sociology, and substantial areas of Marxism—leaned toward the production of books rather than articles. At the same time, by the mid-1970s, the pathbreaking work that could be done with the new quantitative techniques of causalism had been done. There remained only the enormous amount of normal science that the Duncan-Blalock view of the world made possible. New articles within this paradigm were better suited to the research note format characteristic of *Psychological Reports* than to the ever-lengthening *AJS* format; but despite energetic efforts no *AJS* editor, nor any other sociology editor to my knowledge, has succeeded in selling the short form effectively. As a result, the journals were buried under highly competent normal science, at a time when pressures for due process committed them increasingly to judge based on competence rather than on interest or importance.[3]

In many ways the "reality" of whether interesting papers were disap-

3. Thus every new submission in status attainment had its new minor theoretical twist, just as the papers on revolution and population ecology would in the 1980s. The result was a kind of "theory churning" instead of the scientific replication for which Duncan, at least, had hoped. As Bidwell said to his editors at the *AJS* lunch in 1974, "Obviously the editors must take great care that acceptance not occur too frequently among the many manuscripts that are competent but little more."

pearing was less important than the definitions of and reactions to the supposed phenomenon. Outsiders tended to attribute the disappearance of great papers to editorial timidity. As one reviewer wrote on an addendum:

> It has occurred to me that with the pressure for space on the "major" journals in sociology, if one reviewer has any qualms, that is death for a paper, and the whole thing becomes too much a matter of chance or who gets the manuscript. Too bad. Also there is probably a pressure toward orthodoxy, which has made our journals so dull and sterile. (1980)

The reviewer quoted above continued his remarks to the young author rejected in just such a split decision:

> There are two kinds of papers which seldom appear in journals: very poor ones and, unfortunately, the best ones ever written. Yours falls in the latter category, so do not be surprised by any difficulties you may face. Really good work is almost invariably rejected because (1) the reviewers are too ignorant to appreciate its significance (the usual case) and (2) it threatens the interests of persons established in the field.

Indeed, even some editors believed such an explanation. The editor of another top sociology journal wrote to Bidwell in 1978, seeing a combination of timidity and weak submissions:

> In essence, it's the problem of editorial timidity compounded by the reality of the prosaic nature of submitted MSS which is, in turn, a function of graduate training. How do we judge pieces? The clearest and simplest criterion is sophistication in collecting, reducing, and manipulating data. Lacking that, we reject. Blessed with it, we're inclined to accept despite the absence of a generative quality in its substance. . . . Our impulse is to accept pieces that close an issue rather than ones that open up issues. Other things equal, I think it more important that a manuscript be stimulating although wrong [rather] than right and dully terminal—or terminally dull.
>
> It is not a case of being too well trained in methods of research. That can scarcely be the case. It is rather a matter of being too poorly trained in other realms, particularly in theory.

But Bidwell and Laumann found several things wrong with thinking their timidity was the problem, quite aside from their own self-knowledge. For one thing, the idea that stodgy establishment professors killed revolutionary papers was suspicious indeed. Murderers tended to be young. One referee, herself a former journal editor, spoke for many people when she wrote to Laumann in 1980 about the dilemmas of the overworked reviewer:

> I could pass on a manuscript to a junior colleague or senior gradu-
> ate student who could do just as well as I in weeding out the im-
> possible papers. The problem is with the potentially salvageable
> and ultimately worthwhile papers. My juniors, like most others,
> tend to be arrogant and snotty, and I would feel a responsibility to
> at least monitor the comments they sent to the poor authors, but I
> would not be able to spot a paper that might be revised into a real
> contribution without going through the whole process myself.

Most experienced editors seemed to agree that young people were more closed-minded than their elders.

But more important, editors could not publish what did not get sent to them in the first place. One other highly ranked sociology journal in 1980 (and perhaps other years) simply advertised for good papers, sending a general form letter to all recipients of National Science Foundation grants:

> When the fruits of your NSF-funded research materialize, we'd be
> pleased if you'd chip off a paper or two and try it out on [X]. What
> we need, (as you know) is a paper written with the parsimony of
> poetry, the lucidity of E. B. White, and one that has the stunning ef-
> fect of a new world view. PS Quite seriously, we are interested.

Even referees wondered where the good papers had gone. One regular referee wrote to Bidwell wondering:

> Am I getting an unusually weak batch of manuscripts, or am I un-
> usually critical, or is the rejection rate at *AJS* as high as would be
> demanded by the quality of the manuscripts I have been seeing?
> (1978)

Bidwell replied:

> I hope you won't be too distressed by the quality of the manu-
> scripts that we send to you. What you are getting, I am afraid, is a
> pretty good sample of the universe of quality.

But while some referees wondered why they never got interesting papers, others felt that a paper's degree of "interest" was an irrelevant or illegitimate consideration. Only competence should matter. One referee declined to review a manuscript, saying, "The whole topic of this paper bores me, and I suspect I would be less than impartial," as if there were no chance that his boredom was a responsible and important judgment. Another wrote, protesting an acceptance letter that did not require the revisions he suggested:

> As the other reviewer points out, it is an elegant and interesting article, but it is a little too thin and too vague as written. I applaud the fact that AJS accepts essays and I hope it continues doing so. AJS's standards are, however, extremely strict. . . . I am therefore disturbed by an editorial decision which does not quite respect the sense of the reviews.

Laumann replied:

> The problem is in distinguishing the "clearly deficient" from the "competent but stimulating." All too often the issue rests almost entirely in the eye of the beholder.

Thus there emerged a complex calculus in which some people identified quality with interest, some people saw quality as orthogonal to interest, and some people thought interest was irrelevant altogether. But everyone seemed to agree that quality and interest were in short supply. By the beginning of the Laumann years the *AJS* was openly asking its editors to beat the bushes for papers.

As editor, Laumann continued the Bidwellian moral structure. But his correspondence focused on it less: everyone now knew how to behave. Laumann devoted more of his attention to formulating self-conscious standards for publication, with an eye to codifying the search for interesting work:

> Only in the event of exceptional major, innovative contributions have we very reluctantly agreed to publish a manuscript in two parts. In general we would like to avoid papers which are essentially exegetical of the published writings of theorists, though on occasion we have published such papers.

> This paper would not survive a normal AJS review for publication in its present form because it is so heavily descriptive and appears to lack adequate linkage to the broader sociological literature.

> Our policy is to publish *original* research, contributions of an empirical, theoretical, or methodological nature. We do not publish review essays. . . . Obviously the line between these two sorts of contributions may not always be self-evident.

> While we have no inflexible policy on these matters, we generally see ourselves in the market for original empirical, theoretical and/

or methodological papers rather than "state of the art" or pre-scription pieces.

I add, of course, that the paper would have to break new ground. . . . Longstanding journal policy states that we publish only original scholarly contributions (as distinguished, for example, from essays that review a literature or that summarize work published elsewhere).

Given our diverse readership, we are most responsive to manu-scripts that announce important new results or advance a distinc-tive formulation that goes beyond "normal science" contributions to a particular specialty area.

Many of these quotes come from letters to authors who asked Laumann for a preliminary opinion, something he gave much more frequently than had Bidwell. As they make clear, he referred papers out for being too spe-cialized, too unscholarly, and too standardized. The result was to produce a journal with a specific niche, particularly by contrast with the *ASR*. It was in many ways the niche that had been described by Burgess in his document of 1936. On the positive side, Laumann's general message helped the *AJS* attract innovative papers. On the negative side, the insistence on something new (and a similar insistence elsewhere) led to much "theory churning," in which authors sought to dress up minor changes on established ideas as im-portant innovations.

At the same time, the business of disciplining the whole scholarly process went on steadily. By Laumann's time there was emerging an explicit system for rating referees in terms of turnaround time, "black hole" coeffi-cient, agreement with other referees, and so on. There was also a blacklist of bad referees, mostly made up of famous people who looked obviously appropriate but did terrible work. The "teaching" motif was now stan-dard, even normative. When one reviewer wrote in wondering whether she was not "overreviewing" because her reviews were so much longer than those of other referees, Laumann replied:

I only wish more referees were as conscientious and helpful as you are in assisting their colleagues to improve their work. Our pur-pose in sending the referee copies of the other referees' comments is precisely to encourage them to raise the standard of their own contribution as well as to give them some sense of the convergent validity of their judgment.

The policy of sending all comments to all referees had begun in the mid-1970s under Bidwell. The teaching was now to take place *between referees* as well as between referee and author. We are a long way from the Blau-model journal in which an elite judges itself and its juniors.

By the Laumann era, there were also clear policies about where to find referees—in citation lists of published work. They were then tested out and retained if they did a good job. Purging people from the referee list was a regular and routine matter. There were occasional write-in volunteers, most of whom sent a vita and a letter describing their interests. (A few of these went on the list.) And organizations (nearly always of women sociologists) sometimes sent in long lists of potential referees.[4] But the central criterion for referees continued to be that they have some sense of how a referee ought to behave, an experience most effectively acquired by adverse personal experience. Therefore the published literature was the best place to look for well-behaved referees who would not be, like the graduate students noted above, "arrogant and snotty." This method of finding new referees of course speeded the disciplining of the referee pool very effectively.

The attempt to meet all the conflicting moral and emotional obligations of the *AJS* had distinct costs. The major one was a further increase in bureaucratization and scrutiny. Throughout the Bidwell and Laumann years the percentage of submissions for which revisions were invited rose slowly but very steadily from less than 10 percent to over 15 percent. It has risen further since, sometimes hitting 25 percent of submissions. Because of the higher acceptance rate on revisions (about 30 percent in the Bidwell years, it rose to nearly 67 percent in the early Laumann years and has settled at about 50 percent in the past decade), authors nearly always wanted to accept the invitation to revise. Therefore, for many referees papers came twice. As early as the 1980s, the *AJS* was having major problems with turn-downs from substantial numbers of ad hoc referees who felt overworked. In 1983–84, for 30 percent of manuscripts four or more reviewers had to be asked in order to get the necessary two responses. Papers for which no revisions were required have now fallen to a trivial handful, at present fewer than ten in the average year.

Business Matters

The *AJS* continued in the modern era its role as a major cash flow item for the University of Chicago Press. Unfortunately the Press is unwilling to release its current and recent budget data. But I can report here some figures from data that happened to be in the *AJS* records themselves.

4. When the ASA Committee on the Status of Women in Sociology sent Laumann a list of 116 names with résumés in 1982, it included quite a number of eminent women who had refereed for the *AJS* for many years.

In 1981, for example, the journal sold $250,000 in subscriptions, accepted $18,000 in advertising, and enjoyed a few other, minor sources of income (submission fees, reprints, and single-copy sales), for a total income of $282,000. Against this were set off manufacturing costs of $85,000, editorial expenses of $45,000, postage of $15,000, promotion of $10,000, and a host of other expenses totaling about $195,000. The Press took $59,000 as its overhead. The overhead costs reflected directly billed hours of production, editorial, and advertising staff, plus business and subscription office costs prorated by the *AJS* proportion of the total Press subscription list. In the end, the journal was deemed to have a net profit of $28,000, a very handsome 10 percent on revenue. By comparison, the *ASR* makes a "paper profit" of several hundred thousand dollars but has quite different budgeting conventions. Oddly enough, where the University of Chicago Press originally saw the ASA as a captive market on which to support its journal of sociology, the ASA now uses its journal program (with a largely captive [in normative terms] market of members) as a cash cow that supports organizational activities. Overall, the ASA journals contribute a large surplus to the organization, even though only two or three of them actually make money.

As any reader knows, the University of Chicago Press promotes the *AJS* with gusto, indeed abandon. In a typical year (1980), *AJS* promotional brochures and samples appeared in thirteen Press booth exhibits, ranging as far as the Frankfurt Book Fair and the Council on Social Work Education, in addition to the usual ASA, American Political Science Association, and American Anthropological Association venues. But as parts of other exhibits (e.g., the American Association of University Presses), the same materials appeared at another twenty-six sites, including a conference on the redefinition of public and private spheres in Montreal, the Kansas Social Welfare Association meeting in Wichita, and the Great Lakes History Conference in Grand Rapids.[5]

The *AJS* as an Institution of Time

In summing up the history of the *AJS*, I would like to return to the theme of change and continuity that has underlain earlier chapters. As I

5. The Press also pushed the *AJS*, at least early in the recent period, to carry general purpose (nonscholarly) advertising. This had not been urged since the very early days of the journal. But when Peter Rossi began his 1957 putsch attempt, the Press was clearly pressuring on this matter. Helen Hughes wrote with blunt sarcasm to Rossi (7 January 1958): "You will be interested to know that this is not the first time the press has raised the question of our carrying advertising for hotels, railroads, office supply companies, and so on. . . . I think the *American Anthropologist* looked cheap of late years with its advertising of plane and railroad excursions and hotels in the Southwest."

have several times noted, the most important continuity of the *AJS* is physical. The journal *looks* like a single thing throughout its century of existence. That said, it has had in fact several different social and cultural
natures during its various periods.

The *AJS* began as a personal statement, by one man, of his vision of a set
of ideas that could and should be pulled together into a system. Those
ideas—reformism, formal study of society, historical reflection—gave a
loose unity to a set of cultural artifacts grabbed from diverse sources in
fairly haphazard ways. Small was not, in the modern sense, a member of a
discipline. Rather, he and his peers were trying to found a discipline; the *AJS*
was a useful tool in that endeavor, just as the University of Chicago Press
found the American Sociological Society a useful marketing tool for its own
aims of outreach and profit. For Small and his colleagues the *Journal,* like
the new sociology departments and the national association, was an institution aimed at anchoring a type of inquiry (as yet unclear in any detail) in
a particular institutional setting (the newly transformed American university). What they desired to found was not necessarily what resulted, of
course. Small did not by any means want reformism to disappear from sociology.

The middle period *AJS* built on that foundation. But like the ASA in
the same period, it separated itself from the reformist tradition, stressing a
"scientific ethic" that eased that transformation, even though it opened the
door to a statistical paradigm that would ultimately become the tail that
wagged the sociological dog. Albion Small's *AJS* was retrospectively redefined (by people like H. P. Becker [1930, 1932] in his survey of topics) into
the prodromal stirrings of a formal academic discipline, muddied at times
by explicit reformist work and historical vagueness. Controlled by a small
group of close friends, the middle period *AJS* embodied a cohesive vision of
what doing sociology was—the vision whose ultimate form was described
in chapter 2—but did so not through a set of fixed practices or routines, but
rather through the common project of sharing judgments of work. As the
reviewing of this era shows, even fairly serious differences were ignored; editors trusted colleagues for manuscript judgments that took expertise for
granted and moved beyond competence to questions about papers' interest
and importance.

The primary group that supported the middle period *AJS* consisted of
members of a discipline, to be sure, but one that was in decline for much of
the period, threatened by depression and war. Moreover, having finally stabilized as a social structure in the 1930s, sociology at once began the
process of fractionation that produced subdisciplines (and their journals)

steadily right down to the present. The *AJS*'s other crucial context—the department—remained fairly stable for much of the middle period but underwent crisis toward the end. Indeed, the Rossi-Blau transformation of the *AJS* grew directly out of the quantitative triumph of the late 1950s.

That transition, as I have argued, also reflected a number of other forces: the sudden expansion of disciplinary numbers, the generational transition to the younger products of a more highly professionalized era, the rise of a more strongly scientized ideology of investigation. In such a context the *AJS* was available to serve new aims. As a social structure, the *Journal* stayed relatively constant under Blau; it was still based on personal trust. The main change was the shift to double-blind reviewing with its strong presumption of shared disciplinary norms, another aspect of the ideology of scientism. But even this new technique still rested, from the editor's point of view, on personal trust. The transition period indeed brought a full and formal regularization of the review process, although Blau retained Hughes's autocratic approach to editorship. The transition *AJS* was thus a hybrid, founded on the idea that the formal rationality of duly processed reviews would couple directly with shared norms of scientific behavior. This presumed a disciplinary unity that was in fact merely that of a single paradigm.

Although growth slackened slightly in the 1960s, by now the absolute numbers of sociologists were so large that even slower growth once again overturned the *AJS*'s social and cultural structure. Particularly in the 1960s, growth brought extraordinary diversity, and scientific peer review as envisioned in the late 1950s quickly became something of a mirage. The vast new need for referees underscored the diversity of interests as well as of ability in the discipline. Needing to tame the whirlwind, Charles Bidwell, like his colleagues at other journals, opted for a strong reliance on procedural rationality. In some ways he was forced to this by the new role of the journals in tenure proceedings, as by other ways in which whipsawing academic markets drove all but the most competitive, most needy, and most rationalized submitters away from the journals. By this time the *AJS* was being shaped from outside by the discipline, rather than shaping that discipline as it had done in the early and middle periods.

The *AJS*'s position in the department was new as well. Central to department life throughout the first seventy years of its existence, in the modern era the *Journal* became more and more peripheral. Years might pass without any discussion of *AJS* business in department meetings beyond a perfunctory annual report. This too signified the *Journal*'s control by larger disciplinary structures. All the same, the lines of differentiation between the

AJS and the *ASR* first laid out by Ernest Burgess in 1936 persist in the present. The *AJS* continues to have longer articles, longer reviews, and a generally less formulaic intellectual content than do the ASA journals.

In short, over its long history the *AJS* has maintained a certain internal continuity and lineage of development at the same time as it has found itself structurally constituted out of a changing array of environing materials. The internal lineage of social structure—best captured in the history of editorial processes—runs from personal entrepreneurship to primary group sharing to full-scale bureaucracy. Students have become ever more important in this process (the *AJS* now has as many student associate editors as faculty ones) and faculty less (most members of the "editorial board" [the faculty] function merely as referees). The external lineages bound in with this internal continuity have, as I noted, changed greatly. The typical authors have gone from being editorial cronies to being fellow members of a disciplinary elite on the make (of varying ages) to being the ambitious young of an established discipline. In these material senses, the *Journal* has become an institution of the young. Most important of the changes in social structure, however, is the degree to which general disciplinary norms are now bound into the *AJS*'s main conception of itself as an institution. In part this has reflected the transformation of the department toward eclecticism. But even the long stability of the 1970–90 faculty, which certainly had a strong belief in Chicago exceptionalism, did not bring the *Journal* back under departmental control. Indeed, it was this very generation that cemented the disciplinary—as opposed to departmental— vision of the *AJS*.

The cultural lineages have changed too. Internally, the *AJS* now lives under the sign of procedural rationality as never before. The articles have gotten long and are filled with citations, tables, and other scholarly paraphernalia. Article interest—the central criterion for publication over much of the *Journal*'s life—is a now questionable matter. Editors, board members, and referees all mutter that much of what is published is competent but boring, a complaint that dates at least from the 1950s and extends well beyond the *AJS*. After a brief fling in the Levinsohn years, the *AJS* is once again the "good, gray *AJS*."

All of this signifies an absorption of the *AJS* into the discipline in a way that belies the very language of internal/external. The *AJS* is now part of a general disciplinary cultural apparatus, indistinguishable in all but minor ways from its competitors. Its internal history is now part of that larger history.

There is nothing in the *AJS*'s development that forced this result. *Sociol-*

ogy and Social Research, Emory Bogardus's personal journal at the University of Southern California, died recently after eight decades, even though in 1935 it was considered an alternative to the *AJS* and even though such successful general journals as *Sociological Forum* have been started in the past decade. Of course, like the *ASR, Sociological Forum* was a captive audience journal: official journal of the Eastern Sociological Society, with consequent preferential access to markets both for papers and for subscribers. But the *AJS*—which has lacked such access for sixty years—has survived by husbanding its prestige and becoming a disciplinary rather than a departmental journal.

At risk of repeating myself overmuch, I must underline in closing the mistake we make if we think of the *AJS*'s history as a teleological narrative: "rationalization," "emergence of a scientific discipline," "triumph of due process." From today's point of view, it may look like that. But the only real continuity to the *Journal* is its physical structure and the surface similarity of "getting articles and publishing them." The aims of the *AJS,* its constituents, its place vis-à-vis department and discipline, its complex social and cultural structure: all these have steadily shifted, sometimes in response to external forces, sometimes through internal imperatives. The shifts have never been complete. The rebraiding of the various lineages running around and through the *AJS* is slow and intricate. But they add up to a gradual process of metamorphosis that should make us question the very pronoun "it" with which we so easily denote the central subject of this story.

Thus the *AJS*'s history may look long and continuous, but it is in fact made up of a set of successive presents, each one as evanescent as the last. This means that events could happen in the next five to ten years that could completely redefine its story into "the ending of paper journalism in sociology," or "the prehistory of a journal of opinion," or "the revolution against methodology." That is, today's present is in some senses different. For we can act on it in ways that we cannot act on the presents of the past.

The Is and Ought of Sociological Journalism

The sweeping history of the *AJS* thus brings us to the current present and to some important dilemmas in that present. The reader will have noticed that I have distinct views on sociological journalism. It is useful to set them forth in greater detail. I begin by considering some previous work on sociological journals, then turn toward theoretical issues and eventually to prescription.

Most writing about sociological journals has been animated by two concerns.[6] Of these, by far the dominant one has been with equity. A typical paper concerns the question whether the ASA rule against multiple submissions creates a bias against nonelite journals (Peters 1976). The other, much more muted, concern of the literature has been with intellectual content: a nagging worry that the system is not serving the discipline well, that good work is being ignored, that refereeing is slipshod at best (e.g., Glenn 1976).

Both concerns are long-standing, invoking normative passions that have never left sociology since its emergence in the social welfare movement. They arise in the contradiction between the familiar American values of democracy and meritocracy. Logically, these two values can coincide only when all participants in a system are of equal merit in some sense. Yet no one involved in sustaining a discipline of knowledge can hold such a belief, for otherwise that discipline has no criteria for accepting or rejecting contributions and hence no effective existence as a delimitable thing.[7] In practice, the two values have in fact led to divergent views of the journals. Some commentators are more fearful for democracy and others for meritocracy. Those who fear for democracy see the history of journals as a struggle of equity to overcome elitism. Those who fear for meritocracy see it as a problem of intellectual merit trying to survive the obligation of diversity.

As I have noted, most past studies of sociological journals have been in the equity/elitism tradition. They focus on the effect of an author's rank or

6. In the section that follows, I speak not only as historian of the *AJS* but also as a former chair of the ASA Publications Committee (1993–95). One phenomenon that experience underscored is the great difficulty of finding people willing to edit major journals.

Some papers relevant to this section are the following. Hargens 1991 comments on the numbers of journals and the citation of work in them. Burt and Doreian 1982 tested models of journal norms. A number of authors have written about prestige and citation (Glenn 1971; Teevan 1980; Gordon 1982; Christenson and Sigelman 1985; Michaels and Pippert 1986). Others have studied influential authors (Oromaner 1980). A more focused study of the *AJS,* the *ASR,* and Chicago is Evans 1986–87. The topics literature includes Buehler, Hesser, and Weigert 1972; Champion and Morris 1973; Szreter 1983; Assadi 1987; Kinloch 1988; Murray 1988; and Garnett 1988. A few people have worked on characteristics of authors, usually gender (Mackie 1977, 1985; Ward and Grant 1985; and Logan 1988). There is a small but most interesting literature on various aspects of actual editorial behavior—reviewing, rejecting, and so on (Page 1981; Snizek, Dudley, and Hughes 1982; Snizek 1984; Bakanic, McPhail, and Simon 1987, 1989, 1990). There was an interesting review of ideas about sociological journalism in the *American Sociologist* 11, 3 (1976), including five articles. For an interesting comparison in economics, see the papers in the *Journal of Economic Perspectives* 8, 1, in particular Hammermesh 1994.

7. I am aware that there currently exist bodies of theory that believe meritocracy and democracy are in no sense contradictory. Much as I would like to agree with them, I am afraid such arguments simply redefine both terms—but mainly meritocracy—to serve their own convenience. Calling a contradiction a noncontradiction doesn't make it one.

method or gender or institutional affiliation on the publication of a particular article, rather than on changes in the kinds of authors appearing in journals overall. They usually consider only one journal, ignoring the self-selection inherent in the process of submission itself, self-selection that probably accounts for most of the variance in whose articles appear where.

Since at least the 1950s, the *AJS* editors, however, have been more concerned about merit. In this they have not been alone. Writing of his years as editor of the *ASR*, Page (1981) reports, "In the fifties, according to many of its critics, the *Review* was theoretically thin, overloaded with small-scale research reports, and neglectful of important social and sociological issues—charges with which I agreed." Page turned to solicitation to get papers from scholars like Bierstedt, Goode, Hughes, Kroeber, Merton, Moore, Parsons, and Riesman. But solid, nonanecdotal data on the issue of important work simply do not exist. The definitions are too problematic. (What *is* important?) Selection bias is overwhelming. And finally, the causality is often reversed; what is published becomes important partly because it was published. Given these problems, it is not even clear that the question whether important work has ebbed away from the *AJS* or other journals is well formed.

In discussing the modern *AJS* I have mentioned a number of reasons we might expect a flight of important work from central disciplinary journals. Concern about this issue is by no means unique to sociologists. Economists have recently presented a long list of classic pieces by major authors that were rejected in peer review (Gans and Shepherd 1994). For example, James Tobin's extension of probit analysis to the multiple regressor case was rejected not once but twice by the *Journal of the American Statistical Association*. But in sociology, evidence is less clear. Certainly there were major new sociologies in the 1970s and 1980s that were not launched from journal articles. Fields like historical sociology began with monographs and edited volumes. Areas that *were* launched by journals—a claim one could make for labeling theory in the 1950s and 1960s, for example—were often launched by journals tailor-made to the task (in that case, *Social Problems*). Some fields were hybrids. The new sociology of science had a specialty journal, but was really introduced to the larger discipline by the monographs of David Bloor and others. Network analysis, log-linear analysis, and event history analysis are perhaps the three sociological revolutions made in the major journals in the last few decades. It is striking that all were methodological innovations.[8]

8. White, Boorman, and Breiger 1976; Boorman and White 1976; Goodman 1972, 1973; Tuma, Hannan, and Groenveld 1979.

Another issue for the *AJS* (and other) editors concerns the homogenization of journal articles. Certainly there are changes in editorial processes that might have produced standardization. Teevan (1980) had a large panel of blind judges rate published papers and found that ratings varied more within journals than between them, even though he used six general sociology journals with widely varying ratings on the Glenn (1971) prestige scale. This result suggests one dimension of homogenization. Another indication, if not of homogenization then of processes that could easily produce it, is the emergence of the "revise and resubmit" judgment, a judgment that has become very common in sociology journals in recent decades. Bakanic, McPhail, and Simon (1987) report that 28 percent of articles were given R&R status on first review at *ASR* in 1977–82. But while it is possible that R&R could be a euphemism for standardization, on another interpretation the rise of extensive revision requirements would be producing not sterile homogenization, but rather "high standards."[9]

Thus the empirical evidence that important work and important workers have fled central disciplinary journals and that those journals are becoming more and more routine is quite mixed. It is on the theoretical level that the arguments seem more compelling.

There are, in fact, several plausible theoretical rationales that imply that central, peer reviewed journals would become less and less influential as intellectual sites. One broad group of rationales points to internal processes that transform journals. The most common such argument is Weberian; the gradual rationalization of editorial procedures leads to interchangeability of concepts, of data sets, of findings. Routine practices for reviewing evolve toward standardized criteria for judgment, partly in the name of equity, partly in the name of efficiency. As a result, journals following such practices become less and less favorable to paradigm changing work and more and more favorable to normal science and to the easily "measured" qualities of articles like statistical rectitude. Indeed, in Kuhnian terms, the very definition of paradigm changing work is work rejected by routine judgment in an ongoing tradition. Rejection is a necessary (but alas not sufficient) condition of great work.[10]

A looser argument focuses not on rationalization specifically but on in-

9. As for the issue of area, there is serious evidence of methodological bias in central sociology journals (favoring quantitative work; see Bakanic, McPhail, and Simon 1987), and there was a running controversy about political bias in the *ASR* throughout the 1970s and 1980s. (As a privately held journal, the *AJS* is exempt from such investigations.)

10. As a further corollary, such developments favor those kinds of intellectual inquiry capable of being turned into normal science, at least on the assumption that types of intellectual inquiry can intrinsically possess differing degrees of this capability.

stitutionalizing and routinizing tendencies more generally. Schutz, Berger and Luckmann, and a host of others would regard routine editorial practices as ways for editors to make sense of a complex, unending flow of diverse material. (This certainly describes Bidwell's problem in 1974.)

Pushed to the limit, both arguments hold that routinization must eventually end; fully routinized practices must receive new legitimation or die. This in turn implies that a given journal, or perhaps more broadly a given mode of communication (e.g., journals, books, edited volumes) remains dominant only for a limited time. As its content becomes fatally routine, it must revitalize itself or be replaced by other journals or even other modes of communication.[11] Certainly there is anecdotal evidence for this theory. In the 1960s, for example, instructional "readers" were of considerable influence in many intellectual fields. Indeed, the classics of symbolic interactionism (e.g., Blumer 1969) appeared as such collections of essays, usually intended for teaching. One sees fewer such influential undergraduate readers today, although there clearly are examples (e.g., in gender studies).

A second class of arguments focuses not on internal processes but on differentiation among journals. On a Michelsian argument disciplinary institutions are in the hands of particular elites, who use them to further their own paradigms and interests. This view predicts for journals a limited eclecticism reflecting the interests of the host departments.[12] Similarly, such a theory argues that as hegemony seizes central journals, new ideas will be embodied mostly in new journals or new media. *Social Problems* is the obvious case in sociology, founded by an explicitly antielite social movement. There have been many since. The various area specialty journals reflect a

11. It was David Laitin who suggested to me, based on personal experience, that whole modes of communication go through fashions. He noted particularly the importance of "course readers" in the late 1960s and of edited volumes in political science more recently. I have some question whether this is a random trend or one in fact connected with precisely the massification that seems to me to drive disciplinary change throughout the social sciences in the past half century. See also Hargens 1991 on the subject of the influence of books versus articles in sociology.

12. It also predicts thereby distinctly different fates for the *AJS, Social Forces,*, and *Sociology and Social Research* on the one hand than it does for the *American Sociological Review* on the other. Private journals should fare differently than public ones. (Yet many—perhaps most—people feel that the *ASR* is more routinized than the *AJS*.) On this argument, however, it might be accidental that quantitative, variables-based orthodoxy eventually became the most important single content in the *AJS,* for an elite-based argument should believe that power is its own progenitor. Control of a powerful resource such as a central disciplinary journal should so strengthen a group that it can stand against all sorts of external disciplinary forces. On this argument, the dominant orthodoxy in the *AJS* could as easily have been symbolic interactionism or some other alternative to the (loosely) quantitative mainstream, had such an elite happened to control the Chicago Department of Sociology.

different process, not so much escape from hegemony as simple differenti-ation.[13]

These theoretical views are not the only ones possible, however. By contrast with the two classes of arguments given so far—editorial policies and differentiation/hegemony—one could argue that establishment of consistent, widely accepted norms is a *precondition,* rather than a result, of serious disciplinary communication. In Merton's view, the establishment of a scientific community presupposes establishment of common norms—norms of reviewing, of judging, of writing. (It is thus not surprising that the Columbia-trained Blau and Rossi took a norm-governed view of the *AJS.*) This view denies the very premise with which all the other views begin: in-teresting work cannot be forced out by "excessive norms" because such work is not even possible until common norms appear. The real issue then becomes whether "common norms" means the loose rules of the middle pe-riod of *AJS* history or the somewhat more rigid ones of the recent period.

Curiously, the new sociology of science, although anti-Mertonian, ar-gues for the same things but on a smaller scale. It stresses norms in the guise of local discourses and common understandings. But local norms have dif-ferent implications than global ones do. As a result this framework leads, like the second one above, to an expectation of local orthodoxies—cer-tainly in space, perhaps in time. This theory also expects that the differing politics of the Chicago Department of Sociology on the one hand and the ASA Publications Committee (responsible for oversight of the *ASR*) on the other would lead to quite different outcomes for the *AJS* and the *ASR.* But the data make it clear that for most of their histories both journals have in fact been under the control of the same elites.

A number of these positions might be gathered into an institutional isomorphism argument. As certain journals moved in the direction of nor-mative governance, others had to follow suit. Obviously the "common professions" sources of institutional isomorphism worked strongly in soci-ology in the 1960s and 1970s, the heyday of a new professionalism in grad-uate training. The mimetic side of isomorphism was also evident; annual meetings provided evidence of what others were doing, and imitation was easy. There was also coercion, as in the obvious case of the *AJS*'s being forced to follow the *ASR*'s lead in the matter of manuscript fees. All the same, it seems best to see isomorphic forces as binding the journals together in a system but other forces as starting the process rolling toward rational-ization.

13. Various general sociological journals were also founded, increasing general purpose space (e.g., *Sociological Inquiry* in 1952 and *Pacific Journal of Sociology* in 1958).

It is clear that some of the differences between these various theories hinge on definitions of key terms. What is paradigm changing work? What are "acceptable" levels of normative disagreement? What is "significant" scientific communication? These are in many ways unanswerable questions, particularly since the ultimate judge of them all is posterity. A classic is a matter of becoming, not of being.

But the underlying question remains a nagging one, even if, as I suggested earlier, it cannot be posed in a satisfactory manner. In what sense, at any given time, was the most exciting work in sociology featured in the central journals like the *AJS* rather than in, say, *Social Problems* or *Gender and Society* or in course readers or other books?

This question is the more important as we look toward the future. Paper journals are costly and cumbersome. Many articles in them are unread— certainly by five years after publication, probably by only two or three. Electronic archival databases would serve exactly the same functions as paper journals and can be similarly refereed, as indeed some already are. It may well be that paper periodicals will survive only as evanescent journals of opinion and controversy. It is striking that our colleagues in economics chose in 1987 to launch the immensely successful *Journal of Economic Perspectives,* a journal designed for systematic coverage of particular controversy areas at the broadest professional level. Such a journal was proposed several times to the ASA Publications Committee and was finally accepted in 1997. The sticking point was the obvious fact that such journals succeed only via active solicitation, a policy the committee felt the ASA membership would not accept.[14]

In one sense, then, the basic issue at present is the relative balance of the archival and the controversial functions of journals. But the functions of

14. Hargens's (1991) review suggests that nearly all articles do eventually get cited, rightly rejecting Hamilton's (1991) finding. But Hagstrom does not rule out self-citation, nor does the existence of one citation imply that a paper really need have been published. Electronic journals were first proposed for sociology by John Senders in 1976. I should note that complaints about journals are not new at all. The *Virginia Law Review* published an extensive symposium on law reviews in its November 1936 number, including a hilarious diatribe titled "Goodbye to Law Reviews" by Yale's Fred Rodell. Some quotes: "Exceptions to the traditions of dumpy dignity and fake learnedness in law review writing are as rare as they are beautiful." "In the main, the strait-jacket of law review style has killed what might have been a lively literature." "The students who write for the law reviews are egged on by the comforting thought that they will be pretty sure to get jobs when they graduate in return for their slavery, and the super-students who do the editorial or dirty work are egged on even harder by the knowledge that they will get even better jobs." "Thus everybody connected with the law review has some sort of bread to butter. . . . It is a pretty little family picture and anyone who comes along with the wild idea that folks might step outside for a spell and take a breath of fresh air is likely to have his head bitten off." Rodell's article is well worth a trip to the law library.

the journals are not merely intellectual. Other functions are now perhaps more widespread, more unique to journals, and more important. We must understand these other functions to project the future of journals.

The first of these functions is adjudication. The modal tenured professor of fifty years ago published one article in a professional career. The ASA had about a thousand members, and assuming a career duration of about thirty-five years, there were probably no more than thirty tenure cases a year in the entire discipline. For the purpose of tenure, half of the space in one journal sufficed. Today the ASA has between ten and twelve thousand academic members. There may be as many as three hundred sociology tenure cases each year. But there is only perhaps five times as much journal space even while the modal untenured professor is now trying to publish many articles rather than one. The resulting competition makes journals the unequivocal courts of first instance for professional success.[15]

A second new function is professional education. As I have shown in detail throughout the *AJS* history, there has been a steady movement toward more "responsible" reviewing and away from the instant rejection that was the fate of many papers only three decades ago. Now all but a tiny fraction of papers are reviewed in detail—even papers that are hopelessly incompetent and that have no chance whatever of publication. The journals aim to teach people how to be better scholars.

But the mathematics of universal reviewing are sobering. With perhaps one hundred sociology journals, averaging perhaps one hundred manuscripts a year, and a substantial fraction of articles now typically going through at least one revision phase, the total number of annual acts of refereeing is several times the size of the ASA, not all of whose members are either able or willing to review. As those who edit less prestigious journals know, the result is that most articles are reviewed not by nationally known experts in the fields they involve, but by people of lesser stature, indeed often by those whose scholarly judgment is hardly known at all by editors:

15. Of course, universities could well abolish tenure. On another point, some may feel that journal space has increased in proportion to the number of tenure cases. But all the new journals do not add up to ten times the space of the old. In 1945 there existed the *AJS, ASR, Social Forces, The Annals, Sociology and Social Research, Journal of Educational Sociology, Population, Population Studies, Social Research, Rural Sociology, Public Opinion Quarterly, Sociometry, Journal of Marriage and the Family, Phylon, Journal of Social Studies,* and *Journal of Social Issues,* to name only the majors, ignoring interdisciplinary journals, regional journals, and journals in closely related disciplines. This list also includes only American journals; there would be twice as many if we included overseas journals. For comparative current statistics, see Hargens (1991), who finds 245 sociology journals worldwide in 1990, by a fairly broad count. By Hargens's standards there were probably forty or fifty "sociology" journals in 1945.

graduate students, people culled from the prospective article's bibliography, people suggested by friends in answer to desperate phone calls. Systemwide, most referees are no more skilled than those whose work they are reading. The notion that serious teaching is taking place in such a system is wishful thinking; what we have is, in the most literal sense, peer review. Teaching sometimes happens, perhaps more often than we have any right to expect, and more often at the elite journals, with their greater ability to get stronger scholars to referee. But it is a chance matter. Journals are no substitute for effective graduate training.[16]

Most of us would like journals made up of important, revolutionary work. But like many people, I put my *AJS* directly on the shelf without reading it, just as I do all my other journals. I do that because I know that the vast majority of scholarly work—certainly including my own—is scarcely of revolutionary quality. Somebody will identify the important work for me, and when I need to read it, it will be there on the shelf. Of course it would be there for retrieval in a refereed computer database, and perhaps in that sense to continue publishing journals in the modern electronic age is largely a ritual.

Perhaps the journals are justified by their controversial character. Perhaps their real purpose is argument and excitement. But this too can develop a ritualistic flavor, as the endless thematic panels at the ASA show all too well: yet another session, we say, on "Rational Choice and Historical Sociology" or "Theoretical Presuppositions of Status Attainment" or "The Resurgence of Culture." Indeed, newspapers alone should tell us how easily the sensational becomes the routine.

But one can live with rituals. They remind us who we are. As long as the journals carry out the rituals of archiving and controversy and publish the occasional revolutionary piece, they do what we need them to do. What is much more worrisome than ritualism with respect to basic journal functions is the driving of journal publication by other functions.

I have already mentioned the excessive burdens of our system of "teaching" through the journals, a system that is in fact a delusion. From the problems brought on the journals by tenure, too, there seems to be no escape. Of course we publish far too much. Of course much or most published work is slipshod, mechanical, or vacuous. Yet we can hardly expect our younger colleagues to take the pledge and publish only important, well-thought-

16. The professional education function of journals has been urged repeatedly in meetings of the ASA Publications Committee. I also speak from personal experience as an editor (*Work and Occupations*). The figure of 100 for number of journals is a conservative 40 percent of Hargens's worldwide figure of 245.

out, substantial work when their seniors do not restrain themselves so and when doing so as individuals is suicidal. The place to fight this war is in our own departments' vettings of cases—showing deans that we take intellectual substance more seriously than number of pages. But there too the incentives are against it. Self-denial does not pay in university politics. The tail of tenure will wag the dog of journals until either the demography of academia settles into a steady state or teaching becomes a truly equal criterion for tenure or tenure itself falls.

Yet no institution, however enmeshed in the nets of other structures, is incapable of action or transformation. The Small *AJS* must have seemed so enmeshed—in the social welfare world—to the department that received it in 1926. Yet within five years it had transformed the *Journal* completely. The Hughes *AJS* must have seemed equally hardened, yet in short order Blau and his colleagues remade it as well.

So today. There are undoubtedly actions that could unravel the loose network of forces that appear to hold the *AJS* in place as the senior representative of a discipline that is slowly subsiding into inconsequence. Taking those actions is a matter of understanding where that inconsequence comes from. It derives from our having made intellectual vision and contribution less important to us than other things. Overcoming our intellectual futility is a matter of having a vision of where sociology ought to go and then embodying that vision in print. To that topic I turn in the next chapter.

7   The Continuing Relevance of the Chicago School

The preceding chapter moved us out of the earlier historical and theoretical tone and into a somewhat more prescriptive one. This chapter continues the trend toward prescription and adds to it a polemical edge—inherited from its origin as a platform oration—that jars a bit with the judicious tone of the rest of the book. But the present is open to change in ways that the past is not, and caution seems ill suited to the moment. For I turn here to address what I and many others view as the current near crisis state of the discipline Albion Small and others so bravely built. My reading of this situation takes me back to the territory of chapters 1 and 2, however, for it is my view that themes running through the Chicago tradition provide the tools for building a new era of sociology.

The Chicago tradition is now a century old. Of course, anniversaries are often valedictions. A centennial sometimes shows an association to be moribund, just as a diamond jubilee may reveal a queen's irrelevance and a golden anniversary finds many a marriage dead. But this need not be so. Living social relations celebrate daily, and anniversaries punctuate their excitement.

What then are we to make of a hundred years of sociology at the University of Chicago? Is it simply a time for eulogy? After all, Chicago dominance of sociology is half a century gone. And while the Chicago tradition renewed itself after the war in Goffman, Becker, Janowitz, and their like, many of Chicago's most distinguished alumni since its dominant years belong more to the mainstream than to what has come to be seen as to the Chicago tradition proper: methodologists like Stouffer, demographers like Hauser and Keyfitz, macrosociologists like Bendix and Wilensky. Nonetheless, at the heart of the Chicago tradition lie insights central to the advancement of contemporary sociology. Therefore I do not here eulogize the Chicago tradition. One eulogizes only the dead.[1]

---

1. This essay has sparked a lot of commentary. Surprisingly, helpful comments (and a gratifying amount of fan mail) came not only from people I knew well but also from relative strangers. I have therefore had more help with this chapter than with virtually anything else I have written. The following all contributed substantial comments: Rebecca Adams, Joan Al-

Sociology's Predicament

Obviously, if I think the Chicago school has an answer I must also think there is a question. Or at least a predicament. Sociology's glaring problems—the closing of the Washington University department and the recent close call at Yale—are perhaps less important than the more subtle ones. One of these subtle problems is sociology's failure to consistently attract graduate students comparable in ability to those attracted by anthropology, political science, and economics. However much we may doubt standardized testing and grade point averages, the differences are too great and too consistent to be ignored (D'Antonio 1992; Huber 1992). Another indicator is sociology's replacement as a policy adviser to governments, a role that has been almost completely taken over by economics. We may belittle economists within the security of our meetings, but they alone have the ear of the prince (see, e.g., Rhoads 1978).

Yet another depressing indicator is our fission into disconnected segments. The ASA annual meeting assembles groups that share little in intellectual style, methodological practices, or substantive concerns (see Ad Hoc Committee 1989). To be sure, this is in some ways a sign of vitality; we are open about accepting certain kinds of differences. But our little factions show that in fact most of us are quite reluctant to accept new *ideas;* those who have them are cordially invited to pitch their tents elsewhere, sometimes within the ASA, sometimes outside it. Thus the prospect of rational choice theory's entering sociology sends historical sociologists to the barricades. Postmodernism causes the same reaction elsewhere. Even the fortunes of feminism show the same segmentary complacency. In anthropology, history, and political science, battles rage over feminist theory. But sociology has absorbed the largest concentration of women in the social sciences without the slightest alteration of its intellectual structure and style in response to feminist ideas.[2]

Perhaps most depressing, sociology has lost much of its excitement. We

dous, Margo Anderson, James Coleman, Claude Fischer, Jeffrey Goldfarb, Donald Levine, David Maines, Douglas Mitchell, John Modell, John Padgett, Moishe Postone, and Charles Tilly. This essay was originally the ASA Sorokin Lecture, delivered 10 April 1992 to the Southern Sociological Society. I have slightly revised it but have left the oratorical style of the original intact. After all, one of its main points is that sociology has gotten too sober.

2. On historical sociology see Abbott 1991a. The ASA Section on Comparative Historical Sociology sponsored a 1991 session titled "Rational Choice Theory and Historical Sociology" that was little short of a witch-hunt. On feminism, it is instructive to consult George Ritzer's (1988) contemporary theory text, which has a separate section on feminism written not by Ritzer but by two invited women. The pattern of segmentalism rather than incorporation is painfully clear. See also Stacey and Thorne 1985. Some, however, believe this fission to be general in the social sciences (e.g., Levine 1981).

still attract undergraduates with books like Elijah Anderson's *A Place on the Corner* (1978) or David Halle's *America's Working Man* (1984) or Mitchell Duneier's *Slim's Table* (1992), but we read such books only to teach them and certainly discourage our students from writing them. We are too busy being scientific. Yet even our science has a tired feeling. We subscribe to journals but don't read them. Competition for space so regiments our methods and styles that authors sometimes seem bored by their own material; they simply go through the proper motions of asterisked coefficients, low R^2s, and suitably judicious claims of theoretical advance. Who today would publish Dudley Duncan's analysis of synthetic cohorts in *The American Ocupational Structure,* an analysis he admits with a large rhetorical wink to be so much fiddling around? (Blau and Duncan 1967, 183). What mainstream journal today would publish Erving Goffman's (1956) theory of embarrassment or Egon Bittner's (1967) observations of police on skid row, or Talcott Parsons's polysyllabic exegeses of American life (e.g., Parsons [1939] 1954)?

Perhaps, as theorists often tell us, things are better in their camp. Theory and methods, after all, have very little to do with each other in the discipline today. Studies of joint ASA section membership show very clearly the isolation of the theory section from the empirical mainstream sections, and reference lists witness the loud silence that greets each in the land of the other.[3] But the book-based literature of the theorists hardly improves on the article-based literature of empiricism. It simply affects profundiosity rather than positivism, judging its authors rather by the righteousness of their philosophical assumptions than by the currency of their statistics. And certainly one cannot accuse the theorists of relevance to the empirical mainstream, indeed of relevance to empirical reality at all. Empirical reality seems beneath their notice unless it involves the whole history of nations or civilizations.[4]

In short, sociology has degenerated into formulas—empirical, theoretical, historical. We are no longer excited enough to take risks, to float unorthodox ideas, to poach on each other's turf. We have given up writing about the real world, hiding in stylized worlds of survey variables, histori-

---

3. This separation is pretty clearly shown by Cappell and Guterbock (1986, 1992). I am less confident of Ennis's (1992) more ambiguous results because of the high stress value for the two-dimensional scaling.

4. Thus Giddens sets his criterion in a characteristic sentence (1984, xxvii): "In formulating structuration theory I wish to escape from the dualism associated with objectivism and subjectivism" (as opposed to "in formulating structuration theory I wish to answer the following question"). Alexander's celebrated tetralogy (beginning with Alexander 1982) well illustrates the "theory without empirical referent" school.

cal forces, and theoretical abstractions. How many of us, I wonder, can claim to have spent since college even one full year in some social situation that is not academic?

I believe that sociology's problem is first and foremost intellectual. The external political threats, the difficulties in attracting students, the fragmentation, these all reflect a weakness that is fundamentally a weakness of ideas. It has been a long time since we sociologists saw an idea that got us really excited, an idea that could transform our intellectual practice, an idea that could make us want to read the journals. I think that the Chicago school stands for precisely such an idea: that Thomas, Park, Burgess, and their students had a theoretical insight that leads out of our current difficulties. I wish here to develop that idea, considering its relation to current theoretical and methodological practices and sketching the first efforts of scholars to renew it.

The Chicago Insight

It has for some time been unfashionable to speak of the Chicago school as having had any theoretical ideas at all. A widespread image portrays an empiricist Chicago that never scaled the theoretical heights with Marx, Weber, and Durkheim and that never escaped from melioristic social welfarism. At best, it is felt, the Chicago school began the practice of large-scale research in sociology and contributed fundamental empirical work in areas like urban studies and criminology. (See, e.g., the portrayal of Chicago in Ritzer 1988 or even in more friendly works like Bulmer 1984.)

But Chicago seems atheoretical only because we—most of us—are sworn vassals of the paradigm that displaced Chicago's, what I shall here call the "variables" paradigm. Within that paradigm, and within its interpretation of the European classics, to be theoretical is to make assertions about the relation of abstractions like "gender," "capitalism," "education," and "bureaucracy." Most of us think that such assertions are in fact the essence of serious sociology, whether we are historical sociologists or status attainers or sociologists of gender. Within such a worldview the Chicago school—which never believed in abstractions like "gender" and "bureaucracy"—is by definition atheoretical. But perhaps sociology's current difficulties should lead us to suspend judgment until we can lay out Chicago's theoretical position.

In a single sentence, the Chicago school thought—and thinks—that one cannot understand social life without understanding the arrangements of particular social actors in particular social times and places. Another way of stating this is to say that Chicago felt that no social fact makes any sense abstracted from its context in social (and often geographic) space and social time. Social facts are *located*. This means a focus on social relations and spatial ecology in synchronic analysis, as it means a similar focus on process in diachronic analysis. Every social fact is situated, surrounded by other contextual facts and brought into being by a process relating it to past contexts.[5]

An immediate corollary is that not only do variables not exist in reality, they are misleading even as a nominalist convention. For the idea of a variable is the idea of a scale that has the same causal meaning whatever its context: the idea, for example, that "education" can have "an effect" on "occupation" irrespective of the other qualities of an individual, whether those qualities be other past experiences, other personal characteristics, or friends, acquaintances, and connections. Within variable-based thinking, one allows for a few "interactions" to modify this single causal meaning contextually, but the fundamental image of variables' independence is enshrined in the phrase "net of other variables" and in the aim to discover this net effect, whether through experimental or statistical manipulation. The Chicago view has always been that the concept of net effect is social scientific nonsense. Nothing that happens in the social world ever occurs "net of other variables." All social facts are located in contexts. So why bother to pretend they aren't?[6]

To say that this view has few current adherents is to understate. Most contemporary sociology does not take the location or relationships of a social fact as central. Time appears, of course, but merely as the tick of a clock. People and events are not located in it, variables are. Plots and processes do not run through it, causal arrows do. The same holds even more strongly for space. Most sociological articles presume unrelated individuals, whether workers, firms, or associations. These individuals are "units of analysis," not actors in social relations. Yet throughout the Chicago writings we find diagrams of typical histories of cases—Thrasher's (1927, 70) diagram of gang careers, for example—and we find map after map after map dotted with brothels, schizophrenics, residential hotels, businesses, or whatever else was of interest. Throughout the Chicago writings, we find time and place.

---

5. I mean more here than that social facts are always embodied, always found in particular instances, although that assertion is the foundation for my further meaning. Because social facts are always embodied, they are also always situated in relation to other social facts and other social bodies. It is this location that is intellectually central, not the mere fact of embodiment.

6. I have elaborated this point extensively (Abbott 1988a, 1990, 1992a), as has Peter Abell, an apostate from the variables camp. Abell 1987 is an excellent discussion of these issues.

Of course there are sociologists, some descended from Chicago, some not, who take seriously this location in social time and space. The historical sociologists, although rather causalist in their methodological writing, in practice take temporal location quite seriously. Sociologists of occupations still retain Everett Hughes's Chicago emphasis on temporal process, as students of social movements retain Robert Park's. And of course the microsociologies descended from or confronted by symbolic interactionism—old Chicago's most specific lineal descendant—retain a strong temporal emphasis as well.[7]

As for spatial location, it is the students of communities and networks who have kept that interest alive. To the former it came directly from Chicago, for community was one of Chicago's central concerns. The network theorists, by contrast, derive their interest in location from formal roots. The major approaches to network analysis are associated with mathematical sociologists: clique analysis with James Coleman and structural equivalence with Harrison White. Although both have been faculty members at Chicago, their network ideas owe little to that association.[8]

But in the main, the idea that social facts are *located facts,* facts situated in social time and place, is a strange one in contemporary sociology. Yet the Chicago work is as readable today as it was in the 1930s. And throughout it we find an unrelenting emphasis on the location of social facts in contexts of time and space, an emphasis we have forgotten. Roland Barthes once said, "It is precisely because I forget that I read" (Barthes 1974, 10). I would like, then, to reread some of the Chicago conceptualizations of temporal and social contexts.

Of Time and Place

Earlier chapters have, I hope, made a strong case for the existence of a Chicago tradition that reaches well beyond the limits of the first

---

7. On historical sociology, see Abbott 1991a. In the literature on occupations, it is the concept of professionalization that has kept the idea of process alive. See Freidson 1986 or Abbott 1988b. On social movements, see the excellent review by McAdam, McCarthy, and Zald 1988. For symbolic interactionism, see Rock 1979 and Lewis and Smith 1980, as well as the more recent work of Maines (e.g., 1993).

8. Spatial theories are also reviving today in criminology, following the tradition of Shaw and McKay at Chicago. Of the network theorists, the classic works are Coleman 1961 and Coleman, Katz, and Menzel 1966 on the one hand and Lorrain and White 1971, White, Boorman, and Breiger 1976, and Boorman and White 1976 on the other. For collections, see Marsden and Lin 1982, Wellman and Berkowitz 1988, and Breiger 1990. At least one writer combines the Chicago theme of urban study *and* networks (Fischer 1982 in his study of personal networks). Geography itself is also making a comeback in sociology; see, e.g., Hochberg 1984 and Hochberg and Miller, n.d.

Chicago school. Nonetheless, in this chapter I will base my argument on the emblematic works of Chicago in the 1920s and 1930s.

At the core of the Chicago school were the dissertations and monographs, usually produced under Park or Burgess, on social structures and processes in Chicago and beyond: Nels Anderson (1923) on the hobo, Paul Cressey (1932) on taxi-dance halls, Harvey Zorbaugh (1929) on the Near North Side, Edwin Thrasher (1927) on gangs, Ruth Shonle Cavan (1928) on suicide, Ernest Hiller (1928) on strikes, Lyford Edwards (1927) on revolutions, Walter Reckless (1933) on brothels, Louis Wirth (1928) on the Jewish ghetto, Clifford Shaw ([1930] 1966) on delinquency, and E. Franklin Frazier (1932), Ernest Mowrer (1927), and others on the family. It is a long list indeed.

Now these Chicago writers did not simply argue that social facts have contexts in social time and space and leave it at that. They distinguished what one might call degrees of contextuality.[9] Think, first, about temporal processes. One fundamental concept of the school was that of "natural history." A natural history was a temporal pattern that followed a relatively predictable course. It could be diverted or shaped by environing facts, but its general sequence could be understood as a whole, beyond the contingent details. The clearest example of this concept among the classic works was Edwards's (1927) analysis of revolutions. For Edwards, revolutions unfolded according to an internal logic. They might be diverted or reshaped. They might fail. But the general logic was regular.

By contrast, Thrasher's (1927) analysis saw developing gangs as considerably more open to contextual influence. The availability of resources, the force of competitors, the physical structure of the environment, all these could shape the career of a gang, a contextual shaping that Thrasher clearly thought stronger than what Edwards saw in revolutions. We might call temporal processes with this greater contextual dependence "careers," to distinguish them from natural histories.

Finally, in a broad range of Chicago work contextuality was so important that one could no longer focus on a single process. Instead one must study a whole network of intertwined processes. The most celebrated ex-

9. "Context" has two senses, of which one is more important to my argument than the other. The strict sense, which is my concern here, denotes those things that surround and thereby define a thing of interest. The loose sense simply denotes detail. Acute readers will note that these correspond nicely to the two judgments of the scientific worth of contextual information. If decontextualization is merely the removal of excess detail, then it's a fine thing scientifically. On the other hand, if it is the removal of defining locational information, it is a scientific disaster. I thank Donald Levine for demanding this clarification.

ample of this was Zorbaugh's *The Gold Coast and the Slum* (1929). At first glance—I remember this was my reaction as a graduate student—the book seems like a well-written but somewhat aimless history of Chicago's Near North Side. But with hindsight one can see that Zorbaugh's analysis was the clearest expression of the Chicago school's concept of an "interactional field." The Near North Side was defined by its contextualities; for Zorbaugh, that is, the community's boundaries were the boundaries of the mutual constraints that defined what went on there—some of them geographic constraints, some of them social, some of them economic. The motion of every group within such a community was so dependent on that of the others that there was no point writing about any one of them alone. One could only write about an interactional field as a whole.

In temporal processes, then, the Chicago writers saw three degrees of contextuality: natural histories with relatively little, careers with considerably more, and interactional fields with so much that individual processes were braided inextricably. Note that all these concepts defined temporal *processes*. That is, there was no possibility of taking these social facts out of their *temporal* contexts. What was at issue was rather, *given* a temporal process, how independent it was of *social* contexts.

One can ask precisely the inverse question. Given a set of *spatial* or *social* structures, how independent could they be of *temporal* context? Here the Chicagoans made similar distinctions. The equivalent to the natural history was the natural area. In defining natural areas, Park spoke of the conversion of "a mere geographical expression into a neighborhood, that is to say, a locality with sentiments, traditions, and a history of its own . . . the life of every locality moves on with a certain momentum of its own, more or less independent of the larger circle of life and interests about it" (Park 1925, 6). Here, as in the natural history, is an entity relatively independent of its surround, but defining everything within it in terms of location. Thus, in Anderson's *The Hobo* (1923, 15) there is a little map of the hobo "main stem" on West Madison Street. The social dynamics of the street itself and indeed of the local hobo community are bound up in the arrangement of the stores along the street.

As the example of Anderson makes clear, there was actually a deep implicit relationship between the natural area and the environing city. Hobohemia was created by a certain economic demand (for migrant occasional labor) and by forces of transportation, economy, and social structure within the city. But these forces were constant in the short run, so it made sense to see Hobohemia as a consistent natural area whose relation to the environment, although important, was not contingent but temporarily fixed. Thus the natural areas were social structures, contextually socially determined, but temporarily free of a need for analysis of their temporal context.

Writ large, this kind of thinking led to the ecological analysis of social problems in terms of "disorganization." Various natural areas had various degrees of organization and disorganization; social problems were believed to be directly associated with the latter. This was to be a fundamental strand of Chicago work on mental illness (Faris and Dunham 1939), on divorce (Mowrer 1927), and above all on crime and delinquency (Shaw and McKay 1942).[10]

It is of some historical importance that the natural areas model was relatively conformable with variable-based techniques. As the Chicago school declined, location in a natural area simply became another variable describing the individual. But the theoretical content of the concept was lost in the transfer, so that by the time of Robinson's celebrated attack on ecological correlation and the ecological fallacy (1950) there remained only a shadow reality of the original conception of ecological forces, implicit within the idea of group-level variables.[11]

Often Chicagoans considered natural areas expressly in relation to each other, making the pattern of spatial effects depend on various environing factors. Inevitably this involved a move toward temporality. At the heart of the Chicago conceptual armamentarium—given in Park and Burgess's 1921 text—were concepts like "contact," "conflict," "assimilation," and "accommodation" that described the temporal patterns of reciprocal determination of groups by other environing groups. The situation here was

10. I am taking no position on whether disorganization was a good or a bad concept, the issue that has caused the most spilled ink here (see the various sources cited in Kurtz 1984, 55–57, and especially Alihan 1938). Rather, my concern with the ecological studies of social disorganization is that they took space, connection, and context seriously.

11. The targets of Robinson's article included such prominent Chicagoans as Ogburn, Shaw, and Harold Gosnell of the Political Science Department. As is well known, Robinson's mathematical argument shows that ecological correlations are generally higher than individual ones for artifactual reasons related to clustering on the variables. Many have interpreted Robinson's article as enforcing the individual level of analysis, the decontextualization characteristic of emerging survey analysis. However, Robinson himself acknowledged that his argument did not affect those concerned with true "area-level" measurements (1950, 352); rather, as he said, "Even out-and-out ecologists, in studying delinquency, for example, rely primarily upon data describing individuals, not areas" (1950, 352). (His example was Clifford Shaw.) Robinson thus simply discounted the idea that the rates were indicators of a group-level property of disorganization, taking them simply as individual behaviors. This was of course his theoretical decision, not Shaw's. It is worth noting, in this regard, that like the survey tradition generally, Robinson simply ignored the problems of contagion and diffusion, assuming independent individuals as units of analysis, contrary to the theoretical tradition of ecology.

analogous to that of the careers concept in the Chicago approach to temporal context. Just as there were more important *social* contexts and contingencies in careers than in natural histories, so also did the *temporal*
environment play a greater role in these "area careers" than in natural areas.

Wirth's (1928) discussion of the Chicago Jewish ghettos was of this
"area career" type. The relation of the ghetto to the larger forces of city expansion, to changing patronage of Jewish businesses, and to the temporal
patterns of generational succession and of successive waves of immigration
all shaped the experience of daily Jewish life. Wirth centered his analysis on
the Jewish community, just as in his analysis of gang careers Thrasher
(1927) retained a focus on the individual gangs. But each writer considered
more extensive contingencies than in natural histories or natural areas; the
development of successive Jewish communities was the group's career in a
complex social and geographical space.

In the limit, the range of temporal contexts for a social structure became
so great that again it required leaving the individual case behind and discussing the interactional field as a whole. Zorbaugh's *The Gold Coast and
the Slum* again provides the clearest example, for the idea of an interactional field involves not only a range of social contexts but a range of temporal ones as well. The story of the Near North Side involves not only
long-term processes like changes in economic structure and in the composi-
tion of the immigrant population, but also shorter-term ones like local succession in neighborhoods and even more rapid ones like the turnover of
residents in rooming houses. Spatially, the interactional field involves not
only the large-scale differentiation from and interdependence of this whole
area on the city, but also shorter-range phenomena like the intermingling of
church congregations produced by parishioner mobility and the economic
interdependencies of the various subsections of the Near North Side itself.

Unlike the natural areas concept, the concept of interactional fields did
not make an easy transition to the variables world. Nonetheless, in some
subfields, particularly historical sociology, it is alive and well. Immanuel
Wallerstein's *The Modern World-System* (1974) and my own *The System
of Professions* (1988b) both describe such interactional fields. To take the
case I know better, my argument about professions was essentially that professions themselves are like ethnic groups pushing each other around in
Chicago and that the work that professions do is equivalent to the physical
and social geography of the city itself. The history of professions is then a
history of turf wars. One cannot write the history of any individual profession, because that profession is too dependent on what other professions
around it are doing. One can only describe the field of interprofessional

conflict—the rules, the stratagems, the tricks, the byplays of interaction. Into this field from time to time come larger forces: changes in professional work occasioned by technological and organizational developments that are equivalent to changes in the transportation and economic patterns of the city. These induce yet further cascading changes in the interactional field. And there are rules for the field, much like the political rules of the city. And so on. And so on. Although the filiation may seem distant, my book was at heart an exposition of an old Chicago concept.

We may think then of a three-by-three table in which the row dimension describes increasing degrees of temporal contextuality and the column dimension describes increasing degrees of social contextuality (see table 12). I have essentially made the argument that the Chicago writers nearly always worked in the last (most contextual) row or column, and that these two intersect, in the 3,3 cell, in the concept of interactional field, which presumes multiple levels of social and temporal context. In the concept of interactional field we must, like Zorbaugh, Wallerstein, or me, move away from the level of individual cases and begin to describe the rules and regularities of interaction throughout the field. Contextual contingency is so complex that one cannot study the individual case directly and cannot make predictions of any but the most general sort.

I shall later discuss some other cells of this little table. For the moment I merely wish to emphasize that implicit in this whole focus on context and contingency was a coherent vision of social structure. The Chicago writers believed social structure to be a set of temporary stabilities in a process of flux and reciprocal determination. The social world was made up of actors mutually determining each other in ways sometimes deliberate and some-

Table 12. Context in the Chicago School

		Degrees of Contextuality: Space		
		None	Some	Much
Degrees of Contextuality: Time	None			Natural area (Park)
	Some			Area "career" (Wirth)
	Much	Natural history (Edwards)	Career (Thrasher)	Interactional field (Zorbaugh)

times quite unforeseen. But the cornerstone of the Chicago vision was location, for location in social time and space channeled the play of reciprocal determination. All social facts were located in particular physical places and in particular social structures. They were also located within the temporal logic of one or more processes of succession, assimilation, conflict, and so on. This meant that the Chicago vision was of a social structure embedded in time, a structure in process.

I read this summary with no little irony. Didn't the historical sociologists tell us that the general importance of Marxism in 1970s sociology was that it gave sociologists a way to think about change and process (Abbott 1991a)? Didn't the Weber of rationalization and other processes replace the Parsonian Weber in the same period and with much the same effect? Why is it that contemporary sociology clean forgot what the Chicago school had to say? Why weren't they our "classical sociology?"[12]

In part it happened because the Chicago work lies between the contemporary and the classic. When we read a classic, we ignore the old ideology and odd phraseology in order to focus on that part of the text that addresses the perennial, the permanent, the enduring. Thus we make an important social theorist of Durkheim despite his silly neocorporatism, of Weber despite his penchant for pigeonholing, of Marx despite his preoccupation with a factory system now long gone. But the warm prose of the Chicago school fools one into reading it as contemporary work.[13] Then all at once one is embarrassed by Park's earnest theory of racial accommodation, by Cressey's description of a "tendency to promiscuity" (1932, xiii), by Thrasher's analysis of "wanderlust" (1927, chap. 10). And so one problem is that the Chicago school seems neither old enough to be classic nor yet young enough to be contemporary.

Another problem has been simple snobbery. Chicago writing lacks the Latinate literacy and high tone of the Europeans. Our sociological theorists, like Henry James and many others before them, find the raw insight of American thought too much for their tastes. They prefer European sophis-

12. The standard answer to this question is that Chicago sociology failed to become classic theory because it had no theory and that its empirical work is of mainly antiquarian interest. I have disposed of the first argument above. As for the second, not only is the Chicago work exciting reading today (as I am about to argue), but the Chicago data archives are in fact a rich mine for researchers willing to reanalyze them with current methods. It is nonetheless striking that C. Wright Mills's (1959) denunciation of the 1950s sociological consensus (between "grand theory" and "abstracted empiricism") makes no mention of Chicago sociology, even though one principal theme of his attack is decontextualization.

13. "In these pages," Everett Hughes writes at the opening of his 1928 dissertation on the Chicago Real Estate Board, "we do not observe a dinosaur's bones, for which we must imagine the flesh, but the struggling flesh itself of a living and young institution in the City of Chicago."

tication, having managed somehow to forget the impact of pragmatism—the American philosophy that shaped Chicago sociology firsthand—on European theorists like Habermas (Habermas 1971).

Whatever the reason for ignoring Chicago, the central Chicago concept of locatedness has a peculiar importance for us today, for it can help us reconcile theoretical and empirical work. Most sociological theory, whether Continental or American, contemporary or classic, keeps social facts in their contexts. It concerns process, relationship, action, and interaction. But most of our current empirical work concerns decontextualized facts with only a tenuous connection to process, relationship, and action. A general empirical approach founded on action in context could articulate much more effectively with our general theoretical traditions than do our present methodologies.

This gap between theory and empirical work must be of great concern to every contemporary sociologist. Of course each subarea has its own theorists and theories, as Merton (1948) urged in his celebrated remarks about middle range theory, and these area theorists, as one might call them, are indeed much more closely tied to empirical work than are the generalists. But they work with a vocabulary of ideas about causality, about effects, about contexts, that is implicitly a general theory whether they will or no. And that general theory in fact derives from the decontextualizing methodological paradigm of modern sociology. Let me now consider that paradigm in more detail.

Notes on the Relation of Sociological Methods and Theory

The notion of removing social facts from their contexts did not begin with the decline of old Chicago in the 1930s. In one sense any social count does this, and social statistics after all date from the seventeenth century. Since the coming of the Hollerith machine in the 1880s, statisticians had been able to cross-classify social statistics extensively, a task helped by the invention of correlation in the same period. Cross-classification and correlation were used mainly for description, to say that people of type x were also likely to be y and z. This kind of typologizing is, in a mild way, contextual thinking, since it lumps values of variables into their "contexts" of other variables. But it is already a major step toward decontextualization, because it constructs types from individual variables rather than analyzing them as gestalts or emergents.[14]

---

14. On the history of statistics till 1900, see Stigler 1986. For various related topics, see the essays in Owen 1976 and also Anderson 1989. A valuable source on the history of "causal analysis" is Bernert 1983. For a more recent analysis, see Abbott 1998. A useful general source throughout the following section is Turner and Turner 1990.

The first major exponent of formal statistical methods in sociology was Franklin Giddings, the dominant figure in the Columbia sociology department in the first third of this century and the supervisor of such distinguished students as Howard Odum, William Ogburn, and F. Stuart Chapin. Giddings's *Inductive Sociology* (1901) makes causal understanding the goal of sociology and conceives of causality as a sufficient combination of necessary causes. But after this stirringly Millian introduction, the book moves on to give, essentially, long lists of variables related to various social phenomena, complete with hints on measurement. Sociological laws are patterned after the law of gravitation or the ideal gas law and so are essentially summaries of empirical correlations. In terms of my three-by-three table, Giddings was interested in the 1,1 cell, the cell with minimal contextuality in either space or time. It is also clear that, deep down, his idea of theory was simple empirical generalization. Causality, however interesting in principle, seemed to require a foundation of empirical generalization very much under construction.

The chief contrast to Giddings's methods with their variables and correlations was provided by what were called "social surveys": broad-based field researches on communities, institutions, and social problems, usually conducted by social workers or their ancillaries in the charity organization movement. These were focused studies, generally using multiple methodologies, but always retaining facts in their immediate contexts because the surveyors wanted to figure out why and how particular social problems occurred in order to change them. There were interview studies of workers in particular industries, crime reports interlarding official statistics with descriptions and case studies, and whole community studies involving teams of researchers. *Middletown,* for example, is one of the last great products of the social survey movement (Lynd and Lynd 1929). The survey movement had no theoretical aims. It never aimed to discover, for example, the relation of abstractions like "work" and "commitment to family"—the kind of "law" that was central to Giddings's project—but rather studied (to continue the example) the relation of a certain group of workers to their families within a certain community and a certain industrial context.[15]

At the empirical level, then, the Chicago school was in many ways a hybrid of the social survey tradition and Giddings's "scientific" sociology (Giddings detested surveys [Bulmer 1984, 67]). Although Park and Burgess spent considerable time differentiating their "scientifically guided" work

15. On the survey movement, see the discussion in Turner and Turner 1990 and more generally the various essays in Bulmer, Bales, and Sklar 1991. I discussed this movement briefly in chapter 1 in connection with Deegan's arguments about the Chicago school.

from the meliorism of the survey movement (Bulmer 1984, chap. 5; Turner and Turner 1990, 25), to readers of today the work of the Chicago school reads more like the social survey literature than like the work of the Giddings school.[16]

Yet the Chicago school had theoretical ambition. This differentiated its procedures from those of the survey movement and gave the school's writings a coherence that the products of that movement lack. As I have argued, Chicago theory focused on the locatedness of social facts and the importance of contextual contingencies.[17] This theoretical commitment entailed the Chicago mixture of methods, for if the effects of causes were so shaped by environing factors that no causes had uniform effects, specific theories must be theories about constellations of forces, not theories of individual causes. The fastest way to discover such constellations of forces was by case study, since the sheer combinatorics made studying the matter at the aggregate level difficult. And more generally only the eclectic combination of ethnography, statistics, life history, and organizational history could do full justice to the multiple layers of spatial and temporal contexts for social facts.[18]

By contrast, Giddings's notion of causality—sufficient combinations of

16. Although the Chicago school thus seemed to combine the attention of the survey movement to particular details with the scientific ambitions of the Giddings school, there were few direct links between them. Burgess had participated in a survey (Bulmer 1984, 73; Harvey 1987a, 87), and Park taught a course on surveys, but both thought Chicago research practice was far more systematic. (But see Deegan 1988, which sees a much stronger and more direct link with the survey tradition.) On the "scientific sociology" side, Park and Burgess knew Giddings's work—it appears in their text (Park and Burgess [1921] 1970)—but were quite conscious that he lay in a different tradition (see, e.g., Park's introduction to the text).

Yet Chicago writing certainly reads like the surveys. For example, one may readily compare Ogburn's 1912 Columbia dissertation on child labor laws (Ogburn [1912] 1964) with Crystal Eastman's 1910 *Work Accidents and the Law*, one volume of the great Pittsburgh Survey, and with Everett Hughes's 1928 dissertation on the Chicago Real Estate Board. All three study the rise of regulatory institutions. But where Ogburn focuses on average ages of permitted entry to the labor force across states, considering the increasing uniformity of these ages as the years pass, Eastman and Hughes study actual events in particular contexts. Particular actors are readily identifiable, as are patterns and constellations of forces surrounding particular events. One can follow processes within particular cases (in Eastman's case, in literally gory detail). None of this is possible in Ogburn.

17. Contrary to one common judgment about Chicago, ecology was and is a perfectly respectable genre of scientific theory. Our current notion of theory is so shaped by the variables paradigm that we define theory by conformity to that paradigm. Most sociologists think theory is that which rigorously describes the relation between two variable properties of individual units. As a glance at theories of catalysis or evolution reveals, however, sometimes it is necessary, because of the impact of context on cause, to theorize systems directly in terms of the relations within them. Chicago-style ecology belongs to this branch of theorizing.

18. The eclectic combination was Bulmer's "Chicago Manifold" (Bulmer 1984). Note that the argument about combinatorics implies that the relation of case study and ecology is more an elective affinity than a necessity, something that was forgotten in the great method-

necessary causes themselves conceived as abstractions—drives one to directly investigate the varying properties of independent units. Only if causality depends fundamentally on context does it make sense to pursue the Chicago style of research. For the 1,1 cell of minimal contextuality, there is no need to waste time situating facts. It seems to me, then, that the Chicago school represented a distinct intellectual advance on Giddings's program, since it addressed the complexity of social life but did so within a frankly scientific framework. It replaced a particularly simple version of the variables approach with a much more nuanced contextualist approach.

This new notion of emphasizing context had a distinguished intellectual lineage, evident in Park and Burgess's text. The great European sources were Gustav Ratzenhofer and Georg Simmel. Surprisingly, the chief American interpreter of the former was the oft-maligned Albion Small; Chicago students had thus been hearing "ecological" theory long before the arrival of Simmel's student Robert Park, and they had heard it from historicist sources, much as we today hear similar arguments from historical sociologists like Charles Ragin (1987).[19] To these European sources were added the unique contributions of W. I. Thomas and, via Ellsworth Faris, of George Herbert Mead, who between them provided a social psychology less mechanical and abstract than that of either Durkheim's socialized dope or Tarde's (and Giddings's) knowledgeable imitator. Thomas and Znaniecki's *Polish Peasant* study (1918–20) showed how the complexities of the social environment worked themselves out in individual lives and then rebounded through the individuals to reshape the environment and its institutions. The relation of individual and society was thus itself reconceptualized as one of mutual contexts for each other.

ological debates of the 1930s. Those tended to reduce a whole series of dichotomies to the single contrast of quantitative with qualitative work. See Burgess 1927 for an anguished plea for open-mindedness, ignored in the subsequent debate (covered in Bulmer 1984 and to some extent in Turner and Turner 1990).

19. None of Ratzenhofer's works has been translated, to my knowledge. (Small translated some portions, which appear in his own work and in the *American Journal of Sociology*; e.g., *AJS* 10 [1904]: 177–88). The main source in English is parts 4 and 5 of Small's *General Sociology: An Exposition of the Main Development in Sociological Theory from Spencer to Ratzenhofer* (1905). For Small, Ratzenhofer's central insights were the ideas that not society but the social process was the subject of inquiry and that the social process consisted of a continuing interplay of conflicting interests. Small's contextualist message is especially strong in *The Meaning of Social Science* (1910). For example, in speaking of social causes, Small says: "The part that one of these factors plays at a given moment is a function of the operation of all the other factors at the same time" (1910, 20). Sources on Simmel are so well known that there is no need to cite them. Donald Levine has emphasized to me that Simmel's interest in interaction was highly abstracting, and therefore somewhat decontextualizing (loose sense), and that it was Park who insisted on bringing social forms into complex, contextual interrelation.

In my view, then, the Chicago school made a decisive advance by joining the scientizing and the survey traditions via the central idea of contextuality. In making contextuality the central focus of the Chicago school, I am departing from the tradition that has emphasized the role of the subjective, of values, of intersubjectivity generally, in Chicago writing on social life (e.g., Harvey 1987a, to some extent, and all the historians of symbolic interaction, starting with Blumer himself; see, e.g., Rock 1979). I am arguing that the important aspect of intersubjectivity is not so much its subjective character as its *relational* character. Indeed, I feel that those who see salvation in sociology's new swing to "culture," often linking this trend back to the Chicago school or its line of descent through Blumer, make the same mistake. It is the focus on relations among meanings that matters, not simply studying meaning, which can be and has been done in the most wooden manner imaginable.

In making contextuality the center of Chicago, I am also defining the Chicago focus on process—which many have noted before—as logically correlative with the Chicago focus on place, both physical and social. In doing this, I am of course reading selectively. It is not my aim here to study the school in its full complexity. That has been well done by others, as we have seen. Rather, I aim here to take the school's central idea and return it to the foreground of active sociological consciousness. This is what I mean by reading the Chicago school writings as classic texts.

Subsequent history shows that the Chicago synthesis of contextuality failed rather rapidly. A number of forces drove this failure. Some were institutional. The Rockefeller Memorial money dried up in 1932. Park left Chicago for Fisk University. The university's new president, Robert Maynard Hutchins, was unenthusiastic about social science. But other forces were intellectual, and these are more important.[20]

For one thing, by the 1930s Herbert Blumer was laying the foundations

20. Chicago also, as Martin Bulmer (1984) has shown so well, pioneered the large-scale, externally funded research enterprise in sociology, beginning with the *Polish Peasant* and continuing through the salad years of Laura Spelman Rockefeller Memorial support. There can be little question that part of Chicago's eminence stemmed from this support and from the failure of the dogmatic Giddings (Bulmer 1984, 142) to command similar funding. For related material on (and varying interpretations of) the decline of Chicago, see Bulmer 1984 and Turner and Turner 1990. In studying this decline, it is wise to separate the political decline of the department in the discipline (shown in the founding of the *American Sociological Review* and the "coup" of 1936—a coup in which many young Chicago graduates participated) from the decline of the ideas now labeled as "Chicago school." These are in some ways quite different stories. Joan Aldous made the interesting suggestion to me that one reason for the decline of the intellectual message of Chicago was that people took it too literally, as if the message were the concentric zone theory itself rather than the importance of context and location.

of symbolic interactionism by emphasizing the symbolic, intersubjective side of the Chicago approach and by appropriating Mead's social psychology (some have said in vain; see Harvey 1987a, 161). In the process he attacked earlier, more eclectic Chicago work like the *Polish Peasant* for being unscientific because its categories were not generated directly enough from the data. Blumer thus accepted the scientific aims of sociology but helped further a split within it by conflating on the one hand objectivism, quantitative study, and variable-based approaches and on the other subjectivism, qualitative study, and case-based approaches. (This unification of previously crosscutting dichotomies into an overarching opposition worked itself out in the department in the personal opposition between Blumer and Ogburn, as I noted earlier.) Blumer also missed the point about context, thinking that the central problem with variable-based approaches was their failure to capture the *subjective* ambiguities of the situation rather than their denial of contextual determination in causality in general, of which the subjectivity problem was merely a part.[21]

But the more important force in the decline of Chicago was the rise in the 1930s of opinion polling and market research. This was a much-improved version of the variables paradigm of Giddings. The extreme wing was led by Paul Lazarsfeld. Lazarsfeld favored purely operationalist social science, deliberately ignoring causal processes and theory, for which he had little hope (Turner and Turner 1990, 105, 114). (Coleman [1990, 89] says Lazarsfeld "had a difficult time understanding sociological theory.") His archetypal project was market research on consumer attitudes. Its ultimate aim was not to figure out *why* consumers thought what they thought, but simply to find which product they preferred (see Lazarsfeld and Rosenberg 1955, 396–98).[22]

Decontextualization was central to such a project partly because consumer tastes would change before an adequate contextualized theory of current tastes could be developed and partly because marketers could not hold "other things equal" in the survey and purchase situations. The necessary decontextualization of particular social attributes was then accomplished through the rapidly advancing discipline of sampling, which not

21. For discussions of Blumer's developing views, see Harvey 1987a, 136; Turner and Turner 1990, 67, as well as Bulmer 1984, chap. 10. Blumer's own views are set forth in his celebrated critique of *The Polish Peasant* (Blumer 1939). His attack on the concept of variables was early (1931) and reiterated (e.g., 1956). But because of the other concepts that he often conflated with "variables" (such as "rigor," at times), Blumer contributed heavily to the unnecessary polarization of the time.

22. It is deeply revealing that Lazarsfeld openly stated that the act of purchasing a good was the very epitome of human action (Lazarsfeld and Rosenberg 1955, 389–90).

only separated individuals from their social context of friends, acquaintances, and so on but also deliberately ignored an individual *variable's* context of other variables in the name of achieving "more complete" knowledge of the variable space. Sampling not only tamed contextual effects to mere interactions, it also thereby produced data sets in which the levels of contextual causation were deliberately minimized. This would later enable a whole generation of sociologists to act as if interaction were a methodological nuisance rather than the way social reality happens.[23]

Like Lazarsfeld, Samuel Stouffer, the leader of the moderate survey researchers, believed that only modern survey analysis could produce the building blocks of a discipline (see, e.g., Stouffer 1950). Stouffer had underscored the contrast between survey research and the Chicago school in his celebrated dissertation (1930), which tested the speed and efficiency of four student colleagues as judges of attitudes when pitted against a set of coding protocols. That the protocols produced the same answers in a frac-

23. To my reading, the main text of this period—Lazarsfeld and Rosenberg's (1955) *Language of Social Research*—moved to a fully decontextualized position. Relation between cases makes a brief appearance in a couple of early papers by Leon Festinger and one sociometry paper (by Daniel Goodacre). Relation between variables (context as understood within the variables paradigm) commands only one paper (by Allen Barton). Otherwise the variables paradigm is full blown in dozens of papers, with independent cases, independent variables, and narrative conceived as trends or panel changes in variables. The methodological other for Lazarsfeld and Rosenberg is institutional research and ethnography, of which they say, "In none of these cases could we find systematic analyses of the methodological problems involved"! (1955, 5). Insofar as Lazarsfeld and Stouffer were interested in context it was simply a matter of ecological variables, not of taking the particular location of particular cases as primary. Stouffer's soldiers, for example, were influenced by brigade, battalion, and company effects as much as by personal ones. (And Lazarsfeld was equally interested in "global"— emergent—variables [Coleman 1990, 87].) But the ecological variables always worked through individual units, not as whole structures. I thank John Modell for demanding this clarification.

As sampling developed, random sampling proved problematic. For the clustering of cases in the variable space (and in terms of accessibility to sampling) meant that random sampling provided little information about unusual groups. The answer to this was stratified sampling, in which information about the real clustering of cases in the variable space was used to bypass that clustering in order to sample unusual groups beyond their presence in the population, later resetting their information to its proper proportion through weights. The clustering information thus was not a thing to be investigated but rather a problem in survey design. In theory, the aim was to make information on the unusual cases achieve the same relative error as information on the common cases (where the law of large numbers guaranteed rapid approach to population parameters). But this involved a philosophical assumption that relations in the underlying space were broadly linear, embodied in the statistical practice of making the behavior of parameters under different sampling strategies into the principal criterion for selecting statistics. Otherwise there would be no point in taking the unusual cases at all seriously; one would rather analyze the space directly in terms of clusters, that is, in terms of interaction. On the history of sampling, see Chang 1976 and Hansen and Madow 1976. The fundamental structure of modern sampling stems from a 1934 paper of Jerzy Neyman.

tion of the time Stouffer took as conclusive demonstration that protocols were the preferred approach to social research. But of course by posing the problem as "what is the fastest way to code a variable" he had already designed in his answer. The great issue in the 1930s debate between case studies and survey methods was not over whether surveys could find variables faster; that was obviously true. Rather, it was over whether the concept of variables—the concept of taking social facts out of their contexts—was a sensible one in the first place. About this, Stouffer's elegant experiment had nothing to say. For Stouffer was deeply committed to the idea of variables, as was clear from his later statement that general theory "does not provide us with interrelated propositions which can be put in the form if $x1$, given $x2$ and $x3$, then there is a strong probability of $x4$" (1950, 359). The aim of theory was to provide deductive sources for such testable statements about variables, and if a theory did not provide those deductions, it was too vague to be useful. Variables were the reality.[24]

The practical importance of survey research's operationalism lay in its amenability to the equally operational body of statistical procedures invented by Ronald Fisher and his colleagues in the 1920s. (See Anderson 1989 for a discussion of the increasing dominance of these procedures.) Lazarsfeld himself preferred his esoteric "latent structures approach." But for the less adroit, there were the highly portable Fisherian methods, designed for specific operational aims—in Fisher's case, to decide whether fertilizer did any good on a particular field. (Stouffer had studied with Pearson and Fisher in the early 1930s [Bulmer 1984, 179].) There was no pretense that the Fisherian factorial design could aid causal theory, although conversely it was easier to test hypotheses if one had an effective causal theory. (See Kempthorne 1976 for an overview.) The causal emphasis was to come later (Bernert 1983; Abbott 1998). In the meantime, the main fight between the would-be Fisherians and the conservatives was over the issue of contextual causation. Fisher and most other biometricians had handled contextual effects through experimental design. Even so, Fisherian statistics suffered a brilliant contextualist attack from Jerzy Neyman, who blasted Francis Yates in the mid-1930s by showing that the whole procedure depended on the untestable assumption that contextual (interaction)

24. Stouffer's data-driven character shines through the classic story, repeated to me by both Howard Becker and Charles Tilly, that Stouffer stimulated his theoretical thinking by watching the cards pile up in the slots of the IBM card sorters. His research office had to have extra wiring to support three sorters (Terry Clark, personal communication). Note, with respect to the quote in text, that $x1$, $x2$, $x3$, and $x4$ are not actions (in which case we would have Stouffer proposing generalized narratives) but rather variable properties of individual units of analysis.

effects were well behaved (Traxler 1976). Surprisingly, nothing ever came of Neyman's remarks. (Neyman himself had after all done fundamental work on sampling.) Indeed, brilliant but fruitless attacks on the Fisherian methods for their atheoreticality have continued for decades, the latest coming from Berkeley's inimitable David Freedman (e.g., 1987).

The makers of the new variables revolution saw that by removing social facts from their immediate contexts one could make them accessible to the power of the new inferential statistics. Correlational methods, regression, factor analysis—all the panoply of hypothesis-testing methods became applicable once one made the conceptual leap that "values of variables" were comparable across a wide variety of contexts. Even a hardened contextualist must admit that the combination of survey methods and statistics was radical and exciting. Like the contextualist, interactionist insight that preceded it, it produced an extraordinary flowering of sociology, in books like Lazarsfeld, Berelson, and Gaudet's *The People's Choice* ([1944] 1968), Stouffer et al.'s *The American Soldier* (1949), Berelson, Lazarsfeld, and McPhee's *Voting* (1954), Lipset's *Political Man* (1960), Coleman's *The Adolescent Society* (1961), and Blau and Duncan's *The American Occupational Structure* (1967). This is a very distinguished list.[25]

If you take the time to reread these books, you will find them to be raw, fresh, exciting. On rereading Blau and Duncan one feels the authors' sense of acute excitement. Here is Duncan eager to try the ultimate wrinkle of the variables paradigm, the structural equation approach developed, ironically enough, by a Chicago colleague of Robert Park's—the great biologist Sewall Wright. The book is written, to the great surprise of a contemporary reader, in narrative format. In each chapter the authors walk the reader through what they do as they do it, rather than presenting it in some proper "scientific" or logical order. The authors are therefore present and visible. Their acute disappointment at the shortcomings of their data speaks out again and again. They frankly confess their strong statistical and method-

25. Note that there are works on this list that extend beyond the variables paradigm. *The Adolescent Society* is partly a network book, as were several other major works out of the Columbia department, such as Katz and Lazarsfeld 1955. Nonetheless, in these books networks were seen not as whole structures, but rather in terms of their final connections to the respondent. Katz and Lazarsfeld talk about "sequence" of influence, as Berelson, Lazarsfeld, and McPhee (1954) talk about the "process" of voting. But both of these "narratives" are reconstructed out of information gathered as variables and hence have lost most processual detail. One can see in these works, however, an *attempt* to preserve the concepts of particular social and temporal location within the variables framework. It was only after the revolution of causalism (see below) that even this attempt disappeared. Recall that, as with my analysis of Chicago, I am not concerned with the important organizational contributions of Lazarsfeld and the Columbia department. For a note on these, see Glock 1979.

ological assumptions as well as the ways those assumptions violate reasonable views of the social process. Their apology is simply that perhaps radical assumptions will produce exciting results. And because one is swept up in their excitement, even the unsympathetic reader grants them the assumptions, just to see what will turn up. Like the contextualist paradigm, then, the variables paradigm produced enticing and stimulating works.[26]

By the 1960s, the variables paradigm had built a whole edifice of social analysis. Thanks to Lazarsfeld and others, it had its major anchor in the commercial survey literature—market research and polling. But it had taken over empirical sociology as well. The paradigm reached its high-water mark when Bernard Berelson and Gary Steiner published their summary of "what the behavioral sciences now know about the behavior of human beings" (1964, 3). Most of the "truths" in the book (which was titled *Human Behavior: An Inventory of the Findings*) are in fact bivariate associations, sometimes with one or two controls. There are relatively few references to *why* things happen.[27]

This was soon to change. During the 1960s, sociologists began to accept a probabilistic image of causality that had always been implicit in the structural equation approach. The image of probable causality was borrowed from the physical sciences by Hubert Blalock (1964) and other writers to justify their work. Unlike market researchers and biologists, sociologists using the variables model began to think that their main effects stood for causal forces. Their articles implied that variables like gender, bureaucracy, and income could "do things" in the social world.[28]

26. I am not the first to read Blau and Duncan with a largely literary eye. See Gusfield 1980. Contrasting it with *Tally's Corner*, however, makes it seem quite a different book than it seems here, where I am contrasting it with later works in the status attainment tradition.

27. James Coleman has argued (1990, 91–92, 1992) that sociology became more individualistic because the society around it did. He implicitly locates the methodological change I have noted (toward operationalist and variable-based conceptions) as part of this move toward an individualized, disconnected society. Although the debate is beyond the scope of this chapter, I think, quite to the contrary, that the new individualism of the social sciences was in fact constitutive of societal individualism. In any case, I am consciously pursuing an internalist reading of the discipline here and so disregard his (important and worrisome) argument.

Also, John Modell has correctly pointed out that I have ignored one crucial link between the Chicago heritage and the new standard sociology, that running through human ecology to demography, via people like McKenzie and Hawley. Although space forbids addressing that strand of sociology, it is striking that demography today is thoroughly dominated not by the concerns of theoretical ecology or even by formal demography, but rather by routine applications of methods from the Lazarsfeldian heritage that I am discussing here.

28. For the smoking gun of probable causality, see Blalock 1964. The language can be seen rapidly shifting, over the first few pages of the book, from a concern with actual events to a removed level of variables. See Abbott 1992a and 1998 for detailed analyses of this type of language.

The takeover of causal imagery was by generational turnover. By the 1960s the generation trained under the prevariables paradigm began to disappear. New students learned the methods not as an adjunct to more general analysis or as a quick solution for empirical problems set by the interactionist paradigm. Rather, in true Kuhnian fashion, they learned *from the method* a set of assumptions about social reality that fundamentally shaped their vision of the social world. The paradigm gradually became self-enclosed because its methods negated any social fact they could not comprehend. By the 1970s many sociologists imagined the social world as a kind of general linear reality (Abbott 1988a). The closed nature of the paradigm dominated even theorists in subfields, whom Merton had hoped would prevent such closure. Even a writer like John Meyer, in proclaiming the new institutionalism in organizational studies, insisted on setting it forth in bivariate, decontextualized (other things being equal) hypotheses (see Meyer and Rowan 1977 and Scott and Meyer [1983] 1991).

It was this final move to "causal analysis" that created the real abyss between theory and methods. Men like Stouffer had had one foot in the old and one foot in the new. Stouffer was trained in a department dominated by ethnography but himself moved away from it. He believed deeply in Giddings's type of generalizations and dreamed that one could create deductive theories with decisively testable differences in empirical implications (Stouffer 1950). And Talcott Parsons, with Stouffer at his side at Harvard, believed much the same thing, although he wanted the major effort put into generating the theories, and although by theory he meant something far more abstract that did Stouffer. In the sequel, Parsons's theories never specified any empirical implications, but for the moment the two men supported the temporary rapprochement of theory and methods that got sociology through its great flowering in the late 1950s and early 1960s. A similar, but closer, more synergistic relationship obtained between Merton and Lazarsfeld at Columbia.[29]

---

29. It is useful to see exactly how this articulation worked. A classic example is Berelson, Lazarsfeld, and McPhee's *Voting* (1954), to which we have Parsons's detailed response (1959). What is striking about the Berelson et al. book, to readers used to the language of causalism since 1965, is that each chapter concludes with a long list of bivariate correlations, sometimes with controls. The book concludes with a massive list of these and comparisons with several other studies. The feel of the book is thus highly descriptive, in current terms. Where, we would ask today, is the causal analysis? Moreover, the book feels quite historical in its attention to particular details (and not just because these are old details; it is thus contextual in the loose sense). To be sure, in formal terms process remains only as a nascent panel cause diagram (281) and in the sixteen-fold tables that cross-classify two dichotomies at two time points. But

But causalism went beyond that. Once empirical sociologists began to think that main effects actually represented something more than an analytic convenience, they lost touch with the theoretical foundations of the discipline in real social action. The variables paradigm had begun with Ogburn, Stouffer, Duncan, and Lazarsfeld's fortunate yoking of the new statistics to sociological thinking via the idea of variables. Causalism restricted this bridge to one-way traffic.

As a result, the variables paradigm has never really renewed itself. Today it is old and tired. The intellectual exhaustion I described at the outset of the chapter is in fact the exhaustion of the variables paradigm. After years of distinguished and important work, it has lost its capacity to excite us. In part it lost its excitement through self-absorbed technicality ("formal and empty ingenuity," said Mills [1959, 75]). In part it lost touch with real people, not only as readers but also as objects of analysis. In part, as I have said, it lost touch with social theory, which was and continues to be mainly about social action and interaction.

But perhaps most important of all, the fun is over. Today we never see the big wink from Duncan as he tries yet another far-fetched calculation. We never see a big wink from anybody.[30] Today the sudden rush of new results that inevitably flows from new methods—the overall picture of political life that the new surveys made possible in *Political Man,* for example—is

there is attention to particular political generations and to particular historical processes, and of course there are the three waves of the survey on which the book is based.

Yet the theoretical lessons learned have in fact little to do with the actual results. There are two chapters of conclusions. The first—for the disciplines—correctly situates the book as an attempt to mediate between a psychological and a more historical, structural view of voting. The second—clearly for the general audience—examines the implications of the findings for the normative theory of democracy. It is this second conclusion that is Parsons's sole concern in commenting on the work. Parsons (1959) gives a long interpretation of the various "paradoxes" that Berelson et al. had used, in a somewhat ad hoc fashion, to conclude their book. He weaves these into a theory of the equilibrating functions of the political system. There is thus a nearly complete disjuncture between the "middle range" conclusions with which Merton might have been concerned (chap. 13) and the grand theoretical (Parsonian) ones (chap. 14). This disjuncture allowed Parsons to believe that the work realized an aim he expressed in 1948: "The ideal is to have theoretical categories of such a character that the empirical values of the variables concerned are immediate products of our observational procedures" (1948, 158). The Parsons-Stouffer "articulation" was actually a chasm bridged by a leap of faith. It thus becomes clear how Mills 1959 could attack grand theory and abstracted empiricism as different things even as their practitioners thought they were different aspects of one thing. Note, however, that the link between Merton and Lazarsfeld was much closer, and much longer enduring, than that between Parsons and Stouffer (Coleman 1990, 89).

30. Duncan got the last wink on everyone when he published, as his last major work in sociology, *Notes on Social Measurement* in 1984. *Notes* blew a raspberry at vast areas of current sociological research and methodology, from LISREL (209–10) to occupational scales (194). Unfortunately, it has remained merely a cult classic.

over as well. We can never be surprised that way again. Now we are simply filling in the details. The idea of variables was a great idea. But its day as an exciting source of knowledge is done.

The Future of Sociological Methodology

Now, you might think I am about to say that if only we would read the Chicago school, and hearken to its message, the clouds would lift, sociology would become exciting, policymakers would beat a path to our door, and so on. But that is nonsense. The flowerings of both the Chicago school and the variables paradigm depended—I'm being a good Chicagoan here—on a conjunction of things. It was not just good theory that was involved. In both cases a large body of method and analytic technique lay ready to hand. Chicagoans built directly on the long-standing social survey tradition. The variables paradigm went nowhere until it began to utilize the analytic machinery of the Fisherians. Therefore absorbing the contextualist message of the Chicago classics can do us no good unless there are methods at hand for putting that message into active empirical practice. The good news is that those methods are waiting for us.

Let me begin with desiderata. A methodology for contextualist sociology must put into some kind of empirical practice the basic concepts of the Chicago school that I outlined above. We require ways of discovering natural histories—long, consistent patterns of events. We require ways of parsing careers—complex sequences with substantial environmental determination. We require ways of describing interactional fields. We require also ways of investigating complex spatial interdependence, and of making this spatial interdependence more and more temporally structured, till again we arrive at the description and measurement of interactional fields.

Note that I make no statements about the kinds of data required. A central reason for returning to contextualism is that it would bring together kinds of sociology long separated. As I said before, the historical sociologists often *do* discuss natural histories and careers and interactional fields. Many of those in the interactionist tradition *do* discuss spatial interdependence. And our theorists *do* couch their theories in terms of action, often structured in time and space. In what follows, then, I shall focus mainly on *positivist, formal* methods for contextualism. For they are what the discipline needs most and what, fortunately, seem about to become widely available.[31]

---

31. In this connection, I have been asked several times why I do not deal here with the topic of culture. This is an important question, for culture is a central topic in sociology today (as it should be) and in particular is associated strongly in many people's minds with both social temporality and social geography, both of which are seen as socially constructed. In part I ig-

Table 13. Contextualist Methodological Examples

		Degrees of Contextuality: Space		
		None	Some	Much
Degrees of Contextuality: Time	None	Mainstream methodologies		Network analysis (White)
	Some			Robust action (Padgett) Network games (Abell)
	Much	Sequence analysis (Abbott)	Narrative formalism (Abell, Heise)	Encoding

In closing, then, I would like to discuss some work that begins to develop such methods. I do not mean these new methods *are* in fact the particular techniques that will revolutionize sociology; rather, they illustrate the kind of thinking that will produce the techniques that will revolutionize sociology. Once again, I proceed by considering the heavily contextual cells of my table.

I begin with studies of social context, for these have seen more work than temporal contexts, principally in what has become known as network analysis. Network analysis has substantial empirical results to its credit. Thus, Edward Laumann and David Knoke's *The Organizational State* (1987) uses network analysis to uncover a complex and shifting structure within national politics that is completely unrecoverable through standard

---

nore culture for simple manageability. To enter it into my argument is to move toward general theorizing, whereas my goal here is to restate the Chicago tradition. A second reason is that I do not think that the idea that meaning (causal or otherwise) arrives in part from context is the same as the idea that meaning is inherently multiple or complex. It is the latter that I take to be the central concern of those who question me about culture, in part from their quizzical reactions to my conception of "narrative positivism" (Abbott 1992b. Narrative isn't supposed to be capable of having a single meaning.) I do think culture is a central topic, but I don't dare take it on when I am already embroiled in the battle of contextuality and causality. Like Blumer, some previous readers of this chapter have fallen into conflating variables, quantitative study, objectivism, and analytical rigor on the one hand and interpretation, ethnography, subjectivism, and narrative on the other. (For an example of this conflation, see Richardson 1990.) I am arguing that a common concern for context unites *various* groups with various positions on those other dichotomies. Nonetheless, there is clearly an essay like this one to be written about the disappearance of culture from mainstream empirical sociology.

variable-based techniques. Location is a central theme here, as it has been throughout Laumann's work. The empirical achievements of network analysis reflect an equally powerful set of theoretical foundations, developed largely by Harrison White and his students. Together, the empirical and theoretical sides of network thinking present a more closely unified approach to social reality than anything in the variables paradigm. And of course network thinking has raised the question of contextual determination in ways highly embarrassing to that dominant paradigm, as in White's 1970 book *Chains of Opportunity,* which has shaped studies of labor markets among groups from civil servants to psychiatrists and state police. (See Chase 1991 for a review of "vacancy chain" systems, and the sources cited above, note 8, for general sources on network analysis.)

Some daring investigators are pushing network analysis toward temporal complexity (the 2,3 cell of table 13). Peter Abell (1990a) has begun to combine his formal analysis of narrative similarity with rational choice models of action. The result is a conception of "games in networks." Another example is John Padgett's analysis of networks of connections over the century-long buildup of the Medici political party in Florence (Padgett and Ansell 1993). With methods developed from White's blockmodeling, Padgett traces in elegant detail the slow, often accidental construction of kinship, economic, and political networks that ultimately gave Cosimo de' Medici the capacity for "robust action," action largely independent of controls or coalitions under him (precisely the kind of action none of Laumann and Knoke's organizations could undertake). As in so much of contemporary sociological theory, Padgett's direct focus is on action in structure. (White has written a theoretical book on this subject [White 1992].)

The same sort of methodological development is gradually coming to studies of temporal patterns and contextual determination. A number of theorists have been at work on formal models—particularly Thomas Fararo and John Skvoretz (e.g., 1984). But here too we see the development of practical empirical methods (for reviews, see Abbott 1992b, 1995b).

The first of these are addressed directly to the classical problem of comparison and categorization of narratives across units: the 3,1 cell of table 13, where temporal context is strong but units are basically independent. This is the practical question of whether Park was right in emphasizing natural histories, careers, and other sorts of temporal patterns. My own work in what is called sequence analysis focuses here. I have used scaling techniques to analyze narratives of professionalization among American doctors, showing clearly that local power took precedence over local knowledge (Abbott 1991b). I have also used more esoteric techniques—sequence comparison algorithms from computer science—to analyze careers of musicians (Abbott and Hrycak 1990) and histories of welfare states (Abbott and DeViney 1992). For a review of such studies see Abbott and Tsay 1998.

Others—chiefly David Heise and Peter Abell—have focused on more complex, interactive narratives involving several interdependent actors. Heise's methods (see Heise 1989, 1991 and Corsaro and Heise 1990) arose out of his attempt to code complex, ethnographic narratives in consistent ways. These methods produce logical structures to complex stories that can be compared across instances of one type (arguing with a policeman, say) or between types (arguing with a policeman compared with, say, academic seminars). An elegant example is Griffin's (1993) analysis of lynching. Abell (1987, 1990b, 1993) has taken a different approach (emphasizing mathematics rather than logic) to a somewhat similar coding of complex narratives. Abell's studies of consumer cooperatives show how surprising similarities of outcome emerge under narrative (and causal) conditions that seem strikingly different. Other writers (Padgett 1981, for example) have tried still other techniques.[32]

In their critics' eyes all of these studies, those emphasizing temporal context as well as those emphasizing spatial context, suffer from a crucial flaw. They lack "causal analysis." They do not tell us "what are the crucial variables." But that is their whole point. Causality as it has emerged in sociology since 1965 is so much reification. Social life is no more, in fact, than recurrent patterns of action in recurrent structures. These methods, each in its own way, converge on the direct analysis of patterns of social activity in temporal and social context that were at the heart of the Chicago school. They tell us what are the crucial *actual patterns*, not what are the crucial variables. The latter are a figment of our unsociological imagination.[33]

32. The reader will note that I have left undiscussed the 3,3 cell—heavy on both temporal and social context. This is in part because I feel no one has achieved serious empirical analysis there. Indeed, it may be impossible without simulation. But more important, it reflects my judgment that the unification of the temporal line of contextualism (the narrative positivism of Heise, Abell, and myself) with the social contextualism of White-type network analysis requires some profound theoretical work. Most important, I feel that the temporalists have to overcome the teleology implicit in their narrative comparisons; after all, the past isn't "really out there somewhere." I think this problem can be addressed through the notion that past narratives are "encoded" in current social structure. But that is a matter for an article or book of its own, not for a short paragraph here. Some readers may worry that I have also not discussed event history analysis and the model of social reality implicit in it, since those seem quite temporally oriented. I have in fact written an article on that subject (Abbott 1990) and so slight it here.

33. It is striking that empirical social science's original stronghold—market research—is the strongest locus of noncausal analytic techniques like scaling and clustering. Marketers bet

Like Park and Burgess, like Ogburn and Stouffer, workers in these new contextualist paradigms have found much of their methodology outside sociology itself. Harrison White and Peter Abell have put their physics Ph.D.'s to good use in formalizing contextual structures. I have borrowed principally from biology and computer science. Charles Ragin's (1987) qualitative comparative analysis—a variables-framework version of contextualism—comes originally from electrical engineering.

While some of these borrowed techniques require serious mathematical training, the large set of problems involving classification of temporal or spatial patterns do not. As it happens, work on classification of complex patterns makes up a substantial fraction of the current computer science literature. These dynamic programming methods for pattern matching have widespread application in biology, computer science, cognitive psychology, and related fields. They are without question the most general set of techniques currently under development in data analysis of any kind. Since they can be applied to patterns of several dimensions, they will ultimately be applicable to comparing networks just as I have used them to compare narratives. (For a current overview, see the sources cited in Abbott 1993.)[34]

Imagine if we could tell a policymaker not just, "Well, if you put x amount of money on that problem the problem will grow 15 percent less than it otherwise would have next year." But suppose we could say, "Well, if you put x amount of money on the problem, then a and b might happen, and if a happens then perhaps c, but if both a and b, then c is quite unlikely, and since c is necessary to d, where you're trying to go, then you can't solve your problem by this approach unless you can avoid b." Imagine if that

---

millions on scaling analyses (multidimensional scaling was after all pioneered by the marketing group at Bell Labs under Joseph Kruskal), while sociologists, with the conspicuous exception of Edward Laumann, never publish them. There is of course an extensive literature on causality, of which Marini and Singer 1988 is a useful review. Sociology has most of the same problems with causality that medicine does. Its original models sought individually necessary causes, for its aims were often operational, and as in medicine, the narrow neck of an individually necessary cause provides absolute operational control. In medicine this kind of causal thinking works for yellow fever but not for arthritis or cancer. Such complex diseases demand analyses of complex pathways leading to common outcomes. Looking for causes in such cases boils down, as Marini and Singer note (1988, 355), to finding "insufficient but nonredundant parts of an unnecessary but sufficient condition." That is the reality of "causal analysis" in sociology today.

34. My faith in these new analytic techniques reflects their direct focus on pattern, on relationship, on context and connection. These techniques can look directly at any sort of pattern, including the complex patterns, interactive in time and space, that old Chicago made central to its sociology. On seeing these methods, one can realize that in part old Chicago died because its theory was too far ahead of its methods. For these are the quantitative methods that Park and Burgess would have seen as ideal for scientific sociological analysis.

were not just a thought experiment that we all can and do carry out in interpreting regression results but were a direct result of standard methods applied to data on policy experiences. That would be policy science indeed. The methods are in fact available to produce it. They simply await our imagination.

Sixty years ago, sociology had an intellectual revolution, the variables revolution. As so often happens, the revolution was misinterpreted by many of the participants. Stouffer thought variables were a shortcut to sociological truths that he still understood within the contextualist, interactionist paradigm (Turner and Turner 1990, 107). Ogburn thought variables were a way of making sociology scientific, not a change of paradigm within an already established field.

Today we stand at the end of that journey. The variables paradigm is old and tired. How lucky for us that not only do we have the great interactionist theoretical heritage to rediscover but that, at the same time, a number of sociologists have begun to develop methods for studying action in context, methods that in turn can make use of the vast array of pattern-recognition techniques. Because of this conjuncture, we can now create a "positivism" attuned to the questions posed by our own theoretical heritage. We now have the empirical power to return social facts to their temporal and spatial contexts. We can look directly at social action by particular social actors in particular social times and places.[35]

In my view, then, we are not at all in crisis. Quite the contrary. Sociology stands before a great new flowering. New methods are available for borrowing. Problems for analysis are more pressing and more exciting than ever. Above all, we possess a goodly heritage of both theoretical and empirical work in the contextualist, interactionist tradition, bequeathed to us by the Chicago school. That work provides a foundation and an example for where sociology ought to go. There is then no need to write a valediction of the Chicago tradition. One eulogizes only the dead.

35. Most important, our discipline has the strongest theoretical tradition in social science founded on the idea of interaction and contextual determination. That idea is utterly absent from the conceptual apparatus of our competitors the economists. Game theory is their first halting recognition that maybe the actions of others are consequential for the actions of the self.

Epilogue

I promised at the outset a wearying journey through "thickets of detail, copses of complexity, and forests of fact." And surely no one can gainsay that description: we have read editors' memos and fought dead fights of long ago. Yet I have just played the triumphant guide and pushed aside the last branches to show the glorious prospect of the future.

The reader will have noticed that the philosophy of history assumed throughout this book firmly rejects such a teleological gesture. We have arrived at a clearing, or perhaps a little knoll where we can look around a bit, but woods lie ahead in all directions. To put the matter more fancifully but more accurately, we no sooner enter a clearing than it grows up rank about us. The longer we stay in our little clearing and train our eyes on our surroundings, the more clearly we see that this clearing too is full of previously invisible obstructions. There is no triumphant moment; there is only struggling to reach another present in which to take a breath and look around.

Here I will revisit the several questions raised in the prologue. First, I argued that what we usually call social things—the Chicago school being the instant example—are not so much things as processes, ways of becoming that are characteristic of particular locales in social life. Implicitly in the prologue and explicitly later, I argued that all social things are traditions—lineages was my word—and that the secret of their thingness lies in the way they bind together various preceding lineages in the social process. Directly from these views flowed my second prologue argument, the notion that one can investigate social things only historically. In a deep sense, pure synchronic analysis is meaningless.

My third prologue argument followed logically from the first two: the different lineages or traditions in the social world crosscut one another. Most particularly, the continuity of names should not fool us into believing in the continuity of the named. The endurance of noun phrases like *American Journal of Sociology* and Chicago Department of Sociology, like that of nouns like sociologist or religion, is a transparent scrim behind which the stagehands are perpetually moving the props around. Every time we turn on the backlights of synchronic analysis we see a different setting.

223

My fourth theme concerned the emergence of prescription as a mode of discussion. As we move toward the present, we become more comfortable with prescription, indeed we demand more of it. Let the dead bury their dead, we think, except insofar as exhumation can serve our current debates. I reported various writers' exhumations—not always very carefully done—in chapters 1 and 2. But I have left hanging the issue of prescription more generally, although I have made at length my own prescriptive argument in favor of the central Chicago concept of location.

Where then have we come in terms of these four problems? First of all, we have now the concept of lineage, which I have—sometimes covertly, sometimes openly—tried to substitute for the presentist nominalization of simple nouns. Clearly the social world is perpetually traversed by these myriad lineages, which braid together the various events of social life into the knotted mass of history. Each event takes its place in many lineages simultaneously. Individual lineages achieve their coherence, in my argument, by arranging these events into mutually reinforcing structures. Social entities emerge when this rearrangement is successful and die when it fails. Often, as with the Chicago school, failure of one kind—the end of the first Chicago school as a social reality at Chicago—is exchanged for success of another—the firming up of the Chicago school as a cultural object.

In general the coming and going of this "resonance" has been a crucial organizing theme for the book. For it is only by detailed investigation that we can see this resonance anywhere but in the obvious places—in people and in organizations with nominal continuity. To see it in something as elusive as a "Chicago tradition," we have to recognize how members of that tradition recreate it by arguing with each other in certain resonant ways. But chapter 2 also gave us an interesting vision of resonance failure. The "eclectism" of the Chicago Department of Sociology in the Hauser years did not produce a great flowering or even a coherent department. It was, in fact, a scrim covering a shift in the level of coherence, from department to discipline. In that sense the Chicago department after 1955 was less consequential than before, and hence less thinglike, a mere hollow name unless we accept the reality of Morris Janowitz's resurrection of it.

It has been my aim, above all in the chapters on the *AJS*, to show how rearrangements of lineages—all of them attempting to build certain kinds of resonances—take place. In the *AJS* history, the *Journal*'s continuity was in the first instance physical and nominal, but the other lineages bound into the *AJS*—norms of behavior, concepts of science, primary groups and bureaucracies, old people and young people, Press and discipline—all these shuffled rapidly behind the screen of continuity. All through the history, bits and pieces, sometimes quite major ones, were pushed in and out of the *AJS* as a social phenomenon. The *Journal* was continually remade in a sequence of presents. In a way, the whole "Chicago tradition" is another such scrim. Most of "Chicago" these days isn't in Chicago. It is important also to remember *what* disappears. Reformism doesn't completely disappear from the social world because it got edited out of the *AJS* and bundled out of the American Sociological Association. It was bound into other lineages—into city management, into urban planning schools, into social work, into the politics of the cultural left, and so on. Indeed, it has come back to the *AJS* in the present, for the *AJS*, like all of current sociology, contains much "scientific" writing that is reformist in its choice of subject matter, its tone, and the aims of its analysis. No one today makes a career in sociology by arguing that inequality is a natural state of affairs. (Admittedly the late Bruce Mayhew tried, but with little success.)

The concept of braiding implies that social things—entities, lineages, whatever we wish to call them—are perpetually open to action and that, at least within the constraints provided by the complete pattern of lineage connection across the entire society, any type of rearrangement is possible. To be sure, for any local lineage there seems to be an "outside," a set of "larger forces." For that reason I have not scrupled to use the language of inside/outside. But the outside is in fact a mirage. "External" is merely a code word for all the other entanglements of lineages braided in with the event we happen to be interested in. (These entanglements are not atomic but structured, which is why the economists' concept of market does not offer a way out of our current dilemmas.) The entire social world is made up of local interaction, and even the "largest" of events (e.g., the decline of a whole discipline, or the making of a nation) have to be built or recreated or reversed moment to moment. In such a view, the action/structure problem does not exist, for, as the Chicago schools have argued, in such a view it is the actual details of locations—the network of action and lineage—that determine action's outcome in the future. No structure exists outside the current present, immune to action. The cunning of reason is a Hegelian delusion, like its Marxist stepson the dialectic of modes of production.

To say that all social events are located, and that location has central consequences for their impact, implies that events without location have no meaning, or rather no specific meaning. We can impose—as did the variables paradigm with much short-term success—the idea that locationless events can and should be investigated. But I hope I have persuaded the reader that as a general rule for investigation this is not wise.

The philosophical term for things that have meaning only when their location is specified is "indexicals." The famous indexicals are the pronouns (I, she, they, etc.) and the spatial and temporal relatives (here, there, now, then, before, etc.). But under the Chicago argument made in chapter 7, all events and social phenomena are indexical to some extent. An obvious example is "science." Robert Park thought he was being scientific, as did Everett Hughes in developing a more structured Parkism, and as did Peter Rossi, who thought Hughes in turn knew nothing about science. When Louis Wirth decried "abstractions . . . so abstract that they can no longer be referred back to concrete instances or empirical situations," he said something to which all sociologists before or since would assent, even though his colleagues at the time disputed him (see chapter 2, p. 67). It is thus the locatedness of social events that creates the grounds for indexicality. From it arise both a solidarity that brings disparate events together and a consequent misunderstanding that drives them apart.

Much of sociology responds to the complexities of indexicality by throwing the concept of culture over reality like a gleaming counterpane. Our colleagues in anthropology have indeed made of the culture concept an exquisite fabric, but many borrow it simply to smooth over demanding structural details. One way forward, then, is to consider the structures of indexicality directly. Just as we have here seen the unfolding of indexical events within a single lineage, we can examine that unfolding more broadly, across a whole range of disciplines. How does and how should social science proceed if it is based on what appear to be enduring indexical structures: the opposition of science and nonscience, say, or of positivism and interpretation, or of narrative versus analysis? It is to this systematic chaos of disciplines that I turn next.

Sources and Acknowledgments

There are two unpublished sources for this book, personal communications and manuscript collections in the Joseph Regenstein Library at the University of Chicago. The manuscript work was partly shared with Emanuel Gaziano, with whom I wrote chapter 2. The personal communications (all with me personally), which vary from written documents to informal conversations, are as follows (all positions at the University of Chicago unless otherwise specified):

Charles Bidwell, Professor of Sociology, 20 June 1994
Peter Blau, Emeritus Professor of Sociology, University of North Carolina, Former Associate Professor of Sociology, 17 March 1995
Donald Bogue, Emeritus Professor of Sociology, 30 June 1994
Leonard Broom, former Editor, *American Sociological Review,* 4 January 1993
Leo A. Goodman, Professor of Sociology, University of California at Berkeley, Emeritus Professor of Sociology, 16 April 1994
Joseph Gusfield, former student, Emeritus Professor of Sociology, University of California, San Diego, 5 August 1994
Chauncy Harris, Emeritus Dean of the Social Science Division, 6 May 1994
Philip Hauser, Emeritus Professor of Sociology, 9 January 1993. (I talked to Hauser about *AJS* matters; he died while chapter 2 was in preparation, before I could talk to him about the postwar period generally.)
Donald N. Levine, Professor of Sociology, 23 June 1994
Florence Levinsohn, former Managing Editor, *American Journal of Sociology,* 30 December 1992, 5 October 1998
F. B. Lindstrom, former student, 26 April 1993
Robert K. Merton, Emeritus Professor of Sociology, Columbia University, 15 April 1994
William Sewell Sr., Emeritus Professor of Sociology, University of Wisconsin, 27 June 1994
Ethel Shanas, former student, Emerita Professor of Sociology, University of Illinois, Chicago, 13 July 1994

The following manuscript series were consulted for this book; all are at the Joseph Regenstein Library of the University of Chicago.

Personal Papers

EWB Ernest Watson Burgess Papers
PMH Philip M. Hauser Papers
ECH Everett C. Hughes Papers
  MJ Morris Janowitz Papers
WFO William F. Ogburn Papers
AWS Albion Woodbury Small Papers

RMT   Ralph M. Tyler Papers
 LW   Louis Wirth Papers

Organizational Papers

PP89   Presidential Papers 1889–1925
PP45   Presidential Papers 1945–60
PP52   Presidential Papers 1952–60
PPAB   Presidential Papers on appointments and budgets, 1925–40
 UCP   University of Chicago Press Archives (includes annual reports, abbreviated
         UCPAR)
 MDS   Minutes of the Department of Sociology
 SSR   Papers of the Society for Social Research

The following manuscript collections were consulted but yielded no relevant material: Marion Talbot Papers, C. R. Henderson Papers, Frederick Starr Papers.

Citations to manuscript collections are all given in notes. Since all these collections are organized in folders within boxes, they are cited as follows: EWB 33:2–4 means Burgess Papers, box 33, folders 2–4. (These are the minutes of the faculty seminar discussed in chapter 2.) Certain materials were in the Social Science Division vault. These are cited as SSV. We saw them with the kind permission of Colin Lucas, then Dean of the Social Science Division and currently Vice-Chancellor of the University of Oxford.

With respect to chapter 2, it is important to realize that source availability affects our reconstruction of the past. In particular, the absence of any personal papers of Blumer and Warner and the relative paucity of Hughes's personal material (most of his extensive materials cover his career at Brandeis) mean that we must judge these men through others' eyes. Also, there is no central collection of department minutes from 1939 to 1956. What survives is what faculty (mostly Wirth) happen to have kept.

A further direct source for chapter 2 deserves much thanks. Manny Gaziano and I sent copies of the first draft to six sociologists who had been on the Chicago faculty in the immediate postwar period: Howard Becker, Otis Dudley Duncan, Nelson Foote, Leo Goodman, Alfred Reiss Jr., and Anselm Strauss. All were kind enough to read the document on short notice and provide copious comments. These comments sometimes sent us to new sources, sometimes sent us back to old sources. They often challenged our interpretations. Although problems and differences undoubtedly remain, the chapter is much the better for the help these six gave us. We thank them deeply for their time and concern.

Sources on the history of the *American Journal of Sociology* demand separate comment. The surviving papers of the *AJS* are in several parts.

AJS1   "*AJS* Records 1967–75," archived 1982, twelve cartons
AJS2   "*AJS* Records Addenda 1960–83," archived 1986, nineteen cartons
AJS3   "*AJS* Records Addenda 1983–86," archived 1988, six cartons
AJS4   "*AJS* Records Addenda, n.d.," archived 1990, four cartons
AJS5   "*AJS* Records Addenda, n.d.," archived 1992, six cartons
AJS6   "*AJS* Records Addenda, n.d.," archived 1993, five cartons

None of this is yet organized into folders. I cite simply by the carton number. AJS2.19 means *AJS* Records Addenda 1960–83, carton 19. There is no telling where letters and other materials currently in the *AJS* archives will end up when the files are formally archived and opened. These files were simply pulled out of filing cabinets, placed in boxes, and taken to the library. Materials from various periods are scattered in various places throughout the *AJS* records. Rather than confuse the reader by providing locations that will undoubtedly be changed before the records are opened, I am simply citing all letters in text by author, receiver, and date. In a few places I have used the form (e.g.) AJS1.12 to mean *AJS* first gift, twelfth carton. By contrast, *AJS* 5:112 means *American Journal of Sociology,* vol. 5, p. 112, in the standard format. The year is easily calculated by remembering that the *AJS* began publication in 1895; just add the volume number to that year and you have the date, although since the *AJS* volume year begins in July, your result may be one year later than the actual publication date.

Another common reference in the notes on the *AJS* is to the *Annual Publication of the American Sociological Society,* abbreviated throughout as *Publication.* This was issued by the University of Chicago Press from 1905 to 1934 and renamed *American Sociological Review* (abbreviated *ASR* throughout) in 1936. AJSAR means *AJS* annual report from the given year. Normally these went from the editor to the Press. Additional manuscript information was also presented to the consulting editors at the annual lunch meeting at the ASA.

Throughout the citations, editors of the *AJS* are given by initials: AWB—Albion Woodbury Small, EF—Ellsworth Faris, EWB—Ernest Watson Burgess, HB—Herbert Blumer, ECH—Everett Cherrington Hughes, PHR—Peter H. Rossi, PMB—Peter M. Blau, CAA—C. Arnold Anderson, CEB—Charles E. Bidwell, EOL—Edward O. Laumann, WP—William Parish, MT—Marta Tienda. A few other people are sometimes cited by their initials: William Fielding Ogburn (WFO), Helen MacGill Hughes (HMH), Florence Levinsohn (FL).

Chapters 2 through 6 are overwhelmingly based on documentary sources, since in my view these are more trustworthy than recollection. I have used personal recollection—both from the list above and from the six commenters who read chapter 2 in draft—largely to corroborate documentary materials. In no case have I presented as fact any information resting on one personal recollection and nothing else. Because of that, I have in general omitted direct citation of personal communications.

This is the place for thanks to those who helped dig out the sources. First among these are the staff of the Special Collections Department of the Regenstein Library. One reason so much excellent work is done on the history of Chicago sociology is that the finding aids for manuscript collections already contain so much useful information about the sources. A second acknowledgment is to Assistant Dean Mary Brandon of the social science dean's office, who helped us with divisional sources. Several research assistants have labored on the various parts of this project. The word "labored" should be taken very seriously. Those who worked on chapter 3 found the identities and histories of a thousand of our often obscure colleagues in sources so diverse that I can only begin to list them in the relevant footnotes. I thank these students particularly: Jill Conrad, Emily Barman, and Julian Go. (I did the database programming myself, God help me.) Manny Gaziano, who began as my research assistant, ended up as a coauthor of chapter 2. Angela Tsay developed the database on which chapter 1 is based. The University of Chicago Press helped support these research assistants, as did the Division of Social Sciences, and indeed the College, through research funding provided me in my tenure as master of the Social Sciences Collegiate Division.

References

Abbott, A. 1988a. "Transcending General Linear Reality." *Sociological Theory* 6:169–86.
———. 1988b. *The System of Professions*. Chicago: University of Chicago Press.
———. 1990. "Conceptions of Time and Events in Social Science Methods." *Historical Methods* 23:140–50.
———. 1991a. "History and Sociology." *Social Science History* 15:201–38.
———. 1991b. "The Order of Professionalization." *Work and Occupations* 18:355–84.
———. 1992a. "What Do Cases Do?" In *What Is a Case?* ed. C. Ragin and H. S. Becker, 53–82. Cambridge: Cambridge University Press.
———. 1992b. "From Causes to Events." *Sociological Methods and Research* 20:428–55.
———. 1993. "Measure for Measure." *Journal of Mathematical Sociology*. 18:203–14.
———. 1995a. "Things of Boundaries." *Social Research* 62:857–82.
———. 1995b. "Sequence Analysis." *Annual Review of Sociology* 21:93–113.
———. 1998. "The Causal Devolution." *Sociological Methods and Research* 27:148–81.
Abbott, A., and E. Barman. 1997. "Sequence Comparison via Alignment and Gibbs Sampling." *Sociological Methodology* 27:47–87.
Abbott, A., and S. DeViney. 1992. "The Welfare State as Transnational Event." *Social Science History* 16:245–74.
Abbott, A., and A. Hrycak. 1990. "Measuring Resemblance in Sequence Data." *American Journal of Sociology* 96:144–85.
Abbott, A., and A. Tsay. 1998. "Sequence Analysis and Optimal Matching Methods in Sociology." Unpublished manuscript, Department of Sociology, University of Chicago.
Abell, P. 1987. *The Syntax of Social Life*. Oxford: Oxford University Press.
———. 1990a. "Games in Networks." *Rationality and Society* 1:259–82.
———. 1990b. "The Theory and Method of Comparative Narratives." Manuscript, University of Surrey, Department of Sociology.
———. 1993. "Some Aspects of Narrative Method." *Journal of Mathematical Sociology* 18:93–134.
Adams, R. 1977. "An Organization and Its Uncertain Environment." M.A. thesis, University of Chicago.
Ad Hoc Committee on ASA Future Organization Trends. 1989. "The Future Organizational Trends of the ASA." *Footnotes* 17, 6:1–6.
Adler, P. A., P. Adler, and E. B. Rochford Jr. 1986. "The Politics of Particiaption in Field Research." *Urban Life* 14:363–76.
Alexander, J. C. 1982. *Positivism, Presuppositions, and Current Controversies*. Berkeley: University of California Press.

Alihan, M. 1938. *Social Ecology.* New York: Columbia University Press.

Anderson, E. 1978. *A Place on the Corner.* Chicago: University of Chicago Press.

Anderson, M. 1989. "Expanding the Influence of the Statistical Association." In *Proceedings of the American Statistical Association Sesquicentennial,* 561–72. Washington, D.C.: American Statistical Association.

Anderson, N. 1923. *The Hobo.* Chicago: University of Chicago Press.

Ashmore, H. S. 1989. *Unseasonable Truths.* Boston: Little, Brown.

Assadi, B. 1987. "The Social Construction of Knowledge." Ph.D. diss., Howard University.

Bakanic, V., C. McPhail, and R. J. Simon. 1987. "The Manuscript Review and Decision-Making Process." *American Sociological Review* 52:631–42.

———. 1989. "Mixed Messages." *Sociological Quarterly* 30:639–54.

———. 1990. "If at First You Don't Succeed." *American Sociologist* 21:373–90.

Baldwin, J. D. 1990. "Advancing the Chicago School of Pragmatic Sociology." *Sociological Inquiry* 60:115–26.

Bannister, R. C. 1987. *Sociology and Scientism.* Chapel Hill: University of North Carolina Press.

Barthes, R. 1974. *S/Z.* New York: Hill and Wang.

Becker, H. P. 1930. "Distribution of Space in the American Journal of Sociology, 1895–1927." *American Journal of Sociology* 36:461–66.

———. 1932. "Space Apportioned Forty-eight Topics in the American Journal of Sociology, 1895–1930." *American Journal of Sociology* 38:71–78.

Berelson, B., P. F. Lazarsfeld, and W. N. McPhee. 1954. *Voting.* Chicago: University of Chicago Press.

Berelson, B., and G. A. Steiner. 1964. *Human Behavior.* New York: Harcourt, Brace and World.

Berger, B., ed. 1990. *Authors of Their Own Lives.* Berkeley: University of California Press.

Bernard, L. L. 1909. "The Teaching of Sociology in the United States." *American Journal of Sociology* 15:164–213.

———. 1930. "Schools of Sociology." *Social Science Quarterly* 11:117–34.

Bernert, C. 1983. "The Career of Causal Analysis in American Sociology." *British Journal of Sociology* 34:230–54.

Bittner, E. 1967. "The Police on Skid Row." *American Sociological Review* 32:699–715.

Blackwell, J. E., and M. Janowitz, eds. 1974. *Black Sociologists.* Chicago: University of Chicago Press.

Blake, J. A. 1978. "The Structural Basis of Theory Production." *Quarterly Journal of Ideology* 2:2–19.

Blalock, H. 1964. *Causal Inference in Non-experimental Research* Chapel Hill: University of North Carolina Press.

Blank, R. M. 1991. "Effects of Double-Blind versus Single-Blind Reviewing." *American Economic Review* 81:1041–67.

Blau, P. M., and O. D. Duncan. 1967. *The American Occupational Structure.* New York: Free Press.

Blumer, H. 1931. "Science without Concepts." *American Journal of Sociology* 36:515–33.

———. 1939. *An Appraisal of Thomas and Znaniecki's "The Polish Peasant in Europe and America."* Bulletin 44. New York: Social Science Research Council.

———. 1956. "Social Analysis and the 'Variable.'" *American Sociological Review* 21:683–90.

———. 1969. *Symbolic Interactionism.* Englewood Cliffs, N.J.: Prentice-Hall.
Bodemann, Y. M. 1978. "A Problem of Sociological Praxis." *Theory and Society* 5:387–420.
Boelen, W. A., W. F. Whyte, A. R. Orlandella, A. J. Vidich, L. Richardson, N. K. Denzin, P. A. Adler, P. Adler, J. M. Johnson, et al. 1992. "Street Corner Society Revisited." *Journal of Contemporary Ethnography* 21:2–132.
Bogue, D. J. 1974. "Introduction." In *The Basic Writings of Ernest W. Burgess,* ed. D. J. Bogue, ix–xxv. Chicago: Community and Family Studies Center.
Boorman, S. A., and H. C. White. 1976. "Social Structure from Multiple Networks II. *American Journal of Sociology* 81:1384–1446.
Breiger, R., ed. 1990. *Social Mobility and Social Structure.* Cambridge: Cambridge University Press.
Brumbaugh, A. J. 1948. *American Universities and Colleges.* 5th ed. Washington D.C.: American Council on Education.
Brunt, L. 1993. "Een stad als symbool." *Sociologische Gids* 40:440–65.
Buehler, C., G. Hesser, and A. Weigert. 1972. "A Study of Articles on Religion in Major Sociology Journals." *Journal for the Scientific Study of Religion* 11:165–70.
Bulmer, M. 1984. *The Chicago School of Sociology.* Chicago: University of Chicago Press.
———. 1985. "The Chicago School of Sociology." *History of Sociology* 5:61–77.
Bulmer, M., K. Bales, and K. K. Sklar, eds. 1991. *The Social Survey in Historical Perspective.* New York: Cambridge University Press.
Burgess, E. W. 1927. "Statistics and Case Studies as Methods of Sociological Research." *Sociology and Social Research* 12:103–10.
Burns, L. R. 1980. "The Chicago School and the Study of Organization Environment Relations." *Journal of the History of the Behavioral Sciences* 16:342–58.
Burns, T. 1996. "The Theoretical Underpinnings of Chicago Sociology in the 1920s and 1930s." *Sociological Review* 44:474–94.
Burroughs, E. R. 1920. *Thuvia, Maid of Mars.* Chicago: A. C. McClurg.
Burt, R. S., and P. Doreian. 1982. "Testing a Structural Model of Perception." *Quantity and Quality* 16:109–50.
Camic, C. 1995. "Three Departments in Search of a Discipline." *Social Research* 62:1003–33.
Cappell, C. L., and T. M. Guterbock. 1986. "Dimensions of Association in Sociology." *Bulletin de Méthode Sociologique* 9:23–29.
———. 1992. "Visible Colleges." *American Sociological Review* 57:266–73.
Carey, J. 1975. *Sociology and Public Affairs.* Beverly Hills, Calif.: Sage.
Cartter, A. M. 1964. *American Universities and Colleges.* 9th ed. Washington D.C.: American Council on Education.
Cassedy, J. H. 1983. "The Flourishing and Character of Early American Medical Journalism." *Journal of the History of Medicine and Allied Sciences* 38:135–50.
Castells, M. 1968. "Y a-t-il une sociologie urbaine?" *Sociologie du Travail* 10:72–90.
Cavan, R. S. 1928. *Suicide.* Chicago: University of Chicago Press.
Champion, D. J., and M. F. Morris. 1973. "A Content Analysis of Book Reviews in AJS, ASR, and Social Forces." *American Journal of Sociology* 78:1256–65.
Chanfrault-Duchet, M.-F. 1995. "Biographical Research in the Former West Germany." *Current Sociology* 43:209–19.

Chang, W.-c. 1976. "Statistical Theories and Sampling Practice." In *On the History of Probability and Statistics,* ed. D. B. Owen, 299–315. New York: Marcel Dekker.

Chapoulie, J.-M. 1996. "Everett Hughes and the Chicago Tradition." *Sociological Theory* 14:3–29.

Chase, I. 1991. "Vacancy Chains." *Annual Review of Sociology* 17:133–54.

Christakes, G. 1978. *Albion W. Small.* Boston: Twayne.

Christenson, J. A., and L. Sigelman. 1985. "Accrediting Knowledge." *Social Science Quarterly* 66:964–75.

Coleman, J. S. 1961. *The Adolescent Society.* New York: Free Press.

———. 1990. "Columbia in the 1950s." In *Authors of Their Own Lives,* ed. B. Berger, 75–103. Berkeley: University of California Press.

———. 1992. "Sociology and the National Agenda." Paper presented at the Centennial Conference of the University of Chicago Department of Sociology, Chicago, 2 May 1992.

Coleman, J. S., E. Katz, and H. Menzel. 1966. *Medical Innovation.* Indianapolis: Bobbs-Merrill.

Corsaro, W. A., and D. R. Heise. 1990. "Event Structures from Ethnographic Data." In *Sociological Methodology,* ed. C. Clogg, 1–57. Oxford: Basil Blackwell.

Cortese, A. J. 1995. "The Rise, Hegemony, and Decline of the Chicago School of Sociology, 1892–1945." *Social Science Journal* 32:235–54.

Coser, L. A. 1971. *Masters of Sociological Thought.* New York: Harcourt, Brace.

Cote, J.-F. 1996. "Le réalisme social et l'école de Chicago." *Cahiers de Recherche Sociologique* 26:115–37.

Coulon, A. 1992. *L'école de Chicago.* Paris: PUF.

Crane, D. 1967. "The Gatekeepers of Science." *American Sociologist* 2:195–201.

Cressey, P. G. 1932. *The Taxi-Dance Hall.* Chicago: University of Chicago Press.

Cruttwell, P. [1954] 1960. *The Shakespearean Moment.* New York: Vintage.

D'Antonio, W. V. 1992. "Recruiting Sociologists in a Time of Changing Opportunities." In *Sociology and Its Publics,* ed. T. C. Halliday and M. Janowitz, 99–136. Chicago: University of Chicago Press.

Deegan, M. J. 1988. *Jane Addams and the Men of the Chicago School.* New Brunswick, N.J.: Transaction.

———. 1995. "The Second Sex and the Chicago School." In *A Second Chicago School?* ed. G. A. Fine, 322–64. Chicago: University of Chicago Press.

———. 1996. "Dear Love, Dear Love." *Gender and Society* 10:590–607.

Denzin, N. K. 1995. "Stanley and Clifford." *Current Sociology* 43:115–23.

———. 1996. "Post-pragmatism." *Symbolic Interaction* 19:61–75.

Dibble, V. 1975. *The Legacy of Albion Small.* Chicago: University of Chicago Press.

Diner, S. J. 1975. "Department and Discipline." *Minerva* 13:514–53.

Duncan, O. D. 1984. *Notes on Social Measurement.* New York: Russell Sage.

Duneier, M. 1992. *Slim's Table.* Chicago: University of Chicago Press.

Eastman, C. 1910. *Work Accidents and the Law.* New York: Charities Publications Committee.

Ebert, M. 1952. "The Rise and Development of the American Medical Periodical." *Bulletin of the Medical Library Association* 40:243–76.

Edwards, L. P. 1927. *The Natural History of Revolution.* Chicago: University of Chicago Press.

Ennis, J. G. 1992. "The Social Organization of Sociological Knowledge." *American Sociological Review* 57:259–65.

Evans, R. 1986–87. "Sociological Journals and the 'Decline' of Chicago Sociology: 1925–1945." *History of Sociology* 6–7:109–30.

Fararo, T. J., and J. Skvoretz. 1984. "Institutions as Production Systems." *Journal of Mathematical Sociology* 10:117–82.

Farber, B. 1988. "The Human Element." *Sociological Perspectives* 31:339–59.

Farber, N. 1995. "Charles S. Johnson's *The Negro in Chicago*." *American Sociologist* 26:78–88.

Faris, R. E. L. 1967. *Chicago Sociology, 1920–1932*. San Francisco: Chandler.

Faris, R. E. L., and H. W. Dunham. 1939. *Mental Disorders and Urban Areas*. Chicago: University of Chicago Press.

Faught, J. D. 1980. "Presuppositions of the Chicago School in the Work of Everett C. Hughes." *American Sociologist* 15:72–82.

Feffer, A. 1993. *The Chicago Pragmatists and American Progressivism*. Ithaca: Cornell University Press.

Fine, G. A., ed. 1995. *A Second Chicago School?* Chicago: University of Chicago Press.

Fischer, C. S. 1982. *To Dwell among Friends*. Chicago: University of Chicago Press.

Fish, V. K. 1981. "Annie Marion MacLean." *Journal of the History of Sociology* 3:43–62.

Fisher, B. M., and A. L. Strauss. 1978a. "The Chicago Tradition and Social Change." *Symbolic Interaction* 1:5–23.

———. 1978b. "Interactionism." In *A History of Sociological Analysis*, ed. T. Bottomore and R. Nisbet, 457–98. New York: Basic.

———. 1979a. "George Herbert Mead and the Chicago Tradition of Sociology" (part 1). *Symbolic Interaction* 2, 1:9–26.

———. 1979b. "George Herbert Mead and the Chicago Tradition of Sociology" (part 2). *Symbolic Interaction* 2, 2:9–20.

Frazier, E. F. 1932. *The Negro Family in Chicago*. Chicago: University of Chicago Press.

Freedman, D. A. 1987. "As Others See Us." *Journal of Educational Statistics* 12:101–28, 206–23.

Freidson, E. 1986. *Professional Powers*. Chicago: University of Chicago Press.

Gans, J. S., and G. B. Shepherd. 1994. "How Are the Mighty Fallen." *Journal of Economic Perspectives* 8:165–79.

Garnett, R. 1988. "The Study of War in American Sociology." *American Sociologist* 19:270–82.

Gaziano, E. 1996. "Ecological Metaphors as Scientific Boundary Work." *American Journal of Sociology* 101:874–907.

Giddens, A. 1984. *The Constitution of Society*. Berkeley: University of California Press.

Giddings, F. H. 1901. *Inductive Sociology*. New York: Macmillan.

Glenn, N. D. 1971. "American Sociologists' Evaluation of Sixty-three Journals." *American Sociologist* 6:298–303.

———. 1976. "The Journal Article Review Process." *American Sociologist* 11:179–85.

Glock, C. Y. 1979. "Organizational Innovation for Social Science Research and Training." In *Qualitative and Quantitative Social Research*, ed. R. K. Merton, J. S. Coleman, and P. Rossi, 23–36. New York: Free Press.

Goffman, E. 1956. "Embarrassment and Social Organization." *American Journal of Sociology* 62:264–71.

Goodman, L. A. 1972. "A General Model for the Analysis of Surveys." *American Journal of Sociology* 77:1035–86.

———. 1973. "Causal Analysis of Data." *American Journal of Sociology* 78:1135–91.

Gordon, M. 1982. "Citation Ranking versus Subjective Evaluation in Determination of Journal Hierarchies in the Social Sciences." *Journal of the American Society for Information Science* 33:55–57.

Gouldner, A. 1970. *The Coming Crisis of Western Sociology.* New York: Avon.

Grafmeyer, Y., and I. Joseph, ed. 1979. *L'école de Chicago.* Paris: Aubier.

Greenwald, M. W., and M. Anderson. 1996. *Pittsburgh Surveyed.* Pittsburgh: University of Pittsburgh Press.

Griffin, L. J. 1993. "Narrative, Event Structure Analysis, and Causal Interpretation in Historical Sociology." *American Journal of Sociology* 98:1094–1133.

Gusfield, J. 1980. "Two Genres of Sociology." In *The Rhetoric of Social Research,* ed. A. Hunter, 62–96. New Brunswick: Rutgers University Press.

———. 1992. "The Scholarly Tension." In *General Education in the Social Sciences,* ed. J. MacAloon, 167–77. Chicago: University of Chicago Press.

Habermas, J. 1971. *Knowledge and Human Interests.* Trans. J. J. Shapiro. Boston: Beacon.

Halbwachs, M. 1932. "Chicago, expérience ethnique." *Annales d'Histoire Économique et Sociale* 4:11–49. (Reprinted in Grafmeyer and Joseph 1979 pp. 279–327.)

Halle, D. 1984. *America's Working Man.* Chicago: University of Chicago Press.

Hamilton, D. P. 1991. "Research Papers." *Science* 251:25.

Hammermesh, D. S. 1994. "Facts and Myths about Refereeing." *Journal of Economic Perspectives* 8:153–63.

Hammersley, M. 1989. *The Dilemma of Qualitative Method.* New York: Routledge.

Hannerz, U. 1980. *Exploring the City.* New York: Columbia University Press.

Hansen, M. H., and W. G. Madow. 1976. "Some Important Events in the Historical Development of Sample Surveys." In *On the History of Probability and Statistics,* ed. D. B. Owen, 75–102. New York: Marcel Dekker.

Hargens, L. L. 1991. "Impressions and Misimpressions about Sociology Journals." *Contemporary Sociology* 20:343–49.

Harscheidt, M. 1989. "Biographieforschung." *Historische Sozialforschung* 14:99–142.

Harvey, L. 1987a. *Myths of the Chicago School of Sociology.* Avebury: Aldershot.

———. 1987b. "The Nature of Schools in the Sociology of Knowledge." *Sociological Review* 35:245–78.

Heise, D. R. 1989. "Modeling Event Structures." *Journal of Mathematical Sociology* 14:139–69.

———. 1991. "Event Structure Analysis." In *Using Computers in Qualitative Research,* ed. N. Fielding and R. Lee, 136–63. Newbury Park, Calif.: Sage.

Helmes-Hayes, R. C. 1987. "A Dualistic Vision." *Sociological Quarterly* 28:387–409.

Henry, C. P. 1995. "Abram Harris, E. Franklin Frazier, and Ralph Bunche." *National Political Science Review* 5:36–56.

Hiller, E. T. 1928. *The Strike.* Chicago: University of Chicago Press.

Historical Statistics of the United States to 1970. 1976. Washington D.C.: Government Printing Office.

Hochberg, L. 1984. "The English Civil War in Geographical Perspective." *Journal of Interdisciplinary History* 14:729–50.

Hochberg, L., and D. W. Miller. n.d. "Internal Colonialism in Geographic Perspective." In *Geography of Social Change,* ed. C. Earle and L. Hochberg. Stanford: Stanford University Press. Forthcoming.

Hoyt, H. 1933. *One Hundred Years of Land Use Values in Chicago.* Chicago: University of Chicago Press.

Huber, J. 1992. "Report of the ASA Task Group on Graduate Education." Washington D.C.: American Sociological Association.

Hughes, E. C. 1928. "A Study of a Secular Institution." Ph.D. diss., University of Chicago.

Hughes, H. M. 1972. "Maid of All Work or Departmental Sister-in-Law?" *American Journal of Sociology* 78:767–72.

Irwin, M. 1956. *American Universities and Colleges.* 7th ed. Washington D.C.: American Council on Education.

Jackson, K. T. 1985. *Crabgrass Frontier.* New York: Oxford University Press.

Jackson, P. 1985. "Urban Ethnography." *Progress in Human Geography* 9:157–76.

Jaworski, G. D. 1995. "Simmel in Early American Sociology." *International Journal of Politics* 1995:489–17.

———. 1996. "Park, Doyle, and Hughes." *Sociological Inquiry* 66:160–74.

Jazbinsek, D., and R. Thies. 1997. "Grossstadt Dokumente." *Schriftenreihe der Forschungsgruppe "Metropolenforschung"* FSII:96–501. Berlin: WZB.

Joas, H. 1993. *Pragmatism and Social Theory.* Chicago: University of Chicago Press.

Karesh, M. 1995. "The Interstitial Origins of Symbolic Consumer Research." M.A. thesis, University of Chicago, Department of Sociology.

Katz, E., and P. F. Lazarsfeld. 1955. *Personal Influence.* New York: Free Press.

Kempthorne, O. 1976. "The Analysis of Variance and Factorial Design." In *On the History of Probability and Statistics,* ed. D. B. Owen, 29–54. New York: Marcel Dekker.

Kinloch, G. C. 1988. "American Sociology's Changing Interests as Reflected in Two Leading Journals." *American Sociologist* 19:181–94.

Kornblum, W., and V. W. Boggs. 1986. "42d Street." *Social Policy* 17:26–27.

Kuklick, H. 1980. "Chicago Sociology and Urban Planning Policy." *Theory and Society* 9:821–45.

Kurent, H. P. 1982. "Frances R. Donovan and the Chicago School of Sociology." Ph.D. diss., University of Maryland.

Kurtz, L. R. 1984. *Evaluating Chicago Sociology.* Chicago: University of Chicago Press.

Lal, B. B. 1990. *The Romance of Culture in an Urban Civilization.* London: Routledge.

LaPerrière, A. 1982. "Pour une construction empirique de la théorie." *Sociologie et Sociétés* 14:31–41.

Lauer, R. H. 1976. "Defining Social Problems." *Social Problems* 24:122–30.

Laumann, E. O., and D. Knoke. 1987. *The Organizational State.* Madison: University of Wisconsin Press.

Lazarsfeld, P. F., B. Berelson, and H. Gaudet. [1944] 1968. *The People's Choice.* New York: Columbia University Press.

Lazarsfeld, P. F., and M. Rosenberg. 1955. *The Language of Social Research.* New York: Free Press.

Lebas, E. 1982. "Urban and Regional Sociology in Advanced Industrial Societies." *Current Sociology* 30:1–264.

Lengermann, P. M. 1979. "The Founding of the American Sociological Review." *American Sociological Review* 44:185–98.

———. 1988. "Robert E. Park and the Theoretical Content of Chicago Sociology." *Sociological Inquiry* 58:361–77.

Levine, D. 1981. "A Sense of Unease." Draft manuscript, University of Chicago, Department of Sociology.

Lewis, J. D., and R. L. Smith. 1980. *American Sociology and Pragmatism*. Chicago: University of Chicago Press.

Lincourt, J. M., and P. H. Hare. 1973. "Neglected American Philosophers in the History of Symbolic Interactionism." *Journal of the History of the Behavioral Sciences* 9:333–38.

Lindner, R. 1993. "Literature and Sociology." *Sociologische Gids* 40:4–19.

———. [1990] 1996. *The Reportage of Urban Culture*. Cambridge: Cambridge University Press. First published as *Die Entdeckung der Stadtkultur*. Frankfurt: Suhrkamp.

Lindstrom, F. B., and R. A. Hardert, eds. 1988. "Kimball Young on the Chicago School." *Sociological Perspectives* 31:298–314.

Lipset, S. M. 1960. *Political Man*. New York: Doubleday.

Lofland, L. 1980. "Reminiscences of Classic Chicago." *Urban Life* 9:251–81.

———. 1983. "Understanding Urban Life." *Urban Life* 11:491–511.

Logan, J. R. 1988. "Producing Sociology." *American Sociologist* 19:167–80.

Logan, J. R., and H. L. Molotch. 1987. *Urban Fortunes*. Berkeley: University of California Press.

Lorrain, F., and H. C. White. 1971. "The Structural Equivalence of Individuals in Social Networks." *Journal of Mathematical Sociology* 1:49–80.

Lundberg, G. A. 1929. *Social Research*. New York: Longmans.

Lynd, R. S., and H. M. Lynd. 1929. *Middletown*. New York: Harcourt, Brace and World.

MacAloon, J. J., ed. 1992. *General Education in the Social Sciences*. Chicago: University of Chicago Press.

Mackie, M. 1977. "Professional Women's Collegial Relations and Productivity." *Sociology and Social Research* 61:277–93.

———. 1985. "Female Sociologists' Productivity, Collegial Relations, and Research Style Examined through Journal Publications." *Sociology and Social Research* 69:189–209.

Maines, D. R. 1989. "Repackaging Blumer." *Studies in Symbolic Interaction* 10:383–413.

———. 1993. "Narrative's Moment and Sociology's Phenomena." *Sociological Quarterly* 34:17–38.

Maines, D. R., J. C. Bridges, and J. T. Ulmer. 1996. "Mythic Facts and Park's Pragmatism." *Sociological Quarterly* 37:521–49.

Marini, M. M., and B. Singer. 1988. "Causality in the Social Sciences." In *Sociological Methodology*, ed. C. Clogg, 347–409. Washington, D.C.: American Sociological Association.

Marquand, J. P. 1949. *Point of No Return*. Boston: Little, Brown.

Marsden, P. V., and N. Lin. 1982. *Social Structure and Network Analysis*. Beverly Hills, Calif.: Sage.

Marsh, C. S. 1936. *American Universities and Colleges*. 3d ed. Washington D.C.: American Council on Education.

Matthews, F. H. 1977. *The Quest for an American Sociology.* Montreal: McGill-Queens University Press.

———. 1985. "Ontology and Chicago Sociology." *Philosophy of the Social Sciences* 15:197–203.

Matza, D. 1969. *Becoming Deviant.* Englewood Cliffs, N.J.: Prentice-Hall.

McAdam, D., J. D. McCarthy, and M. N. Zald. 1988. "Social Movements." In *Handbook of Sociology,* ed. N. Smelser, 695–737. Newbury Park, Calif.: Sage.

McCracken, J. H. 1932. *American Universities and Colleges.* Washington, D.C.: American Council on Education.

McNeill, W. H. 1991. *Hutchins' University.* Chicago: University of Chicago Press.

Meltzer, B. N., J. W. Petras, and L. T. Reynolds. 1975. *Symbolic Interactionism.* Boston: Routledge and Kegan Paul.

Merton, R. K. 1948. "Response." *American Sociological Review* 13:164–68.

Meyer, J. W., and B. Rowan. 1977. "Institutionalized Organizations." *American Journal of Sociology* 83:340–63.

Michaels, J. W., and J. M. Pippert. 1986. "Social Science Journal Characteristics and Journal Citation Measures." *Social Science Journal* 23:33–42.

Miller, Z. L. 1992. "Pluralism, Chicago School Style." *Journal of Urban History* 18:251–79.

Mills, C. W. 1943. "The Professional Ideology of the Social Pathologists." *American Journal of Sociology* 49:165–80.

———. 1959. *The Sociological Imagination.* London: Oxford University Press.

Mowrer, E. 1927. *Family Disorganization.* Chicago: University of Chicago Press.

Murray, S. O. 1988. "The Reception of Anthropological Work in Sociology Journals." *Journal of the History of the Behavioral Sciences* 24:135–51.

Neyman, J. 1934. "On the Two Different Aspects of Representative Method." *Journal of the Royal Statistical Society* 97:558–606.

Niemeyer, H. 1989. "Die Biographie." *Sociologia Internationalis* 27:89–97.

Nisbet, R. 1966. *The Sociological Tradition.* New York: Basic.

Oberschall, A. 1972. *The Establishment of Empirical Sociology.* New York: Harper.

Ogburn, W. F. [1912] 1964. "Progress and Uniformity in Child Labor Legislation." In *W. F. Ogburn on Culture and Social Change,* ed. O. D. Duncan, 110–30. Chicago: University of Chicago Press.

Ohm, R. M. 1988 "The Continuing Legacy of the Chicago School." *Sociological Perspectives* 31:360–76.

Oromaner, M. 1980. "Influentials in Textbooks and Journals, 1955 and 1970." *American Sociologist* 15:169–74.

"Organization of the American Sociological Society." 1906. *American Journal of Sociology* 9:535–69, 681–82.

Owen, D. B., ed. 1976. *On the History of Probability and Statistics.* New York: Marcel Dekker.

Padgett, J. F. 1981. "Hierarchy and Ecological Control in Federal Budgetary Decision-Making." *American Journal of Sociology* 87:75–129.

Padgett, J. F., and C. K. Ansell. 1993. "Robust Action and Party Formation in Renaissance Florence." *American Journal of Sociology* 98:1259–1319.

Page, C. H. 1981. "The American Sociological Review, 1958–1960. *American Sociologist* 16:43–47.

Park, R. E. 1925. "The City." In *The City,* ed. R. E. Park, E. W. Burgess, and R. D. McKenzie, 1–46. Chicago: University of Chicago Press.

Park, R. E., and E. W. Burgess. [1921] 1970. *Introduction to the Science of Sociology.* Chicago: University of Chicago Press.

Parsons, T. [1939] 1954. "The Professions and Social Structure." In *Essays in Sociological Theory,* 34–49. New York: Free Press.

———. 1948. "The Position of Social Theory." *American Sociological Review* 13:156–64.

———. 1959. "'Voting' and the Equilibrium of the American Political System." In *American Voting Behavior,* ed. E. Burdick and A. J. Roderick, 80–120. Glencoe, Ill.: Free Press.

Pennef, J. 1990. *La méthode biographique.* Paris: Armand Colin.

Persons, S. 1987. *Ethnic Studies at Chicago.* Urbana: University of Illinois Press.

Peters, C. B. 1976. "Multiple Submissions." *American Sociologist* 11:165–79.

Pfautz, H. W., and O. D. Duncan. 1950. "A Critical Evaluation of Warner's Work in Community Stratification." *American Sociological Review* 15:205–15.

Platt, A. 1991. *E. Franklin Frazier Reconsidered.* New Brunswick: Rutgers University Press.

Platt, J. 1992. "Acting as a Switchboard." *American Sociologist* 23, 3:23–36.

———. 1994. "The Chicago School and Firsthand Data." *History of the Human Sciences* 7:57–80.

———. 1995. "Research Methods and the Second Chicago School." In *A Second Chicago School?* ed. G. A. Fine, 82–107. Chicago: University of Chicago Press.

———. 1996. *A History of Sociological Research Methods in America* Cambridge: Cambridge University Press.

Plummer, K., ed. 1997. *The Chicago School: Critical Assessments.* London: Routledge.

Ragin, C. C. 1987. *The Comparative Method.* Berkeley: University of California Press.

Raushenbush, R. E. 1979. *Robert E. Park.* Durham: Duke University Press.

Reckless, W. 1933. *Vice in Chicago.* Chicago: University of Chicago Press.

Reinharz, S. 1995. "The Chicago School of Sociology and the Founding of the Graduate Program in Sociology at Brandeis University." In *A Second Chicago School?* ed. G. A. Fine, 273–321. Chicago: University of Chicago Press.

Reynolds, M. 1995. *From Gangs to Gangsters.* Guilderland, N.Y.: Harrow and Heston.

Rhoads, S. E. 1978. "Economists and Policy Analysts." *Public Administration Review* 38:112–20.

Richardson, L. 1990. "Narrative and Sociology." *Journal of Contemporary Ethnography* 19:116–35.

Riesman, D. 1990. "Becoming an Academic Man." In *Authors of Their Own Lives,* ed. B. M. Berger, 33–74. Berkeley: University of California Press.

———. 1992. "My Education in Soc 2 and My Efforts to Adapt It in the Harvard Setting." In *General Education in the Social Sciences,* ed. J. J. MacAloon, 178–216. Chicago: University of Chicago Press.

Ritzer, G. 1988. *Contemporary Sociological Theory.* New York: Knopf.

Robertson, D. A. 1928. *American Universities and Colleges.* Washington, D.C.: American Council on Education.

Robinson, W. S. 1950. "Ecological Correlations and the Behavior of Individuals." *American Sociological Review* 15:351–57.

Rock, P. 1979. *The Making of Symbolic Interactionism.* Totowa, N.J.: Rowman and Littlefield.

Rodell, F. 1936. "Goodbye to Law Reviews." *Virginia Law Review* 23:38–45.

Roos, P. A., and K. W. Jones. 1993. "Shifting Gender Boundaries." *Work and Occupations* 20:395–428.

Ross, D. 1991. *The Origins of American Social Science.* Cambridge: Cambridge University Press.

Salerno, R. A. 1987. *Louis Wirth.* New York: Greenwood.

Satzewich, V. 1991. "Aboriginal Peoples in Canada." *Innovation* 4:183–302.

Schwendinger, H., and J. R. Schwendinger. 1974. *The Sociologists of the Chair.* New York: Basic.

Scott, W. R., and J. W. Meyer. [1983] 1991. "The Organization of Societal Sectors." In *The New Institutionalism in Organizational Analysis,* ed. W. W. Powell and P. J. DiMaggio, 108–40. Chicago: University of Chicago Press.

Senders, J. 1976. "The Scientific Journal of the Future." *American Sociologist* 11:160–64.

Shanas, E. 1944. "The *American Journal of Sociology* through Fifty Years." *American Journal of Sociology* 50:522–33.

Shaw, C. R. [1930] 1966. *The Jackroller.* Chicago: University of Chicago Press.

Shaw, C. R., and H. D. McKay. 1942. *Juvenile Delinquency and Urban Areas.* Chicago: University of Chicago Press.

Shils, E. 1948. *The Present State of American Sociology.* Glencoe, Ill.: Free Press.

———. 1991. "Ernest Watson Burgess." In *Remembering the University of Chicago,* ed. E. Shils, 3–14. Chicago: University of Chicago Press.

Short, J. F. 1971. *The Social Fabric of the Metropolis.* Chicago: University of Chicago Press.

Sibley, E. 1963. *The Education of Sociologists in the United States.* New York: Russell Sage.

Skocpol, T. 1979. *States and Social Revolutions.* Cambridge: Cambridge University Press.

Skura, B. 1976. "Constraints on a Reform Movement." *Social Problems* 24:15–36.

Small, A. W. 1905. *General Sociology.* Chicago: University of Chicago Press.

———. 1910. *The Meaning of Social Science.* Chicago: University of Chicago Press.

———. 1916. "Fifty Years of Sociology in the United States." *American Journal of Sociology* 21:721–864.

Smith, D. 1988. *The Chicago School.* New York: St. Martin's.

Smith, W. D. 1979. "The Emergence of German Urban Sociology." *Journal of the History of Sociology* 1:1–16.

Snizek, W. E. 1984. "Casting the First Rock." *Scientometrics* 6:215–22.

Snizek, W. E., C. J. Dudley, and J. E. Hughes. 1982. "The Second Process of Peer Review." *Scientometrics* 4:417–30.

"Social Scientist David Riesman." 1954. *Time* 64 (27 September): 22–25.

Stacey, J., and B. Thorne. 1985. "The Missing Feminist Revolution in Sociology." *Social Problems* 32:301–16.

Stigler, S. M. 1986. *The History of Statistics.* Cambridge: Harvard University Press.

Storr, R. J. 1966. *Harper's University.* Chicago: University of Chicago Press.

Stouffer, S. A. 1930. "An Experimental Comparision of Statistical and Case History Methods of Attitude Research." Ph.D. diss., University of Chicago.

———. 1950. "Some Observations on Survey Design." *American Sociological Review* 15:355–61.

Stouffer, S. A., E. A. Suchman, L. C. DeVinney, S. A. Star, and R. M. Williams Jr. 1949. *The American Soldier.* Princeton: Princeton University Press.

Strauss, A. 1996. "A Partial Line of Descent." *Studies in Symbolic Interaction* 20:3–22.

Szreter, R. 1983. "Writings and Writers on Education in British Sociology Periodicals, 1953–1979." *British Journal of the Sociology of Education* 4:155–68.

Teevan, J. J. 1980. "Journal Prestige and Quality of Sociological Articles." *American Sociologist* 15:109–12.

Thomas, J. 1983a. "Chicago Sociology." *Urban Life* 11:387–95.

———. 1983b. "Towards a Critical Ethnography." *Urban Life.* 11:477–90.

Thomas, W. I., and F. Znaniecki. 1918–20. *The Polish Peasant in Europe and America.* 5 vols. Chicago: University of Chicago Press; Boston: R. G. Badger.

Thrasher, F. M. 1927. *The Gang.* Chicago: University of Chicago Press.

Tiryakian, E. 1979. "The Significance of Schools in the Development of Sociology." In *Contemporary Issues in Theory and Research,* ed. W. E. Snizek, E. R. Fuhrman, and M. K. Miller, 211–33. Westport, Conn.: Greenwood.

Tolman F. 1902–3. "The Study of Sociology in Institutions of Learning in the United States" (parts 1–4). *American Journal of Sociology* 7:797–838, 8:85–121, 8:251–72, 8:531–58.

Traxler, R. H. 1976. "A Snag in the History of Factorial Experiments." In *On the History of Probability and Statistics,* ed. D. B. Owen, 283–95. New York: Marcel Dekker.

Tuma, N. B., and M. T. Hannan. 1984. *Social Dynamics.* Orlando, Fla.: Academic.

Tuma, N. B., M. T. Hannan, and L. P. Groenveld. 1979. "Dynamic Analysis of Event Histories." *American Journal of Sociology* 84:820–54.

Turner, R. H. 1988. "Collective Behavior without Guile." *Sociological Perspectives* 31:315–24.

Turner, S. P., and J. H. Turner. 1990. *The Impossible Science.* Newbury Park, Calif.: Sage.

Van Delinder, J. 1991. "Streetcorner Sociology." *Mid-America Review of Sociology* 15:59–69.

Verhoeven, J. C. 1993. "An Interview with Erving Goffman, 1980." *Research on Language and Social Interaction* 26:317–48.

Wacker, R. F. 1983. *Ethnicity, Pluralism, and Race.* Westport, Conn.: Greenwood.

———. 1995. "The Sociology of Race and Ethnicity in the Second Chicago School." In *A Second Chicago School?* ed. G. A. Fine, 136–63. Chicago: University of Chicago Press.

Wallerstein, I. 1974. *The Modern World-System.* New York: Academic.

Ward, K. B., and L. Grant. 1985. "The Feminist Critique and a Decade of Published Research in Sociology Journals." *Sociological Quarterly* 26:139–57.

Wellman, B., and S. D. Berkowitz. 1988. *Social Structures.* Cambridge: Cambridge University Press.

White, H. C. 1970. *Chains of Opportunity.* Cambridge: Harvard University Press.

———. 1992. *Identity and Control.* Princeton: Princeton University Press.

White, H. C., S. A. Boorman, and R. L. Breiger. 1976. "Social Structure from Multiple Networks." *American Journal of Sociology* 81:730–80.

Wilcox, C. 1997. "Encounters with Modernity." Ph.D. diss., University of Michigan.

Winkin, Y. 1988. *Les moments et leurs hommes.* Paris: Seuil.

Wirth, L. 1928. *The Ghetto.* Chicago: University of Chicago Press.

Wright, R. 1945. "Introduction." In *Black Metropolis,* by St. C. Drake and H. Cayton, xvii–xxxiv. New York: Harcourt Brace.

Young, A. A. 1994. "The 'Negro Problem' and the Character of the Black Community." *National Journal of Sociology* 7:95–133.

Yu, H. 1995. "Thinking about Orientals." Ph.D. diss., Princeton University.

Zorbaugh, H. W. 1929. *The Gold Coast and the Slum*. Chicago: University of Chicago Press.

Index

This book contains at least glancing mention of almost a thousand people. I have limited the names indexed to those who appear several times or are discussed substantially.